Running Theaters

BEST PRACTICES FOR LEADERS AND MANAGERS

DUNCAN M. WEBB

**ALLWORTH
PRESS**
NEW YORK

12 11 10 09   7 6 5 4

Published by Allworth Press
An imprint of Allworth Communications, Inc.
10 East 23rd Street, New York, NY 10010

Cover design by Derek Bacchus
Interior design and typography by Sharp Des!gns, Lansing, Michigan

ISBN-10: 1-58115-393-7
ISBN-13: 978-1-58115-393-4
LIBRARY OF CONGRESS CATALOGING-IN-PUBLICATION DATA
Running theaters : best practices for managers and leaders / by Duncan M. Webb.
    p. cm.
Includes bibliographical references and index.
1. Theater management. I. Title.
PN2053.W36 2005
792'.068—dc22
                                2004021394

Contents

Acknowledgments

I have approached the writing of this book as a research effort designed to inform and educate a broad cross-section of workers, volunteers, and students on best practices in performing arts facility management. Thus, my gratitude goes first and foremost to all of the individuals in the field from whom we collected information and stories through written surveys and interviews. Brief biographies for every person interviewed are presented as an appendix to the book. We were thrilled and grateful to have so many individuals prepared to answer our endless questions not only with straight and informative answers, but also with compelling stories and anecdotes that add real flavor to the book.

I must say that all of the wisdom and insights contributed by the group give me great confidence about the future of the industry. Though the individuals who run facilities are as different as the facilities they manage, I am amazed and impressed at the overall level of passion, intelligence, and foresight exhibited by those who work in these buildings, and hope some of that rubs off on the reader.

Let me also thank a set of professionals for their work as editors of preliminary chapter drafts: Robert Long, Bruce MacPherson, Jack Hagler, Robyn Williams, Joanna Baymiller, Victor Gotesman, Michael Curry, Chuck Cosler, and Bill Reeder.

And finally, I must express my gratitude to the staff at Webb Management Services, who have toiled long and hard on compiling data, analyzing surveys, and constructing the theater list. This includes Sarah Jaycox, Tim Holbrook, and Casey Reitz. Special thanks must go to Michael Chipman. He took responsibility for the transcription of all of our interviews. He translated many of those rambling tales into crisp nuggets of wisdom. And he applied his considerable skills as a writer and editor to add a professional polish to the text.

Foreword

When I was running the Alvin Ailey American Dance Theater, I brought the company to the Herod Atticus, a large Roman amphitheater built into the base of the Acropolis in Athens, Greece. Everyone in the company was thrilled to perform on this historic stage with the Parthenon placed so beautifully above the amphitheater's stone seats. I was less enthusiastic. I simply stood on the stage and noted that the number of seats had not increased in the two thousand years since the theater was erected!

This is just one reason why managing a theater gets more difficult, year after year—it is virtually impossible to increase productivity in the performing arts. Once a theater is constructed, the number of seats is literally set in concrete. Yet the number of performers in any given work remains the same year in and year out. While the automobile industry can find ways to build more cars with fewer people, we still have the same number of performers in *Oklahoma* or *Don Giovanni* as when they were written. Therefore, while expenses rise with inflation, earned revenue potential is capped. Unless one can consistently raise ticket prices enough to cover the rapidly increasing costs, and few theaters can, the gap between earned income and cost becomes increasingly ominous. The challenge to arts managers to fill this gap gets greater and greater.

And the challenges facing those who are in charge of theater facilities go far beyond the lack of earned income growth. As virtually every theater manager seeks to find the growing levels of contributed income needed to fill the gap between expenses and earned income, they begin to compete more intensely and across a wider geographical area with other arts organizations and other not-for-profit organizations. It used to be true that one or a few wealthy families took pride and responsibility for funding the deficit of a major arts organization. Now that is not feasible anymore, as budgets have grown and fund raising requirements have soared.

We face other trials as well. Over the past twenty years, various forms of sophisticated entertainment systems have made it simple to create an in-home theater with easy-to-use recording systems and Internet access; many people have simply chosen to stay home rather than to bear the expense of going to the theater. So the challenge of reaching out to the potential audience for any venue must constantly be met: How do you identify this audience? What combination of outreach, education, partnership, producing, and presenting will prove the successful formula for getting them into the seats?

Anyone in charge of a theatrical venue will encounter physical challenges as well. Rapid developments in technology require the manager to stay on top of what's new, what's necessary, and what's affordable. Those who manage older venues must pay attention to both safety and preservation, while those in charge of new spaces must make sure wish lists and budgets are in balance. And, along with all of this, the manager must also be a leader, skillful at both listening to and influencing his fellow men and women. Loyal, useful boards must be culled and maintained; staffs hired, trained, challenged, admonished, praised, and promoted.

Yes, the need for trained and talented arts managers is deeper than ever before. Yet arts administration is a young field. Traditionally, arts executives "fell" into their jobs, usually after having worked at a record company or having been a performer or director. Formal arts management education did not start until the 1970s and, even now, many of today's senior arts managers entered the field with no training.

So the question is, how can we train current executives and future arts managers for this challenging profession with few rules and fewer good texts? There is probably no better way than to listen to the practitioners who struggle every day to produce great art with limited resources. In creating *Running Theaters: Best Practices for Leaders and Managers*, Duncan Webb has done remarkable research, interviewing a wide variety of managers in charge of regional, campus, and community based theaters across North America. He has elicited the diverse rules and truths these leaders live by as they cope with a difficult environment.

Each arts manager will find his or her own truths as we continue to define this rapidly transforming field. But the insights provided by the current experts will serve as the launch pad as future leaders take theaters hurtling through the twenty-first century and beyond.

MICHAEL KAISER

President of the John F. Kennedy Center for the Performing Arts

Introduction

I am a management consultant to people who build and operate theaters. I decided to write a book on the management of performing arts facilities in North America for several reasons. First of all, there are no books or guides for theater managers, boards, and students that are specifically about facility management. Second, I wanted to do the research that might help us understand how theaters succeed on an operating basis. And finally, I wanted to understand how individuals respond to the complexity and shifting pressures of being a facility manager.

This book is offered for the benefit of those who work in theaters, volunteer in theaters, fund theaters, or are students of theater management. We will cover a broad range of topics, from the marketing and programming of performing arts facilities to their physical maintenance, from the particular issues surrounding operating historic facilities to those issues associated with facilities located on college campuses. Within a number of these areas, we will address the role of technology. We will wrap it all up with thoughts on some of the broader trends we've observed in the field and some words of inspiration from successful facility managers.

All of us at Webb Management Services spent a year collecting stories and insights from people in the field. These pages are filled with their views on what it takes to successfully operate a performing arts facility. We also felt it was important to share different approaches and opinions expressed on best practices, which, for our purposes, are defined as a practice or behavior that leads to success. It is fascinating to see how managers approach different problems in different ways, but it is also fascinating to see a series of overarching themes: the complexity of the job, an increasingly outward focus, changing audiences, and the impact of technology on the performing arts.

I should explain the focus on theater managers in North America. Though most of our work is in the United States, I did get my start in the arts in Canada, and I can say with some confidence that the difference in facility management practices between the two countries is small, and getting smaller. But going beyond North America is another question. We have worked in several countries in South America, and it is clear that the way those theaters operate is fundamentally different, given their economic structures, the role of government in the arts, tax laws, marketing practices, administrative skills, and the role of theaters in society and culture. Not having any significant experience with theater managers in any other countries, we would not even hazard a guess as to the validity of our research beyond this continent.

Looking at theaters in North America raises an interesting question: How many are there? First of all, we are not interested in theaters controlled by a producing organization, which excludes lots of smaller facilities controlled by theater companies, as well as some dance spaces and even a symphony hall or two. We are interested in facilities with multiple users, where there is a management organization in place that activates a building with some combination of rentals, presented events, producing, and community programming.

Even with that qualification, it is not easy to establish how many theaters there are, simply because there is no comprehensive inventory. There are lists of performing arts centers, historic theaters, and campus theaters, but no comprehensive list exists that pulls it all together.

Who could resist a challenge like that? We decided to take it on, and so, through the first half of 2004, we assembled and combined lists. We started with existing lists of facilities from organizations like the International Society of the Performing Arts (ISPA), the American Performing Arts Presenters (APAP), and the League of Historic American Theaters (LHAT). Then we contacted state and local arts councils and agencies, working through them to collect facility directories. Here are a few highlights of that research:

- We have identified approximately 3,500 performing arts facilities in Canada and the United States that fit our definition of "theater": a performing arts venue with multiple users and a management organization.
- Let's accept that this is an incomplete list, as there are certainly facilities tucked away in various communities. Most are probably smaller or school-based facilities that are available to community-based groups on an occasional basis.
- Let's also accept that the number of qualifying facilities is a moving target. There are new and renovated facilities coming online all the time, as well as other facilities that disappear, or at least go dormant, on a regular basis.
- Here is the split of capacity on those facilities where capacity information was available:

> Less than 250 seats 14.9%
> 250-499 seats 20.0%
> 500-999 seats 22.5%
> 1,000-1,499 seats 13.0%
> 1,500-1,999 seats 8.8%
> 2,000-2,499 seats 8.3%
> 2,500-3,499 seats 7.4%
> 3,500 + seats 5.1%

- Here is the age range of facilities for which that information was available:

> 1800-1899 . . . . .6%
> 1900-1929 . . . . .24%
> 1930-1959 . . . . .19%
> 1960-1989 . . . . .29%
> 1990-2007 . . . . .22%

- Here are the states with the most theaters. We also show each state as a percentage of the entire list, and each state's percentage of the total U.S. population.

	NUMBER OF THEATERS	PERCENT OF LIST	PERCENT OF U.S. POPULATION
California	499	15.8%	12.0%
New York	277	8.8%	6.7%
Illinois	271	8.6%	4.4%
Ohio	117	3.7%	4.0%
Texas	112	3.6%	7.4%
Florida	104	3.3%	5.7%
North Carolina	104	3.3%	2.9%

- Here's the same exercise for the Canadian provinces with the most facilities:

	NUMBER OF THEATERS	PERCENT OF LIST	PERCENT OF CANADA POPULATION
Ontario	147	40%	38%
Manitoba	55	15%	4%
British Columbia	49	13%	13%
Alberta	35	10%	10%

- Finally, we noted that 13 percent of the facilities in North America are on a college campus.

The other interesting variable is that there are many different models for the operation of performing arts facilities. They are managed by governments, the private sector, educational institutions, facility management companies, and arts organizations. For our analysis, we are interested in all of these models. Not all of our topics will be relevant to all facilities, but there is a lot of common ground. Off we go!

Chapter One

The Theater Manager's Job and the Operating Context

What does it take to run a theater and to do it well? Or, to put it another way, what is the job description for a successful theater manager? Here are a couple of ads from ArtSearch (TCG's "National Employment Bulletin for the Arts"). I've taken out references to specific facilities:

Executive Director: An award-winning performing arts center is seeking a highly qualified arts leader to continue its growth as a major regional arts institution. The executive director oversees, directs, and assures high quality in all operations and functions of the Center, in accordance with the bylaws and reporting to the Board of Directors. The executive director will: direct a sixty-person staff; develop and administer an annual budget of $1+ million; oversee financial and legal compliance and reporting; oversee events, resource development, marketing, and grant writing; provide local and statewide leadership and advocacy for the Center; build relationships with artists, arts organizations, business, government, education, media, members, donors, and program users; and serve as chief spokesperson for the Center.

General Manager: Center for the Arts seeks enthusiastic, self-motivated individual for senior staff position. Responsibilities include (but are not limited to) coordination of facility use with in-house and outside rentals of the

theater, gallery, and meeting rooms; daily operation of facilities and personnel; budget creation and administration; artist contract negotiations; educational program development; strengthening and developing board and staff;
building local private, corporate, and business contributions; and developing
a strategic plan for the next step of the Center's growth.

Both ads go on to suggest the necessary qualifications and experience to
undertake the position, which tend to include a postgraduate degree; experience in a similar position; great communications and grant-writing skills;
knowledge of computers, technical theater, production, and marketing; and the
ability to present a positive public image of the facility.

It's all a little overwhelming. How could one person have all of those skills
and attributes and be able to do all of those things? And how could a person
ever be trained to take on such a job? Well, the answer is that there are
people who are qualified and capable to undertake this work, and they have
gained all sorts of skills and training from many areas of the arts and entertainment industries that have allowed them not just to survive as facility managers, but also to flourish.

Common Elements of Facility Management

The language in these job postings is often a bit over-the-top, and I suppose
that's an effective way to discourage all but the most serious of candidates.
But it does accurately suggest that the job has many elements that are all quite
different and demanding. Let's consider those elements that would generally be
common from facility to facility.

Facility Management

The job starts with the basic responsibility that one has for a physical space,
and all that that entails—the condition and maintenance of the structure and
systems, a whole set of liability issues, and the need to be a good neighbor.

Activating the Facility

The next element is activating the facility, that very challenging effort of bringing programs into the facility, generally under one of the following categories:

Presented Events

These are events purchased by the facility or an organization associated with the facility, promoted locally, and presented in the facility. There is a huge and sophisticated industry devoted to touring arts and entertainment programs that are available to facility managers. We will devote a good deal of chapter 3 to presenting and what it means to facility managers.

Arts Organization Rentals

Theaters are often activated by local arts organizations that are themselves the producers or presenters of the work. For this kind of use, the facility establishes rental arrangements, providing access to the facility and related services for a fee. These are very important programs and are often the reason that the facilities were developed in the first place.

Education Programs

It's important to separate education programs from other kinds of presented and rental events in a facility. Whether it's hosting the Missoula Children's Theater on tour, the local symphony adding a special school performance, or running a teacher-training program, the building often plays a role in developing and promoting educational programs in the community. On a practical basis, facilities recognize that educational programs are attractive to funders in both the public and private sectors. And fundamentally, education is the key for nonprofit facilities, since their incorporation as a 501(c)(3) tax-exempt organization depends on their having an educational mission.

Produced Events

These are events created by the facility itself, such as a play or a dance or an opera whose creation is driven by the same organization that manages the building. This is not universal, but we will see that more and more facilities are moving away from renting and presenting toward a more active role in the creation of the work.

Other Community Uses

Finally, there are all of those other rental events that activate the facility and help pay the bills, from corporate meetings to wedding receptions. While these events tend not to be intrinsic to the mission of the building, they are important as a means to strengthen the relationship between the building and the community while improving financial performance.

The real challenge for the theater manager is finding a balance between all of the competing needs and uses of the space. Starting in the late 1980s and early 1990s, this balancing act became a major challenge for managers of most larger performing arts centers, as communities became increasingly obsessed with the need to book *Cats*, *Phantom of the Opera*, and their offspring, often at the expense of local performing arts organizations. The frenzy has subsided somewhat, but the facility manager still faces considerable pressures on who and what gains access to the stage.

Managing Staff and Board

Once you have a building and a program, there is the need to build and maintain a staff and volunteer organization. Both halves of this equation present significant challenges to managers. The staff of a theater tends to be a committed and tight-knit group that works very hard for very little money. There is also a tremendous diversity of skills and people needed to run a theater, from the worn-out, late-night technical director to the flashy, breakfast-meeting development director. The manager has an amazing challenge: to try to bring this group together to work as a team for rewards that are less about money than they are about other kinds of personal satisfaction. Then there is the board—a group of volunteers brought together as keepers of the mission, overseers of the operation, and fundraisers. The amount of time and effort that goes into the care and feeding of the board is often a great surprise for facility managers.

Marketing and Fundraising

Next are the functions that represent the two halves of revenue generation—the earned income that comes with successful marketing, and the contributed income that comes with effective fundraising. The other common element is that both fundraising and marketing depend on detailed information about customers and prospects. And with the emergence and advancements of technologies that allow managers to capture and use information about their customers for the benefit of fundraising and audience development, the relationship will become even more important.

Community Relations

Twenty years ago, who would have thought that theater managers would have to become community relations experts? The ability to understand, reach out to, and work with other elements of a community has become a critically important part of the job. Partly, it's a matter of survival; theater managers have come to understand that they must prove themselves to be a fundamental part of the community, not just a place where exclusive elites dress up and mingle. But it also reflects a growing awareness that what goes on in a theater can have a profoundly positive impact on a community, whether that relates to downtown revitalization, improving the quality of life for all citizens, attracting companies and workers to a community, or building cultural tourism. And it is the manager who is ultimately responsible for reaching out to the community and making the theater responsive to and supportive of broad community goals.

General Management

Finally, there are all of those other parts of the job, including the preparation and management of budgets, the purchasing of materials and supplies, relationships with suppliers and customers, and all of the day-to-day responsibilities that come with being the boss.

We will go into greater detail in all of these areas in the following chapters. For now, we can certainly suggest that the job of facility manager is both complex and dynamic. And we can also suggest that successful facility managers have their own approaches to the job.

It is interesting to contrast the job description of the facility manager with that of managers of producing organizations. In producing organizations, one usually finds an artistic director to deal with the creative output of the organization, and an executive director as its administrator. One generally reports to the other, or there is an uneasy partnership reporting to the board. But for facility management, there is only one leader, and that person must take responsibility for both artistic and administrative decisions. In fact, the combination of these responsibilities may be the thing that makes this such a challenging and rewarding career. And, as we will see in the following chapters, the ability to manage both sides of the organization may be the thing that sets some of our facility managers apart.

Different Operating Models

The major reason why the job of managing facilities can be so different from building to building is that the context is often different, with different sorts of owners and operators. Theaters can be owned and operated by local government, an arm's-length agency of government, an educational institution, a private nonprofit, or a commercial organization. And, in many cases, the owner is different from the operator. Each of these various models affects the job of the facility manager. A city-operated facility is bound to involve a lot of bureaucratic wrangling. A manager in a private nonprofit will be much more engaged in fundraising. And the manager of a campus facility may spend the majority of his or her time balancing access to facilities between teaching programs and performances.

As we suggested earlier, there is no preferred model for the ownership and operation of facilities. Different models work better in different communities and under different circumstances. Our task is to consider the job of facility manager in any form of ownership and operation. And we will take the position that the commonalities between the models outweigh the differences.

Evolutionary Management

It is also important to stress that the way that performing arts facilities are managed can and should change over time in response to changing circumstances and opportunities. Some facilities change operators as they grow. Other facilities switch back and forth from private- to public-sector operation as economic and political circumstances change. And in other cases, the mission of the facility changes.

The very first theater I was involved with as a volunteer was the Theatre Centre in Toronto. A group of five experimental theater companies had come together in 1979 to run a theater above a Greek discothèque. In those early days, the space was managed as a cooperative. Over the next few years, we began to separate the management of the space from the groups that used it. We built a separate board and pushed the organization toward a role of attracting and incubating new groups as the original ones matured and moved on to their own spaces. Twenty-five years later, the Theatre Centre is still at it. It has moved eight times over the years, but still acts as a home for a series of emerging producing companies. Over those years, the form and mission of the operating organization has swung back and forth, pendulum-like, from a skeleton staff that serves a set of specific users to a larger and more proactive organization that encourages and supports a much broader group, creating an identity that transcends the specific users. The great challenge has been trying to build such identity without owning a theater, moving from space to space as leases expire and costs escalate. But the organization has certainly succeeded in supporting and nurturing dozens of organizations from an emerging level to an adolescent one, at which point they can be pushed out of the nest.

Facility Management Companies

I mentioned in the introduction that one of ways that facilities are managed is through contracting a facility management company. There are several companies around the country that are hired, usually by local government, to manage performing arts centers. One example is Professional Facilities Management (PFM), based in Providence, Rhode Island. This is an interesting company, a for-profit subsidiary of the nonprofit organization that manages Providence's performing arts center. Norbert Mongeon is CFO of PFM, and has played a significant role in building the enterprise. Here he describes how it works and why it works, as well as why the industry is not dominated by national facility management companies:

Most of the management crew has been with Providence Performing Arts Center since 1983. By 1989 we were looking for opportunities to take our skills and apply them elsewhere. So we launched a management company, and started doing work in Lowell and Springfield, Massachusetts. Then we branched off in 1991 to Fort Myers, Florida, and 1993 to Coral Springs, Florida, and then in 1996 to Skokie, North Chicago, Illinois, and we started booking the Vilar Center in 1999 out in Colorado.

We're not in Lowell anymore, but we're about to start a co-presentation arrangement in Waterbury, Connecticut, with the Palace Theater. Our usual approach is that we come in and offer to take the "headache" of running a facility away from local government. So we are entirely responsible for the building. We get some sort of a subsidy and a management fee, and, if we're profitable, we split the bottom line with the entity that actually owns the facility.

It works because these entities don't really want to be in the business of running a theater. I think they are relieved to be able to hand off a facility to someone else who can deal with the things that come along with it—not just facility maintenance. It is a unique business, and it is not something that municipal entities deal with well. It also requires more wheeling and dealing than municipal entities are used to, or in many cases have the flexibility to be able to accomplish. So basically you set up an arrangement that is arm's-length and that could be fruitful from a public relations standpoint by generating a lot of activity in the facilities, as well as from a financial stand-point. Assuming the entity that is running it is successful, this is win-win for most public entities.

The reason that we're not running fifty theaters right now is that we are concerned about getting too big, but also because there are limited opportunities. Theater management is very different from arena management and convention center management, which are now dominated by just two companies. Theaters are very expensive to build relative to the revenue that they generate, so they require significant fundraising machines behind them, and fundraising always comes down from the board, and so you need a strong board, and you usually have boards that take ownership of the building. So they are much less likely to release control of that facility to an outside entity. If they are going to raise all that money every year, they want to know that they are calling the shots in terms of managing the building, so it's much less likely that they are going to turn around and release control of that facility to a management company.

Facility management companies are interesting and are sometimes a good option for facility owners. But they are not about to dominate this sector and, in any event, they face the same challenges as other types of facility managers. So, from this point on, we'll consider facility management skills, challenges, and practices from the perspective of the individual manager or leader in a performing arts facility, whether he's working for government, a nonprofit, a college, or a facility management enterprise.

The Scale of Operations

As noted in the introduction, there are performing arts facilities of vastly different shapes and sizes. We often think first of the multi-hall performing arts center, but there are a number of very successful one-room centers managed by very small organizations. One great example is the Astor Theatre, a 102-year-old theater of 358 seats in the town of Liverpool, Nova Scotia (population 30,000). The Astor is a successful hall with local renters, a presenting program, school programs, an annual theater festival, and weekly film screenings. The hall is managed by a full-time staff of one. Chris Ball is the manager, marketer, technical director, and fundraiser. As he says: "I am the guy selling you the ticket, and then running back around and taking it from you." Here he explains how he arrived in this position:

> I was working at the paper mill, and got disenchanted with my job and quit. I started volunteering my time here at the theater, and when the position came up, the board of directors knew I had the interest and asked me if I wanted the job. I took it, and gave myself a crash course on the arts. The hardest part was that I had no concept of how to book a show. I had no concept of dealing with agents and managers. I knew absolutely nothing walking in the door.
>
> Now, I should say that the theater at that point was in such bad shape that anything I could do would have been an improvement. It was about a month away from closing when I started, as it was severely in debt. The managers had

lost interest, the board of directors had sort of lost interest, and I didn't know what I was getting myself into. Since I had no other job waiting for me, I decided I wasn't going to let it close. And actually I think it was kind of a benefit not having any kind of an arts background because I invented everything as I went along. I found out what worked and what didn't and created my own way of running the theater, and it seems to have worked.

At the other end of the spectrum, at least in Canada, is the National Arts Centre in Ottawa, a huge complex with performance halls ranging from a 2,300-seat multipurpose hall to a 175-seat black box theater. The organization includes its own orchestra, a dance company, English- and French-language theater companies, and educational programs. And then add to that its mandate to serve a national constituency! Peter Herrndorf is the president and CEO of the organization:

> We are national in character. I think it's exhilarating, but it adds a level of complexity to the task. I'll give you a case in point. Last year we did the first Canadian production of *Copenhagen*. It was a collaboration between the National Arts Centre and the Neptune Theatre in Halifax. So we presented the show in Halifax, we presented the show here in Ottawa, and then transferred it six months later to a commercial theater in Toronto. So that gives you an idea of the range of things we will do. We will commission material, we produce, we coproduce, we present, we transfer; we do all of it. We are an organization that has a great many creative and entrepreneurial balls in the air all the time.

The differences between the Astor and the National Arts Centre are vast. But they are still both in the business of selling tickets, soliciting support, and caring for facilities.

Multiple Facilities

One of the recent trends is that managers are being required to manage multiple facilities in a community. Steve Loftin is the president and executive director of the Cincinnati Arts Association, which runs three separate buildings in Cincinnati, Ohio: Cincinnati Music Hall, Memorial Hall, and the Aronoff Center for the Arts. Loftin says that the management merger of those three facilities came about during the early 1990s, when plans were underway for what would become the Aronoff Center. The 125-year-old Music Hall had been run by a separate nonprofit corporation, and the group of people interested in building a new performing arts facility decided it would be in the best interest of Music Hall and the new facility to merge administrative efforts. They formed a joint organization to assure that the new hall would not jeopardize the Music Hall in programming or fundraising.

The management of that joint nonprofit established parallel priorities for both facilities, and as new staff came online, they were given administrative responsibilities for both halls, including marketing, fiscal management, and organizational administration. "It was clear that there would be some cost-saving opportunities for some things that could be combined, as well as broadened opportunities for facilities rentals when you could market more than one facility," says Loftin.

The new Aronoff Center for the Arts in downtown Cincinnati opened in October of 1995 with a full administration and operations staff, and both halls have been managed since then under a joint organization. During that process, Memorial Hall was also brought under the joint management with Music Hall and the Aronoff Center. Memorial Hall is an historic theater that had fallen into disrepair, so a local organization decided to oversee its cosmetic renovation and then find an operator. Joining the management structure already in place for the other two facilities was an easy choice, since Memorial Hall was not as sophisticated a facility as the other two, but it filled an important niche in the city's performing arts venue inventory. Loftin believes this kind of multiple-facility merger makes sense:

> I'm sure there are exceptions, but it is so difficult in any environment for a single performing arts entity to succeed. You have to make ends meet from a physical standpoint, but there is never enough fundraising, there is too much expense, and there is never enough manpower. Hall management always requires a lot of pieces, including presenting, rentals, resident companies, concessions, merchandise, and ticketing. It is all of those things combined, and any one of them is vital to the final solution of how to run a building. When you collaborate among various facilities, there is an incremental savings and

an incremental increase in efficiency. Joining two halls under one management umbrella may not be fully half as expensive, but they are certainly not as expensive as one plus one. Moreover, I think that community leaders are looking for collaborators—people making the most efficient use of resources—and if you can have one less accountant, one less marketing person, and one less operations manager in the whole scheme of things, then the money saved can be spent on the upkeep of the facilities, programs, or user subsidies.

Rae Ackerman works for the city of Vancouver as their manager of civic theaters, meaning that he is responsible for the 2,929-seat Queen Elizabeth, the 2,780-seat historic Orpheum, and the 668-seat Vancouver Playhouse. As he says, the combination of like facilities is a good thing:

If you've only got one building you are stuck, but with three buildings you've got some flexibility. We have open dates in different buildings. If someone comes along, she can come to us and say, I need a big theater. Well, I've got two. What night is your show? We can look at either theater. We don't have a date here, but we have a date there, so we can move stuff around that way. That's a lot more interesting. When this organization added the Orpheum, it did not add any staff. We could add another theater now and all we would need is another stage door person, maybe a couple of stage technicians. Once you have the infrastructure to run one theater, it doesn't make a lot of difference to add two or three or four more.

It Was Not Always Thus

Thirty years ago, the job of running a performing arts center was very different and much simpler than the one we've started to describe. Facilities usually survived with a small operations staff and a manager principally concerned with booking rentals. What has happened?

- Local arts audiences want to see the best shows and artists in the world, requiring facility managers to become much more adept at picking and promoting touring entertainment.
- Performing arts facilities face intense competition from other activities

competing for shrinking leisure time, requiring facility managers to market their programs in a much more aggressive and targeted fashion.

- Performing arts facilities are much more expensive to build and operate, raising the stakes of the enterprise.
- Public-sector support has been largely replaced by private-sector philanthropy, which is extremely competitive.
- Communities that support performing arts facilities do so with the expectation that these facilities will contribute to the life and prospects of the community on an ongoing basis.

What all of this means is that we are describing a kind of job that did not really exist thirty years ago. So, part of our challenge is to imagine what the job might be like thirty years hence. In the following chapters, we will examine the increasing complexity of facility management and how it might develop in the future.

Chapter Two

Facility Operations

Performing arts facilities are large, complex, and potentially dangerous places of public assembly. In addition, they are often grand and architecturally significant showplaces in the community, seen as a point of pride and a community gathering place. So the job of facility manager starts with responsibility for the physical care and maintenance of a structure, and the safety of those who come through its doors.

In this chapter we will address how performing arts facilities are operated and maintained. Let's split the discussion (as we often split the building) into two elements: what happens in front of the stage (front-of-house operations) and what happens onstage and backstage (backstage operations). We'll also address the issues of capital planning and safety, then hear some opinions on what's coming in the area of technological innovations and performance equipment.

Front-of-House Operations

There are several key elements to front-of-house operations. They are public safety; the management of the box office, ushers, and house staff; food service; and the physical maintenance of public areas.

As an introduction to this discussion, let me relate the experience of the New York Philharmonic in Avery Fisher Hall. The Philharmonic, one of the great orchestras in the world, is a rent-paying tenant of Avery Fisher Hall, which is managed by Lincoln Center, Inc. The orchestra has always had a contentious relationship with the building and building management. There have been well-publicized complaints about the acoustics of the hall, and repeated attempts to correct these problems. In 2001, after almost forty years in the building, it was clear that physical improvements were required. Thus, improvements to the Hall were budgeted to be a part of the Lincoln Center Redevelopment Plan. Internally, members of the Philharmonic staff and board began discussions about how they might approach the redevelopment project as an opportunity to redefine their relationship with the building.

It was in that context that we were hired by the Philharmonic to analyze the operational and financial aspects of taking over the operation of Avery Fisher. It was a very interesting assignment, as it allowed us to consider how a more dominant role in the facility might affect the operating budget, as well as the fundraising demands on the organization. But the most interesting and revealing part of the work was our consideration of how the Philharmonic, as manager of the building, might affect the quality of its customers' experience when attending a concert.

To address that issue, we assessed the quality of house operations, the box office, the physical maintenance of the space, and food service in the building. And we compared it to the operations of other large halls. We determined that while the building was operated in a satisfactory manner, there were shortcomings and compromises that affected the quality of the experience of Philharmonic patrons. The training and dress of ushers was inconsistent and a bit sloppy. The box office staff was generally overburdened and somewhat prickly. Food service (concessions and the restaurant) could have been more abundant and better quality. And the basic appearance of public areas and the state of repair in areas like public restrooms was not what it could be. It could not be said that Lincoln Center was being negligent in any way. They were simply managing scarce resources (human and financial) as best they could. And we could not say with any certainty that the Philharmonic could suddenly step in and achieve a higher level of customer service for the same amount of money. But is was clear that the Philharmonic could take on these responsibilities and upgrade the experience of customers through better service, and that there would most likely be a positive financial return to the organization as ticket sales rose, renewal rates improved, and donations grew along with the level of patron satisfaction.

The recruitment, training, and management of staff is at the heart of these customer satisfaction issues, affecting the level of public safety, box office operations, house staff, and food service. For some facilities, the big question is the extent to which volunteers can be employed in these areas and still provide a high level of service. From our research and observations in a number of facilities, the issue is not whether the staff is paid or volunteer, but how well they are trained and managed in the areas of safety and customer service. We will come back to these issues in chapter 9.

Another interesting debate in performing arts facilities is the question of providing more and better food service for patrons to enhance their experience and potentially contribute to the financial operation of facilities. Having a meal, drink, or dessert before or after a performance is often seen as an intrinsic part of the experience. And as we will review in chapter 12, dining activity creates tremendous economic impact on the community.

For facility managers, the question is how much of this food service should be inside and managed by the building, as opposed to outside or contracted to another operator. Most of the facilities we've observed and managers we've interviewed have stressed the importance of high-quality concessions and the inclusion of catering facilities in the building. The presence of a large ballroom is also important. Steve Loftin, of the Cincinnati Arts Association, says:

> We do have a significant kitchen at the Aronoff Center that could produce mass meals quite well, but the center itself doesn't have really good function spaces. We have three smaller function spaces, but we don't have that 200-to-300-seat-or-more ballroom that could utilize a full kitchen component. As such, it has been difficult to hold large events. We did have a caterer on hand that had control of the kitchen during the first several years, but it frankly couldn't make a go of it. It wasn't a profitable situation for the caterer, so that kitchen has essentially gone unused. Now, in the Music Hall we have a ballroom, about a 17,000-square-foot space, and it's extremely busy with many kinds of events. Really large and high-end functions happen there all the time, so it's a perfectly natural combination to have that kind of facility integrated.

Including a full-service restaurant in a performing arts facility is a daunting prospect. Restaurants are very expensive to develop and maintain. They require different skills from facility management; they add all sorts of health and public safety issues to the building. Most facility managers are very leery about starting a restaurant. They would much rather support other restaurants in the area (reaffirming their role and value to the community), or simply lease a space to a restaurant operator. But in some cases, performing arts facilities have operated restaurants.

Mark Light says that adding a restaurant to his new facility in Dayton, Ohio (the Benjamin and Marion Shuster Performing Arts Center) has been a positive addition for the overall audience experience. "A restaurant is an amenity," says Light. "It is a good idea if you can tolerate the risk. We wanted to open this 130-million-dollar project, and we thought the customers would want to have a restaurant here, so we built one. If it survives it will stay open, and if it doesn't, it will become a bar. That is not the general experience of most performing arts centers. It's not really an optimal answer to put the restaurant in the actual building, but eating out is part of the experience of going to the theater, and if there are not restaurants in the neighborhood, an in-house restaurant certainly adds to the customer's experience."

Backstage Operations

Backstage operations, which technically start at the front of the stage, represent a totally different set of challenges for facility managers. There are the dangers and occupational hazards associated with any industrial workspace. There is all of the technological complexity of performance equipment systems. And then there is the frantic world of production, with all of the magic of performance created for audiences blissfully unaware of the chaos behind the curtains.

Theater consultant Jack Hagler has observed the backstage operations of numerous theaters over the years. He knows a well-run theater when he sees one:

> When I go into theaters, I am usually asked to look at the backstage operations and the backstage equipment. I can tell if there is someone there who

knows what he is doing with regard to the stage and the stage equipment, not only from the condition of the equipment, but also from his proper or improper use of the equipment and in casual conversation with the stagehands. The manager's knowledge, or lack of knowledge, about backstage operations may affect the backstage functionality to some degree, but generally it does not affect the theatrical production. If the manager is trained in technical theater, it usually does show up in the attitude and performance of the stagehands and in the quality and condition of the equipment. If the facility manager is not trained in technical theater, it may or may not show up backstage—it just depends on the personality, training, and sometimes the credibility of who is working back there.

That said, I do think it's important for a theater manager to understand what's going on backstage. The backstage area is inherently dangerous because it is really an industrial work area with overhead lifting and movement in three-dimensional space. Managers who aren't trained in technical theater may not fully appreciate that the backstage area is an industrial workspace.

Hagler points to a common problem. Many facility managers have a limited technical background, so in these buildings, you often see a figurative wall of separation between the technical folks and the operations and management folks. There is a technical director who spends eighty hours a week plugging away on the stage, and everybody loves her because she works so hard, so whatever she is doing must be great, but God only knows what it is. Robyn Williams of the Portland Center for the Performing Arts agrees that this lack of training is a problem:

I worked in one facility where a union guy called me and said, "We've got a really serious maintenance problem on your stage." When you are not backstage all the time, you assume your crew is working hard and everything is safe and done well and the crew is full of great, hard-working people. But I got over there and what I saw was atrocious, really frightening. I asked the staff, "How can you just let this happen? This is Basic Stagecraft 101." The response was, "Well, nobody really told us it was a problem."

So a big part of the problem was that these folks had never continued their education in the industry. That is one reason I am a big proponent of sending our theater people to the Listing Dimensions International and U.S.

Institute of Theater Technology Conferences, so that they know what is happening in rigging and lighting, and so that they know all the health and safety issues of the theater—and not just the technical people, but all of our staff. When we are in a budget-cut mode, the travel and training for my staff is the very last thing I cut, because even with my background, I can't be running around inspecting rigging systems myself. You can try to make sure that your folks are doing their jobs, but really, your best defense is having a highly trained staff.

The point here is that backstage familiarity helps facility managers come to terms with issues surrounding safety, liability, and equipment maintenance, and that leads to creating a maintenance program, which Hagler says is essential:

Most of the larger markets and some midsize markets have a maintenance program in place, and those programs include not only the lighting fixtures and audio systems, but also, and most importantly, the rigging systems. Manual rigging is the least technologically advanced system of any of the theater systems, and the least understood. It is also the most dangerous because installing, maintaining, and operating it is all overhead lifting. That is where I see a lack of maintenance programs or any kind of inspection program in place. I think all of the systems should be inspected, not only for safety but also for operation, so that the manager can budget and plan for proper maintenance and future improvements. I think there should be an annual procedure in place to review the systems for safety and planning.

The good news, according to theater consultant Charles Cosler, is that there is general improvement over the past decade in the quality of backstage operations and in the technical direction in theaters. He says,

We had a funny situation at the Shays Buffalo Theater where a professionally trained young man was brought in as the technical director, but then ran afoul of the guys in the union, who were old-school and accustomed to work rules that enabled them to do as little work as possible. This guy was young and enthusiastic, and he wanted to get on with the work and do good work rather than be a slave to work rules, which caused a lot of friction.

There is also the issue between the unions in larger cities working alongside younger people who have been college-educated and who don't have the blue-collar mindset that most stagehands have about work. But the younger people also haven't been working for many years and don't fully understand that the work of putting on a show is hard—very hard and labor intensive—and at some point, if you continue to do it, you have to learn to pace yourself. You can't kill yourself on every single production, or you are just going to burn out. That is something that the older hands know and the younger ones don't.

Something that you see in a well-ordered work place is a combination of older and younger men and women, and there is a sort of reciprocal compensation between the ages: The older ones may not have the physical strength or ability any more, but they know a lot and they can see immediately how to cut corners and make things easier, while the younger guys do more of the heavy lifting.

Capital Planning

Estimating the capital requirements for performing arts facilities is a complicated effort. One must estimate the life of structural elements and systems in the building, laying out and prioritizing the replacement of these items. Some are more discretionary than others, and the rate of technological advancement affects the redundancy and need to replace performance equipment systems. Facility managers have different approaches to the problem, and while there is not one singular, superior approach to capital planning and maintenance, what became very clear to us in our interviews is that the important thing is to have a plan—any plan—in place from the beginning and to keep that plan up to date.

So what constitutes a good plan? Robyn Williams, executive director of the Portland Center for the Performing Arts, says that the first step is to establish priorities, even though donors and patrons may disagree with those choices:

It's really easy to want to do all the fluffy things that the audience sees, such as new carpet and painted walls and all that sort of thing. Sometimes you have to put those on the back burner and spend money on less sexy things, like a new chiller or a roof.

I wouldn't say that just because you go in and see something wrong, it means that the building is being badly maintained. It may just be inadequately maintained. For example, when I first came to Portland, I was surprised at some of the things I saw in the facilities. So, one of the first things we did was create a capital plan. It was not complicated, but you have to understand where your deficiencies are and prioritize those.

We decided first to address those severe maintenance problems that could have long-term effects on the facility. Well, one of our donors had given us $1.5 million for the renovation of Keller Auditorium, and he wanted to know when the lobby would get all spiffed up. I explained to him that first we wanted to address safety, security, and infrastructure issues. Next came the needs of our arts organizations, so we spent a lot of money upgrading sound and lighting systems. After all, people come to see the art, so it was important that they had the tools to really do their craft well. Our last priority was the front-of-house stuff—the carpet, the paint, and the art on the walls.

Once the plan is in place, it is important to establish a system of review so that the plan can continually evolve to meet the needs of the facility and its users. Anita Scism, executive director of the Walton Arts Center in Fayetteville, Arkansas, says:

Our Center's plan gets updated every year by our facilities department, so we know in advance what is going to happen. In the very beginning, when we built the Arts Center, we developed a forty-year replacement plan in order to get an endowment for those plans. That is working so far. We also have a long-term maintenance endowment and a routine maintenance endowment set up in such a way that these programs are funded in perpetuity.

To fund these plans, a number of managers set up an escrow account in which to set funds aside. James Brown, the executive director of the Civic Center in Oklahoma City, describes his replacement account:

All income from equipment rentals go back into that account, with which we buy new equipment annually. I started with that plan, but I have learned to constantly update the plan. Something that happens in all city-owned venues is that it is hard to compete with police and fire. You are going to lose every time if you have to compete with them for funding. This way, we constantly have state-of-the-art equipment. With user groups, we go over and above the expectations to serve them—we contact them every year and ask for a wish list.

The technology for sound and lighting equipment takes frequent replacement just to keep up, setting aside the issue of deterioration. But our capital plan and escrow account makes it so that when an equipment need falls under the equipment replacement domain, we buy the instruments. That way, we are always on top of the techno curve.

Rod Rubbo, president and CEO of the Cultural Center for the Arts in Canton, Ohio, has a capital replacement plan, but he also allocates annual funds according to specific needs presented to him by a committee made of representatives from all of his resident companies:

We look at their internal needs. They need a new toilet and a new sink and the walls painted, etc. We allocate funds to that, and then our maintenance staff and building superintendent, working with local contractors, deal with that area. We have two other areas that we allocate funds to. One is emergencies, where we put a budget figure toward possible emergencies as needed. Then we have special nonemergency repairs, but they come up outside of the budget area and you just need to deal with them, so we allocate funds to that as well.

Rubbo also has specific accounts set aside for long-range planning issues:

We used to do a five-year plan, but now we do a three-year plan because things are changing so much faster. We have what we call the Category One area, which is about $75,000 a year for high-priority things. Then we look at Category Two, which includes about $100,000 for larger capital projects, like if the Canton Ballet would like a new studio, or we need to add an office, etc. We try to prioritize them and bite one or two off in a given year, but a lot depends on the timing around raising funds in the community. We only go to the community for the largest capital items. For the smaller stuff, we draw from our internal resources.

Safety in Performing Arts Centers

Safety in performing arts facilities is an important topic, and one that has been well covered by various doomsayers. These are complicated issues, as a theater is both a place of public assembly and an industrial workspace. Charles Cosler is a theater consultant who has been helping in the design and planning of new performing arts facilities for twenty-four years. In the course of his work, he has seen many safe and unsafe theaters. Here he offers a harrowing anecdote:

> We were involved in a project in rural North Carolina where the building caught on fire just as it was being finished. The fire department had never been in a stage house, and they had no idea how to deal with the situation. They walked into a stage house that was full of smoke, they couldn't see anything, and they had no idea how the rigging worked. All they saw was that the main curtain was in the air and on fire, so their instinct was to cut it down and get it on the ground where they could deal with it, not knowing that it was counterweighted and that the minute they cut it off of the pipe, the pipe would fly up and the counterweight would crash down on the other side. That is exactly what happened. Sprinklers were going off and there was smoke damage in the stage house, but luckily, we had a fire curtain that operated properly, so the damage was limited to the stage alone.

The point of the story is that the situation could have been avoided with proper training. As Cosler says:

> The fire department should have been brought in as the project was being completed and been allowed to develop a fire plan for that building. Now, when we get toward the end of the project, I usually send out a letter to the architect and the owner saying we recommend that they get the fire department involved in visiting the new facility and developing a fire plan for it.

According to Robyn Williams, it is vital to keep the staff up on current trends in health and safety issues in the workplace, staying on top of what's happening in the field. This practice prevents an organization's staff from becoming so absorbed in their own work that they miss important industry safety issues as they arise. Williams has also instituted regular safety check-ups for the facility. In Portland, there is a safety committee that completes regular inspections on basic facility operations. Additionally, an outside inspector is brought in every two or three years to check up on the rigging system and submit a written evaluation. Williams says this practice was instituted because "even if your staff is really good, when you look at something over and over again, it is easy to not see problems."

Let's not dwell on the problems, but rather introduce a process whereby facility managers might develop a successful safety program. Here are some highlights from an article written by Jerry Gorrell in *Theatre Design and Technology Journal*[1]:

- A well-developed safety program is at the heart of any safe operation, whether that operation is a touring company or the activities in a specific facility. Some might consider having a safety program that covers only the "important things." While a partial safety program might seem better than having none, it is like a child's blanket: It makes us feel warm and cozy, but in a real emergency, it isn't much help. Generally, in a partial safety program, only the easy things get covered—the real problems are avoided, and the most serious hazards are ignored.
- A safety expert can be very helpful when you are developing your safety program. First, he or she can identify hazards that might be invisible or seem inconsequential to the people who work in your theater every day. Second, a safety expert can guide you through the maze of codes, regulations, standards, and recommended practices that become more numerous and complicated each day. And third, a safety professional will not accept the kind of short cuts and rationalizations we so often use in the theater: "this is art"; "it takes too long"; "it costs too much."
- A safety program will:
  - Ensure the safety of all persons working or entering the area
  - Meet your moral obligations to fellow human beings
  - Meet your regulatory and legal obligations
  - Save you money
- A safety program must cover the process and needs to emphasize avoiding shortcuts. Most accidents (about 92 percent) involve unsafe behavior, and

most of this risky behavior involves taking shortcuts with such things as body mechanics (lifting, for instance), not using the proper equipment (a ladder that's too short), or failure to use proper personal protective equipment.

- Your safety program must comply with regulations in the Occupational Safety and Health Act (OSHA) of 1970. In addition, if you are in a state with its own job safety and health program, the safety regulations adopted by your state apply to your facility. (State regulations may be more restrictive than federal regulations, but they may not be less restrictive or provide a less-safe working environment.)

- Your safety program should include the most recent safety standards and guidelines. Many of the OSHA regulations were adopted over twenty-five years ago, and some of the specific standards referenced by OSHA regulations—for instance, standards approved by the American National Standards Institute (ANSI)—have subsequently been revised or replaced. Additionally, simply meeting the OSHA regulations is not enough. There is a large body of safety information, procedures, accepted practices, and recommended practices that have been developed by manufacturers and trade associations like the American Society of Safety Engineers (ASSE) that should be followed as part of any safety program.

- The process of developing a theater safety program involves several steps:
  - Defining the scope of the plan (defining which areas and people are covered)
  - Obtaining the management's statement of policy with regard to safety
  - Assigning responsibilities to various levels of managers and employees
  - Conducting a hazard study or inspection
  - Responding to any hazards identified
  - Writing a safety manual
  - Keeping records
  - Once the plan is in effect, enforcing it

- The final consideration is the competent person. A competent person is one who is capable of identifying existing or predictable hazards in the surroundings or working conditions that provide an unsanitary, hazardous, or dangerous environment for employees. The competent person has authorization to take prompt corrective action to eliminate these conditions. OSHA frequently cites employers for failure to have a competent person at the work site. This is also frequently cited as one of the most common factors in accidents. Look closely at the people supervising the activities that take place on the stage. Do these people have formal training or education in the area they are overseeing? Do they have enough experience to supervise the activities for which they are responsible? Remember, after an accident, you, your qualifications, your associates' qualifications, and your safety program will be placed under a microscope. An effective safety program and proper training and supervision of all stage personnel may save you from that examination and, most importantly, save someone from being injured or killed.

NOTE

1. Gorrell, Jerry, "Safety Program Development for the Theater," *Theatre Design and Technology* (Summer 2000).

Chapter Three

Programming Theaters

Some years ago, the following quotation appeared in the *New York Times*:

Having a dark theater on Main Street is like having a corpse in your living room. It's dead and it's there.

It's a rather blunt way to make the point that nothing is more important in a theater than getting the lights on the marquee and a show on the stage. And it turns out that nothing is more challenging and satisfying for facility managers.

In chapter 2 we introduced the types of activity that generally occur in a theater and the challenge of balancing all of these demands on a space. In this chapter, we will focus on three key elements of programming—presenting, producing, and rentals—and how facility managers balance those often-competing interests.

Presenting

To begin with, let's be clear on what "presenting" means. Presenting means buying a show that already exists and bringing it to a facility. You pay an artist fee and other related costs. You take responsibility for promoting the show locally. And you collect the box office proceeds from the event, hoping that those direct revenues exceed your out-of-pocket costs.

Facility managers approach presenting in many different ways. They can allow a separate organization to become the presenter in a venue, collecting rental income from that organization and assuming minimal risk. They can contract with an organization that is a supplier of product to bring shows to the facility on the basis of shared risk. Or they can simply be a buyer of shows from various different sources, assuming all of the risk. There are variations on these approaches. In fact, some facilities do a combination of all three. They might have an arrangement with a local nonprofit to be the presenter of touring Broadway musicals, have a deal with Columbia Artists Management to bring a set of classical musicians to the facility, and then do separate bookings of touring children's programs.

Whatever the arrangement, success in presenting basically boils down to the following:

- The ability to gain access to good touring product
- The ability to pick the right shows for the market
- The ability to negotiate a good deal for the show
- The ability to promote the show effectively

Let's work through each of these challenges.

Access to Product

Presenting includes many different types of programs. For larger theaters, one generally thinks first of touring Broadway musicals. But there are many types of programs and presenters who activate theaters across the continent. There is touring dance, classical music, and opera. There is more popular music and entertainment, from traditional to contemporary music, and all of the entertainers whose names alone attract audiences.

These are very complicated times for presenters and promoters of touring entertainment. On the one hand, there is an incredible amount and variety of product that is available. And with improved communications technologies, it's a lot easier for facility managers to know what's out there and what's working in other markets.

Doug Sheldon of Columbia Artists Management speaks to these changes:

When I started in this business, not one institution in the arts had a fifty-two-week calendar or a fifty-two-week contract for its performances. That didn't really come until the end of the1960s and beginning of the 1970s. So, we saw dramatic changes in growth and increases in the business in the 1970s and 1980s, far surpassing anything else in the history of the arts here. Now we are seeing an era that forces us to rethink our management, and there is going to be a shakedown. My feeling is maybe we don't have quite as many of the truly great performers, but I think that is also an ebb and flow—it's generational. I do think the general level of talent appearing on the classical music stage is higher and higher in its level of purpose and training; we're not lacking for good artists. We have tons of good artists.

On the other hand, there are challenges for presenters and promoters. Key among these is the concentration of ownership of touring shows, venues, promoters, ticketing, and talent managers under the corporate control of Clear Channel Communications. This publicly traded corporation is also the largest single owner of radio stations and billboards in the United States.

To understand how this happened, we need to work backward a bit. In August 1999, Clear Channel acquired SFX Entertainment, which was itself a publicly traded corporation led by Robert Silverman. SFX was built over a decade through aggressive acquisitions all over the United States, fueled by cheap access to capital and an ambition to become the largest provider of live entertainment in the country. By 2000, there were divisions of the company devoted to music, theater, family entertainment, sports marketing, athlete representation, motor sports, multimedia entertainment, and television. These pieces were assembled from many of the most successful facilities, promoters, agencies, and service providers in the country. And then, with the acquisition by Clear Channel, suddenly there was a huge corporation in a position to control the delivery and promotion of live entertainment in major markets all over the country.

The prospect of the live entertainment industry being so completely controlled by one provider has many in the world of facility management uneasy. Harking back to Economics 101, monopolies can be viewed as a bad thing because they generally reduce the supply of product available in a market, increase the cost of that product, and, given the lack of competition, allow the quality of that product to decline. Not that all of these things have yet happened, but there is significant anxiety in the industry that some might happen. And there have certainly been negative impacts, as expressed by one facility manager who wishes to remain anonymous:

> I think it's absolutely dreadful. Most people I know think of Clear Channel as the evil empire. Their business practices are demonstrably predatory, and in every major market, they now constitute a vertical monopoly. They control access to the principal advertising media, they control the stages, and they control the talent. I can't see how that's good for the public, good for the arts, good for the artists. I've heard one too many stories about how they want a cut of your parking revenue. It's more and more and more all the time.
>
> But I really do think that it is having a homogenizing, risk-averse affect on the performing arts in the country, and I can think of very few things worse than self-censorship in that way. If we had a Justice Department worth its salt, Clear Channel would be broken up.

Judy Lisi of the Tampa Bay Performing Arts Center takes a more balanced view of the situation:

> I have both positive and negative views on Clear Channel and its impact. The tough part is how powerful they are. It's hard to go the independent route, because they control markets and they control product, which is difficult if you are an independent, particularly as it relates to touring Broadway.
>
> But one thing Clear Channel did in the 1980s, when it was Pace Entertainment, was to stabilize the road for Broadway, because in those years, it was common for a tour to cancel after only two or three promoters couldn't do the dates, which caused the tour to collapse, and then everyone down the road would be hurt. Producers couldn't put tours out for forty-eight weeks. There were years in the 1980s where there could be only six shows out in one year, and then if the show collapsed, you were left with huge holes. But because of their emphasis on subscriptions, they really did stabilize the road tremendously.
>
> So I think it's a mixed bag. There are two ways of viewing it. As to the quality of the work, I believe that the creative and technical advances of the

last twenty years by people like Cameron Mackintosh have really increased the quality of what's on the road, and audiences now expect that. You could put junk out there, but people know junk, and it just isn't good enough anymore.

Perhaps the best news for facility managers is that we've been through this before and that, as per those previous occasions, monopolistic control of the industry is not easily maintained.

In the 1890s, Klaw and Erlanger was a theatrical management firm that drove the development of the Theatrical Trust (or Syndicate), which came to control the touring theatrical and entertainment industry. By 1903, they controlled eighty-three first-class theaters, including twenty in New York City and Brooklyn. They developed "partnerships" with many of the leading actor-managers, and were in a position to intimidate local papers that dared to print negative reviews of their productions.[1]

The demise of the Syndicate was brought on largely by public reaction to their ambitions and the efforts of emerging competitive groups. Ironically, it was the Shubert Organization that led this charge, and then went on to assume that same level of monopolistic control that they had fought earlier.

In 1950, the United States Attorney General filed an antitrust lawsuit against the Shuberts and their partners claiming that they were eliminating fair trade. The lawsuit charged that the Shuberts controlled "practically all of the theatrical booking in the United States and operated or participated in the operation of forty of the most desirable and necessary legitimate theaters in the country." The Shubert Organization remains a major producer and presenting organization, but they have been replaced by Clear Channel as the dominant player in the industry.

So, who knows where the Clear Channel phenomenon is headed? On the one hand, presenters want to be able to bring high-quality programs to their markets, and are thus reluctant to enter into exclusive relationships that limit choices (as well as raise costs and threaten quality). On the other hand, there would be nothing worse than having no product to bring to the theater.

Picking Shows

Assuming your facility has some access to product through a range of producers, nothing is more crucial than the actual choice of shows to be presented in the market. And after generations of trying, facility managers have not solved the fundamental riddle of knowing (at least with any certainty) what will sell in their market, which creates tremendous stress and uncertainty. Some facility managers take a very systematic approach to choosing shows, doing their research and making informed decisions. Others are much more intuitive, relying more on their own subjective views of possible programs. And others worry less about how the market will respond, preferring to make their selections in terms of their mission and mandates to bring great work to the community.

Doug Sheldon talks about selling artists today versus forty years ago:

Today there is so much emphasis on the box office, the budget, and finances. That now plays a huge role in what people decide and why they decide to buy it and put in on their stage. I don't mean that it didn't play a role before, but it didn't play as much of a role because they basically knew that they would have a given amount of dollars in income or gifts. Now they don't know. Now they are guessing, but they do know that from week to week they have serious financial problems to manage, so selling is a harder business today. It's almost always harder; when they are in doubt, they are searching for something new because they have to figure out how to reach the public through the media they have available to them. And publicity sometimes is more important than how good the art is.

The other problem is that awareness of classical artists is less today than it was twenty years ago. I don't think that is true of the great artists, but that's only the top 10 percent. Then there is the 20 to 25 percent of the field made up of young artists that you can find a way to maneuver in or out of the field. But then there's the remaining 65 percent of the artists. That's where most of the struggles are, the bread and butter of the industry: not the introduction of new artists or the stars, but the core group in the middle.

And this is where most of the mistakes are made, because the awareness of this group is so low among the general population. One of the top five orchestras told me they were going to reduce their artistic budget, and if such and such a star wanted to play for a reduced fee, then they would engage that person. If not, they wouldn't hire him; instead, they would find a young artist, rather than use a mid-level professional.

So how important is it that the executive director has a strong point of view about programming? Here is Jeff Rosenstock of the Queen's Theater in the Park:

> The founder of the Arena Theater once said that if the theater must have a point of view, it might as well be that of its director. And I have a certain philosophy about plays, being a humanist and feeling like I try to touch people's souls and have people walk out with a certain level of fulfillment. I do think my choice is somewhat implicated, but I think in terms of programming, you go with your gut and see as much as you can and read as much as you can. I find I can't see everything—I've got a family, I've got to be at my own theater—but I know the prejudices of the critics. I know how each of the critics works, and I've seen enough plays that they've seen, so that I can say so and so is not going to like that.
>
> But I also like to listen to my audiences with half an ear, because although I don't want to cater to the audiences, I have to be realistic. I'm always trying to book an act where I'm likely to cover artists' fees and other direct costs with box office proceeds, so I'd better have an audience in the theater!

The Nuyorican Poets Café is a cultural institution on the Lower East Side of New York City. It was founded in 1973 as a place for the expression of local culture, starting with the spoken word. Over the years, it has grown and evolved into a presenter and programmer of extraordinary work, with an amazing level and diversity of programs. On any given week the organization might be hosting a poetry slam, a screenplay reading, a hip-hop concert, a modern art exhibition, and a theatrical production. All of this in one big, open room with a small platform stage at one end and a bar at the other end. To me, there are several keys to their success:

- They are always evolving, changing what they offer, and somehow making it work in that space.
- They remain absolutely authentic and responsive to their community, which is first and foremost their neighborhood on the Lower East Side of Manhattan.
- They are proactive in their programming. They don't just wait for shows to come to them, but send their staff of discipline-based curators out into the community for programs that fit their mission.

- Finally, with that big bar at one end of the room, they have a strong and steady source of earned income to supplement low ticket prices for most of their programs.

Carmen Pietri-Diaz is executive director of the Café. She talks about programming:

> We are very aggressive, but it has gotten to the point where we don't have to do that much scouting—artists and production companies are beating a path to our door. At the same time, it is absolutely critical to stay connected locally. It's very time-consuming because every time I go out, even if it's to run a quick errand, I have no idea when I'm going to get back because I run into people all the time and I want to know what they are doing, or they want to know what we are doing. And I want to bring their ideas back to the Café. I pick a lot of brains just going to get a cup of coffee.
>
> We don't have artists come in and sign a contract and say you are going to perform exclusively for the Nuyorican Poets Café and tie them down to one venue. We totally encourage them to go out and visit different venues and take what they've learned here, take it out there and share it with the rest of the public, share it with other artists, and I think they appreciate that. They come back and they bring other artists, they encourage other artists to come to the Nuyorican. Those artists who go out and make it big tend to remember us. Many of them have come back to do things for us. Last year we had our first building fundraiser, with Reggie Gains and Savion Glover donating performances.

Another key is an inherent conservatism on the financial upside of shows. Michael Currie of the American Theater in Phoebus, Virginia, says:

> For the thirty years I've been in the business, I always budget at 60 percent attendance, so that when I'm doing the annual budget with the city and my board, I will say, This is what I project our revenue to be. It's never above a 60 percent projection, because that way, if the reality is above, it makes us look good. If it's below, I've still got a little bit of a push. One of my great mentors taught me that years ago when I first started. Just don't budget at 100 percent because you think Marcel Marceau is going to sell out. There is no guarantee.

Eric Fliss, manager of the Colony Theater in Miami Beach, describes a good presenter:

A good presenter is someone who is interested in the art—interested in the artistic integrity of the artist—and it's not necessarily about how the show is costing me X amount of dollars, and I need to make a buck on this show. It's somebody who is interested in making an artistic statement by bringing that artist to that community.

The other part of being a good presenter is, when you are bringing an artist into a community, to create a way for that artist to connect with either the local artists or the residents in that community. So it's not just going to that show and seeing the person's work and then that person leaves; rather, how can you exploit the presence of that artist in the city—can you have a master class or a lecture? To me, the presenter who understands the unique opportunity of bringing that artist into the community and then making a connection outside of the actual show is doing a good job.

Negotiating the Deal

My separation of the issues of picking shows and negotiating the deal is somewhat deceptive in that the choice of a particular show often depends on the deal that brings it to the theater. Still, let's proceed with their separate consideration a bit longer.

Negotiating, like picking shows, is not a skill easily taught. Fundamentally, it requires a confident person who can play the game of working with producers, booking agents, and promoters to get the show he wants for the price he can afford. It's interesting that most of the facility managers we've interviewed take the view that their superior negotiating skills and strong relationships with the field have allowed them to get a better deal than their peers for touring programs.

Here is Jeff Rosenstock of the Queens Theatre in the Park on booking shows:

I have a 500-seat theater, so I've found that I cannot book the acts that I want early on, because they are going to want to play larger venues where they charge a higher fee. They'd rather be in a 2,000-seat house charging $25,000, than in a 500-seat house making a third of that. But I'm patient and I also know that every dance company tries to promise its dancers X number of weeks of work, and that there are weeks where they have a dark week, so working in my theater and generating some income is better than paying the dancers and generating no income.

We also are close to New York City, and there are artists that want to get New York reviews or visibility; thus, they need our space when they did not get into the Joyce Theater, or into BAM, or another major venue, but they still want to be in that New York metro area to try out a show. If you are in another part of the country, I think dollars do talk, and I think it's important to pick the companies that you want, to make the investment financially in those companies, and then to build a season around them.

I've found everything is open to negotiation. I'm amazed that artists I couldn't get two years ago, I can get a year later. I may try a different agent or a sub-agent, or be patient, or have a colleague call up. There are no rules in this game, except that you must develop a good reputation.

Promoting the Show

The final challenge is promoting the show effectively in the marketplace, which requires dedicated marketing staff to deliver a compelling message through appropriate media in order to reach audiences with a high propensity for purchasing tickets. Let's reserve this discussion for the next chapter, when we work through all of the elements of audience development.

Producing

Producing is different from presenting in that the facility takes additional financial risk in exchange for the opportunity to shape the product for their market. This can take several forms, depending on how active the facility is in creating the work. To make that point, here are stories from three Judiths— Allen, Daykin, and Lisi—on their versions of producing.

Judith Allen is vice chair of the North Carolina Blumenthal Performing Arts Center and was president of the operating organization from 1990 to 2003. She, along with a group of other performing arts facilities, has been investing in touring Broadway musicals:

In the past, presenters picked off the shelf of what was out there, no matter what it was—not only Broadway shows, but things like the *Three Mo' Tenors* or *David Copperfield*. We all chose what we felt our community would want. We didn't get involved in the creative or the producing part of anything because the product was there and because we were not trained in producing, investing, or partnering in any way.

Several years ago I joined the National Alliance for Musical Theatre, and it was the best thing that could have happened, because I really learned about producing. Not just the idea of producing, but the actual investing, how it happens, how do we produce shows—royalties, licensing, all of the things that most presenters didn't have because they didn't have to worry about the inner workings of the shows they booked. Now presenters are starting to realize the value of networking and of understanding and knowing producers.

Well, as a result of that knowledge, a group of people got together and started talking. And that was the beginning of the Independent Presenters Network, which included producers. And why is that important? You can produce anything and put it in your theater or put it in New York, but if it doesn't have a life after that, you are missing an opportunity.

Our education led us to become direct investors in Broadway productions, such as *Thoroughly Modern Millie*. We did it because we wanted to be part of the process. We wanted to have some say in when we got the show. We wanted the production to survive. And we wanted credit. So we invested in the Broadway production and again in the touring production, and we earned income on that investment as well as provided a great show for our customers.

Now we're working on *Bombay Dreams*. The producers have come to us, and we are working on an investment in the Broadway production, appropriate billing, right of first refusal for the first production that goes out, and the opportunity, if we want, for a prorated investment in that and a guarantee of X number of weeks. That never would have happened twenty years ago. We didn't have a circuit. We didn't have booking agents. It's a lot more advanced today. So now things are going to another level. And if we can do it for Broadway, I think we will soon be able to do it for other types of productions.

Judith Daykin retired from her position as executive director of City Center in New York City in the spring of 2003. Perhaps her greatest achievement there was the *Encores!*, an annual set of three almost-fully-staged productions of older American musicals. Judith tells a great story about the conception and ongoing success of that program:

> The genesis of *Encores!* was the Gershwin Festival we tried at the Brooklyn Academy of Music. We did a concert with all of the music from two musicals in one interminable evening—it was insanity. But the fact that people sat there and lapped it up suggested to me that there was a hunger for it. We were really clear about what we wanted to do, and we needed to be unique. We couldn't be a replication of what had gone on before, so we needed original orchestrations, a full cast and full ensemble, all adding up to a very expensive package. My philosophy from the beginning was: We are going to do it all the way or not at all, because otherwise, what is the point?
>
> In addition, it was clearly mission-driven. We lost a quarter-million dollars the first year, and struggled with the decision of whether or not to move forward. And we elected to go forward—City Center was in the pits at that time. When I got here, we had a deficit of about $700,000, we couldn't pay the vendors, and so on. I've just been going through the files, finding stuff from the original days where we would take old documents and use the backside of them—that is how desperate we were. We knew we could no longer count on dance, which had long been the mainstay at the house to carry us forward. The dance companies were dying right and left, cutting back on the length of their seasons, and that part of City Center's history was over. Maybe not over, but certainly a diminished relationship from the fifty-two years we had before. But we had to go forward with some kind of imaginative programming. And that was *Encores!*

Judy Lisi, president of the Tampa Bay Performing Arts Center, talks about the two ways that her organization goes beyond presenting into producing:

> First of all, I invest in quite a few Broadway shows. I like to be a player in the field, both because it helps me get the shows that I want, and because Broadway means a lot to my market. And I do think it's important to be part of the process and to have your institution be known as part of the process. Unlike other businesses, Broadway as a field doesn't have any research and development. So if we are going to look at it and say we want these shows, we have to try to help figure out where these shows are going to come from, and

I think we have an obligation to be part of it and support it if we can. Investing doesn't give me a big voice in how the show comes together, but I can get the shows earlier if I want to. And if I'm lucky, I can make money on those shows.

Secondly, we started an opera company here. There wasn't one in Tampa, and so I really felt that one of the things we do for our community is make sure our community has accessibility to the great art forms. You know, great opera doesn't tour; it's too big. And there is a lot of inferior opera. It's one of the few art forms you can't book in. So we produce three operas a year. And I must say, the quality is pretty extraordinary. I'm pretty happy with it. And I have a great artistic director. It's all within my organization. I think this could be a new paradigm for performing arts facilities. It is very hard right now to start any professional producing arts organizations, you know. In the sixties and seventies there was money for them, and there just isn't any more. But because it is under our aegis, I don't have all of the extra administration, marketing—all of these extra costs. It's just producing it. But I can use the staff here to do all of that other development and advertising and manage it. So, all the money goes right to the art form. And I think this could be a way for other performing arts centers to do things that they don't have in their own communities.

We also produce other shows here. We produce about three to four plays a year, and I produce a new small musical every year for one of my smaller 300-seat theaters. There is a gap in the community because we have no regional theater company. So I'm working with another local theater company. I commission them to do the plays, I work with them, and they are doing really nice work here. That has grown very nicely. Then we do a small musical every year in our 300-seat theater, and we put it on our Broadway series subscription and people love it—it's their favorite thing every year. But again, because I have a hard time finding product for that 300-seat theater, the only way to do it is in a long run, so I can advertise and keep the production values at a very high quality, which works really well.

Rental Activity

For many theaters, rental activity is the dominant form of programming. It doesn't tend to generate headlines and publicity like big-name presented events, but it is often the bread and butter that proves the value of the facility to the community.

When we are conducting feasibility studies for new or renovated facilities, we spend a good deal of time and effort understanding how local groups can activate facilities. And it's not just a matter of marking them down for a certain number of days and nights in a new space. Many groups fail in new or larger facilities. And lots of facilities struggle because of the weakness of those local arts groups. But in many other cases, new facilities are the catalyst that propels local arts organizations to higher levels of performance and success. In our experience, the key is often how organizations prepare for new facilities, and how ready they are to capitalize on the advantages that new or improved facilities present. We'll come back to this issue in chapter 8.

Let's here consider the ongoing relationship between local arts organizations and facilities. That relationship is often defined by how often local or regional arts groups are in the facility, renting space for performance, rehearsal, and other support functions. It is a fairly straightforward relationship for groups that are only occasional users, but a more complicated one for more active groups that depend on access to facilities on a regular basis.

Bruce McPherson, executive director of the Eisenmann Center in Richardson, Texas, describes levels of uses and users in his new facility:

> There are organizations that are considered primary users. They are Richardson-based, which gives them cheaper rates. It's a three-tiered rate scale. One is just for city of Richardson groups that existed before this building opened (and participated in the design process). It includes the Richardson Symphony—the largest of the groups—and Chamber Music International, an organization that presents chamber artists from around the world. On the second level are a few dance companies, including Dallas Repertory Ballet; the library's lecture series; and Richardson Community Band. All in all, I'd say ten or eleven Richardson-based groups use this building on an ongoing basis. And then everyone else is on the third level.

Often, local groups who are heavy users of a particular facility seek a "resident" status, which generally means some preferred access to facilities and cheaper rent. Kelly Shanley, general manager of the Broward Center in Fort Lauderdale, describes their definition of resident groups:

Our resident companies are the Florida Grand Opera, Miami City Ballet, Symphony of the Americas, and the Gold Coast Jazz Society. Each is presenting a series of the traditional arts in the building, so despite the fact that they are presenting similar series or the same series in Miami and also possibly in Palm Beach, this doesn't mean that they are not our resident company and we don't feel a sense of ownership. As a result of them being in those other markets, we probably do fewer total performances and dates with them than a resident company would normally do in the place they reside, but we also don't have to entertain as much rehearsal time. As a result, we are more active in attended activities rather than rehearsals and load-ins, which is good.

Here's Judith Allen on resident groups and her relations with them:

The problem that often occurs is that the citizens are usually told that a new building is meant for groups like the symphony and opera, and they don't understand anything about presenting. So those groups and their supporters feel that they should have right of first refusal in the facility. That squeezes out the performing arts center and its programs.

So in order to mitigate that, I put everybody in the room together and say the following: "In the beginning was the world, and the world stretched from the second week of September to the second week of May. That's thirty-five bookable weeks. And God also created only thirty-five weekends, and I can't do one thing to change it. Now I need four weeks in that booking season for Broadway shows. I am not going to say anything. You guys need to sit here and look at the calendar and create a template, and make sure that you spread my weeks out properly, because I don't want only Christmas and Easter. And if you don't, I'm going to triple your rent."

Well, that speech worked in both of the facilities I've managed. And both places are still using that template today.

One of the constant challenges for facility managers is determining the cost of accessing facilities for local and regional groups. Most facilities scale their rental groups according to some combination of the following criteria:

- Is it a for-profit or a nonprofit organization?
- Are they from the local community or away?

- Will they rent facilities for the presentation of a public program or for a private one?
- On what day of the week will they rent?
- Will the space be used for performance or for rehearsal?
- Have they gained "resident" status in the facility?

Facilities tend not to use all of these criteria, choosing to publish rates based most often on type of user and day of the week. But most facility managers also reserve the right to adjust rental rates based on other criteria and special circumstances. These are important judgment calls on the part of the manager. There are certainly cases where discounting the rent can help an emerging organization, generating goodwill and long-term benefits to the facility. But too much of that leads quickly to the erosion of earned revenues and the accumulation of deficits, which ultimately hurts all users.

Money is often the source of tension between facilities and users, but there are even more fundamental issues. Rae Ackerman talks about the constant challenge of maintaining relations with the resident organizations:

> I am the evil landlord. That is how I introduce myself. They all think they own the building and I know they don't, so that defines the nature of the relationship. It is variable. Mostly we do pretty well, but I've got a meeting next Tuesday with the general managers of the big four resident companies. I have no idea what the agenda is. I'm assuming that I am not doing something they think I should do or do differently.
>
> I've been on the job for thirteen years, and a lot of my work is keeping those relationships on track. It doesn't get easier or harder—it's variable. When I arrived here, my first meeting with the group of the resident companies was one in which I sat at the table while sixteen people screamed at me for two hours. They hated what I represented. They hated the relationship. I did a strategic planning exercise that included all of them and the commercial presenters that were dominant at the time. Everybody was included. And I came back and said, This is what you told me you wanted me to do and I'll do my best to do it, and they all said, Great. So we had a pretty good relationship, and we've gone on from there. I think it's been mostly pretty good. But as I say, there are irritants that will come up from time to time, and I assume I will hear about some of them in the next week.

For performing arts organizations dependent on access to performing arts facilities, there is a lot at stake. Following are highlights from a conversation with an executive director of a ballet company resident in a performing arts center. This gives a strong sense of the challenges from the user's perspective:

On the positive side, we enjoy a much-reduced rental rate. We could not afford to use the facility without that. And it's tough for the building. They are city-owned, run by a city organization, and have lots of fiscal constraints as well. They have certain benchmarks that they have to meet, so a lot of their rentals are financially driven.

As a resident company, we enjoy the status of being able to have the lowest rental rates that they can afford. The problem is that because of the financial demands on the building, we are looked at as expendable, or we are looked at as an organization that may have to move if in fact the commercial venue can come in and bring in more cash flow. For next year, we have been asked to move because *The Lion King* is coming in. And that's very frustrating.

So we don't have control of our own destiny. If we have a grievance, there is a formal grievance process that is very cumbersome because it is a city organization. If there is a problem, I go to the facility manager. He really has the final say. If I don't like what he says, then it really is very tough to fight because it then involves City Hall. And it's usually not worth it.

And there are other challenges: We don't control the front of house, we really don't control the back of house, we are a tenant for the days that we are there. So we are subject to the rules and regulations of the theater. Probably one of my biggest surprises out here is that we sign an agreement saying we are liable for anything that happens to that theater, whether it was the Ballet's fault or not. So from a liability standpoint, it is very risky. And we have limited ability to influence the level of service that our customers get.

I also go crazy about the user fee, which is a fee on every ticket. So they make more money the more tickets we sell. It is a flat amount of $1.50 per ticket, which is not that much, but it does add up. And I would bet if you surveyed our patrons, they wouldn't know that it wasn't going to the Ballet.

Out of all the disciplines, ballet may be under the most pressure in performing arts facilities. Virtually all major companies make most of their earned income off the annual production of *The Nutcracker*. But now a series of performing arts facilities are putting up competing holiday shows or, even more dramatically, bumping *The Nutcracker* from their building in favor of a show presented by the facility. This has happened for the 2004 Holiday Season at the Wang Center in Boston, where the Boston Ballet is being bumped in favor of the Radio City Music Hall touring holiday show. Norbert Mongeon of PFM articulates the challenge for facility managers:

> If you are a building manager and you take a position to blow off your ballet company and there is no other place for them to go in the community, you may be putting them out of business. Here, Trinity Rep covers 60 percent of its budget with revenues from *A Christmas Carol*. Now, if I did a competing *Christmas Carol* over here at this building, I would be the pariah of the community.

Perhaps nothing provokes more grumbling on the part of facility renters than the mention of user fees. Most facilities charge a base rental fee for access to facilities, and then add additional charges for such things as:

- Use of the box office
- The rental of additional or special performance equipment
- The use of technical labor to bring in and run shows
- Event security during the time of performance

Complaints from users tend to revolve around how expensive these extras are and how they add up quickly, well beyond the resources of the organization. From the facility manager's perspective, there are no easy options. Groups renting facilities should be using the professional services and equipment of the building. Rental rates that automatically include all of these extra costs would most certainly dissuade many users from coming to the facility. So the challenge for managers is to design a package of mandatory and optional charges that is clear and fair to users while still ensuring that the facility is used safely and professionally.

Even more insidious than user fees is the increasingly common practice of placing a surcharge on tickets, whereby the facility collects a fee from the ticket buyer, not the facility renter. Sometimes the fees are a dollar amount added to the ticket price or simply a percentage premium. They usually have worthy-sounding names like "Facility Maintenance Fee" or, for a historic structure,

"Theater Restoration Fund Contribution." In any event, they represent an additional indirect cost to users, as their customers are obliged to pay more to attend performances.

Civic, Corporate, and Private Rental Activity

One of the most significant recent trends in facility management is the discovery that corporations, individuals, and groups love holding special events in theaters, and the exploitation of that fact by astute managers. Here is Bruce MacPherson talking about corporate use of his new facility in Richardson, Texas:

> Our building is called the Charles W. Eisemann Center for Performing Arts and Corporate Presentations. The reason for that name and the focus of the design has to do with where we are situated in Richardson, the heart of the telecom corridor. We wanted to encourage corporate use of the facility, so it was part of the program. It is much easier to adapt a corporate use into a performing arts environment than it is to make an arts group work in a corporate lecture hall.
>
> Across the street from us is a brand new hotel and conference center, and our proximity to that allows us to work in tandem with them to accommodate larger conferences and events.
>
> We also have a meeting banquet hall with 3,150 square feet that is totally outfitted for all AV systems. It also has a nice hardwood floor, wood finishing, and fabric inset panels for acoustics. That room can double as a small recital space for string quartets and piano recitals.

The financial impact of this activity can be very positive. Reviewing the financial records of Avery Fisher Hall a couple of years ago, I observed that while corporate events represented only 15 percent of the dates on the calendar, they accounted for almost 60 percent of the rental income in the hall! But, according to Judith Allen, the financial impact of this activity is only part of its value:

> The money you earn is secondary in importance to the fact that a performing arts center is the center of the community. And the only way you can be a

center of a community is to provide access. So the primary reason for corporate meetings, weddings, bar mitzvahs, spelling bees, schools, etc., to come is because those people need to understand that they have access to their center. And then I achieve my financial goals as well.

Balancing Local Rentals and Touring Presentations

One of the great programming challenges is the need to balance rental activity with touring programs. Here is Kelly Shanley of the Broward Center on that topic:

> I think we do balance it; others would certainly say that we don't. Right now, I would say this building contains the perfect mix of resident companies and Broadway shows. We can accommodate all the resident companies with the desired number of dates that they want, along with Broadway, perfectly well in any given season. The only difficulty comes when they don't get the day of the week they want, or their schedule in the other buildings conflicts with the ones here. So Broadway isn't always the problem. Their schedules conflicting with each other can be the problem, and their schedules in the other buildings can be the problem. Some like to say that Broadway kicked them out, because that is safer. Of course, we remind them that Broadway is among the only activities in this building that is not subsidized and therefore is subsidizing them, but they don't like to hear that either. The truth is, right now they can all be accommodated just fine.

For Linda Shelton at the Joyce Theater in Manhattan, the difference between renting and presenting is more subtle and gradual, with an in-between approach:

> To be a successful programmer, you have to be in touch with your audience and be on top of what's available, whether that is traveling to see things or having relationships with other presenters. For us, the original idea was to have everybody treated the same, and everybody would be part of that program. Then we realized that we wouldn't be able to get an event that would be different or provide another kind of attraction, particularly when it came

to foreign artists or new groups who didn't quite get why they had to rent the theater. We thought that if we want to keep the programming at a certain level, we're going to have to start presenting, so we added the presentation program into the whole concept a little bit later.

We are the home for many New York groups, and the ones that can afford to rent usually do, but sometimes we'll take some financial risk. Sometimes a company is trying something new and they can't take the risk of the whole thing, or maybe they're extending their run from one week to two weeks or something riskier.

A company that can use its marketing and fundraising techniques to its best ability can do well at the box office; these companies don't want to be presented. They want to go out and say, We are self-presenting at the Joyce, and we need X amount of dollars. I think the groups can probably raise more if a funder knows that he is taking the risk.

We use the word "curatorial" to imply that we are after the highest quality. It implies a selection process. We get almost two-thirds more applications than we can accommodate, so we have to be very selective.

An Approach to Programming

We have worked our way through a number of opinions and insights that suggest how the world of programming is both important and complicated, challenging and rewarding. So let's finish this chapter by laying out an approach to programming. The question is: How do you decide what to do in your theater?

1. **Relate to the mission**. For a nonprofit organization, all planning and decision-making must start with a review of the organizational mission. Whether it's deciding on a particular show, setting a season, or establishing rental rates, it all begins with careful consideration of how those decisions are consistent and in line with the mission.
2. **Understand the market**. As so many of our facility managers have said, an understanding of the market is critical. Whether it comes through research, experience, or something you feel in your bones, there must be a strong sense of what might work and what might not. Of course, it must be accepted that no one can really predict how a particular show will do.

There are too many variables. Markets are always changing. And there are so many issues beyond the control of the facility managers. But you still have to try.

3. **Determine an appropriate level of artistic and financial risk**. Given the uncertainty of programming choices, it is critically important for an organization to understand what level of risk is acceptable for the organization. Tom Webster, who runs the University Theater at the University of Montana, has a very small budget allocation from the university, and limited ability to raise additional funds. He can't afford to lose money on many presented events. So his choices are based not so much on the upside, relevance, or interest in the community, but rather on minimizing downside risk with shows that virtually guarantee an audience.

4. **Programming decisions are artistic decisions first and foremost**. The facility director is both impresario and steward of the artistic character of the venue through its programming choices. Arts management consultant Victor Gotesman says, "The creative process of program selection is at the heart of what makes a building tick. The programming mix and the diversity and variety of artistic events, coupled with the quality of artistry and program content, are tangible artistic considerations in program selection. How to select a program that will attract, satisfy, lead, and/or challenge an audience with a high level of artistic excellence is the key challenge facing all facility directors and programmers."

5. **Assess local demand**. Consider the nature and level of demand on the part of local and regional groups for access to facilities while also considering their ability to pay rents and related charges.

6. **Set goals and objectives**. After a look at the mission and the market, and after coming to terms with one's tolerance for risk, the facility manager is in a position to set broad goals and objectives for programming. It is here that one should take a point of view on how the building will be activated with some balance of local and touring product, how local programming and organizations should be supported, how and from where touring programs should be attracted, and how much of the organization's resources should be devoted to these efforts.

7. **Secure sources of product**. The next challenge is securing product for the facility. For rental, education, and other community programs, this means building relationships with producing organizations and other users. It

also entails the creation of operating policy that considers "resident" status and other means to tie a creator of programs to the facility. On the presenting side, it is a matter of finding and booking shows, whether through another organization, with some form of contractual relationship with a producing organization, or simply as a buyer of shows from various sources.

8. **Identify additional rental opportunities**. Assess the demand for rental space on the part of corporate, civic, and private renters of facilities, and the ability of the facility to accommodate that demand without compromising presenting and arts rental activities. Set rates and fees to maximize the financial return on this activity, which also supports the concept of community access.

9. **Set a financial plan**. With additional knowledge of what's to be put on and by whom, the facility manager is in a position to forecast financial performance. This is more important and more difficult with presenting, particularly on the revenue side. But is absolutely critical to planning.

10. **Set a marketing plan**. To support the generation of earned revenues from programming, the facility manager must set the marketing plan. We will spend more time on this particular challenge in the next chapter.

11. **Set a fundraising plan**. The other element of financial planning is consideration of how programming choices affect (or are aided by) fundraising. Presenting tends to attract more corporate partners, as we will discuss in chapter 7. But there is also the issue of how the support of community-based groups and education programs attracts additional philanthropic dollars to the facility.

Laying this out with numbered points suggests a very linear and straightforward approach. But that is not necessarily so, since, for example the marketing and fundraising plans affect the financial plan, which then affects how product is secured for the facility. In particular, it is important to recognize how markets and audiences evolve over time, and what role the programmer can play in bringing them along. Here is Randy Vogel, performing arts center administrator for the new Mesa Arts Center:

> As a programmer, you've got some educating to do. You have to develop audiences, bringing people into the building, educating them about what you are

going to do, and developing a trust with your audience. Imagine being a seventy-five-year-old person who has never been to a real arts center before. And you are sold tickets to the Tibetan monks and their throat singing, for which you paid $40 a ticket. And this was your first experience at the arts center. Are you coming back? Not likely.

Finally, I would like to include a great quotation from Joseph Golden's book, *Olympus on Main Street.*[2] Golden wrote the feasibility study for the Civic Center of Onondaga County, then became the project manager and ultimately the executive director for the Center. He wrote a great book about that experience, full of stories and advice on facility development and management. Here is his unvarnished view of programming:

A philosophy of programming poses a moral issue that managers may wish to consider: Is a facility merely housing, or can it be a force that alters a community's vision of itself? The bias of what follows is undisguised: If a facility does not seriously attempt to fulfill both its mechanical (night-filling) and moral (soul-stretching) roles, it is a failure; it does not deserve to be built. If built, it will deserve all the criticism it will receive as a perpetuator of tunnel vision and elitism.

NOTES

1. Fields, Armond and L. Marc Fields, *From the Bowery to Broadway: Lew Fields and the Roots of American Popular Theater.* (London: Oxford University Press, 1993), 175.
2. Golden, Joseph, *Olympus on Main Street: A Process for Planning a Community Arts Center.* (New York: Syracuse University Press, 1980), 67.

Audience Development

For our purposes, "audience development" means attracting customers to theaters and the events held within them. There is a broad set of activities designed to build awareness and support for the institution in the community. Let's leave that for chapter 12, when we address community relations. For now, let's focus on the effort of putting "bums in seats." For nonproducing theaters, this includes shows that are presented by the facility itself and shows presented by local organizations, the promotion of which might be supported by the facility.

This is an area of profound challenges for facility managers, given the following:

- Competition for consumers' share of time and brain space is intensifying. Targeted and provocative advertisements bombard people daily from all directions, and marketers must rise above the clutter to be noticed.
- Commercial marketers are mounting large campaigns using multiple channels with sophisticated planning, compelling messages, and huge outlays of capital.
- Nonprofit arts marketers are often recent arts administration graduates with limited skills and experience (and a meager salary), or long-time arts

publicists and promoters with limited knowledge or inclination to explore the new frontiers of marketing.

- All nonprofit arts organizations struggle with the decision of how much to invest in marketing. For a mission-driven enterprise, a traditional marketing approach ("give the consumers what they want") must be subservient to the larger issues of what is created/presented and why.

The marketing of arts events is becoming more difficult, more expensive, and, given the overwhelming quantity of promotions thrown at consumers, potentially less effective. Rather than simply working through the fundamentals of marketing, let's focus on some of the more pressing issues and look at how successful facility managers respond to those challenges and opportunities.

Developing a Marketing Focus

Often, the first step for performing arts marketers is to promote a marketing focus in the institution. In addition to her work as director of marketing for New York City Opera, Claudia Keenan Hough teaches marketing in New York University's graduate program in performing arts administration. One of her major efforts is bringing a marketing focus into the nonprofit sector. She says:

> Commercial organizations are more marketing-centric than performing arts or nonprofits in general. We are not a smart business model. A lot of arts organizations spend between 18 and 20 percent of earned income on marketing, which is not much money, especially in a city like New York, where you are really held hostage by the *New York Times*. In order to compete, we must spend more money, and because the market has changed and people are buying much closer to the date of the performance, it requires more frequent advertising. With advanced sales you can be more leisurely, but now you need to be in the customer's face every minute of the day before each performance to encourage them to make that last-minute decision. It's a lot more expensive. And, unfortunately, many organizations cut marketing budgets when times are tough.
>
> But the more basic challenge for the marketer is to get involved earlier. Almost every marketer I know is given the season with instructions to "go sell

it." And that marketer needs to say in advance, "I need to be a part of the planning process. I need to help inform the decisions that we are making." You have to assert yourself. You have to let those people know that you are doing this for the benefit of the organization, and your input is imperative in advance, before they decide on the season.

It all sounds very straightforward, but what Keenan Hough is suggesting has been a very hard sell in the performing arts. Forty years ago, such talk was heretical. For pioneers like Ellen Stewart, the founder of La MaMa e.t.c. (experimental theatre club) in New York City, it was never about marketing:

> We got some audiences when I started, but it wasn't about that. I stood on one corner and tried to get you to see our shows. And when you got to 321 East 9th Street, some steps were missing on the staircase going down to the basement. So you had to climb down, and we didn't want the lights on because we didn't want the police to know what was going on. So you'd have to skip two steps, and someone at the end would be waiting and give you a chair and . . . then when you opened the door, there would be a flood of lights. And I'm telling you, if we had ten people, that was glory, hallelujah.

Performing Arts Audiences

Understanding performing arts audiences and predicting their behavior is a significant challenge. Extensive studies on the size, characteristics, trends, and behavior of performing arts audiences have been done, but there is still much more art than science to understanding audiences and predicting their behavior.

Probably the best recent research on performing arts audiences is within "The Performing Arts in a New Era," a major study completed in 2001 by the Rand Corporation, with major funding from the Pew Charitable Trusts.[1]

Chapter 4 of the study, Audiences for the Performing Arts, reviews past research on audiences and summarizes some of the key concepts. Following is a summary of some of those concepts and their relevance to performing arts facility managers.

Levels of Participation

We measure participation in the performing arts in terms of the absolute level of consumption (total attendance), the rate of participation in a given period (the percentage participating), and the frequency of participation (number of performances a year). Levels of participation, measured by recent studies like the NEA's Survey of Public Participation on the Arts, suggest that the audience for the performing arts is significant and has grown slightly over the last fifteen years.

At the same time, that participation varies tremendously by discipline. Those who participate via the media (e.g., listening to the radio), attend events (e.g., going to a show), or actively participate (e.g., taking a dance class) do so at very different levels when broken down by discipline. While almost 25 percent of adults will have gone to a musical theater production in the last year, only 6 percent have gone to the ballet and 5 percent to an opera performance.

The Characteristics of Participants

Here we identify the sociodemographic and other characteristics associated with participation. The study confirms that the level of educational attainment is the key predictor of participation in the performing arts; those with higher levels of education are much more likely to participate and attend than others. It is not clear why education drives participation, but it is due to some combination of factors including exposure to the arts as a child and having taken arts courses during school years. Early exposure to arts seems important, but several recent studies suggest that classes taken during college have a stronger effect on participation than classes at earlier levels. Education also helps individuals deal with the abstract (important for the appreciation of work of many art forms), and highly educated people may be more interested in the social dimensions of participation.

Factors That Influence Participation

Finally, we search for factors that influence demand, such as sociodemographic changes, changes in taste, changes in practical issues like the supply of programs and their cost, and changes in the stock of experiences that consumers have with the performing arts. The most important idea here for performing arts facility marketers is that you must sell a much broader experience than simply the performance itself. Consumers are attracted to some events and repelled by others based on how they found out about the performance, how easy it was to purchase tickets, how easy it is to find a parking spot, the ability to have a meal or drink in conjunction with the performance, the courtesy of facility employees, the ease with which seats were found, and so on. Thus, successful facilities are able to influence much more than the quality of performance and then have the ability to sell all of the elements of a positive experience to potential consumers.

One of the most contentious and difficult choices for performing arts marketers is how to promote events both to active attendees of the performing arts and to nonattendees. The Rand Report relates that the distribution of participation is highly skewed, in that a relatively small percentage of total attendees account for the vast majority of all visits. It is helpful to sort the overall population into three categories: those who rarely, if ever, attend; those who infrequently attend; and those who are frequent attendees. The report goes on to say:

> The literature offers two slightly different explanations for this phenomenon. The economics literature, for example, suggests that the more knowledgeable people are about the arts, the more likely they are to participate, because they gain more satisfaction from a given level of consumption than do people who are less knowledgeable. The leisure literature, on the other hand, tends to view this phenomenon in more psychological terms: A small fraction of the participants in leisure activities become serious "amateurs" for whom the activity becomes an end in itself. In either case, this phenomenon helps to explain why the term "addiction" is sometimes used to describe the attraction of art lovers to the arts.[2]

The idea of addiction may be related to an interesting emerging theory: that audiences seek a combination of entertainment and fulfillment in return for their attendance at events. In addition, it is important to find out whether potential consumers seek to participate on their own or with others. In this way, it is easier to imagine how aficionados are most likely to be those who seek fulfillment from their social participation in events, whereas occasional attendees are those seeking entertainment in a social setting.

There is certainly a strong argument to be made for active promotion to active attendees who are already informed and inclined to attend. Arts organizations are generally able to reach out to them directly, with direct mail and other channels such as advertising in carefully chosen publications. The problem is that the competition for active attendees is very intense and, given some of the broader demographic trends described earlier in the chapter, it is an older and ultimately shrinking segment of the population.

There are also advantages in targeting occasional attendees. It is a much bigger group, and the fact that they have already attended means that they are relatively aware, informed, and perhaps inclined to attend. But this is a much tougher group to find, with many competing interests and activities vying for a place on their calendars.

Finally, there are the rarely-if-ever attendees, the group most difficult to reach, to inform, and to convert into audiences. But, taken from the perspective of mission and long-term viability, sometimes this becomes the vital segment. According to Robyn Williams of the Portland Center for the Performing Arts:

> In order to increase your audiences, you want to get the folks who don't normally set foot in your building to come in. Position your facilities as more of a community player or community center so that people will come downtown into the building. Eliminate that scare factor. Help them realize it can be casual and fun, that it's not stuffy or intellectually hard to understand. Also, any way you can get kids into your building to have a good time and create good memories for them, it just increases the chance of having them as your future adult audience. Those are critical steps in audience development.

The Rand Report identifies the following key trends for performing arts marketers:

- More people are attending the performing arts at present, but rates of attendance remain stable. This means the same types of people are attending the same programs with the same frequency, but there are simply more people in that group through population growth.
- Participation through the media is growing, meaning that more people are content to experience the arts through means such as television and radio.
- There is a greater desire among consumers for flexibility in how they

participate in the performing arts. This confirms a recent but powerful trend away from subscriptions and toward single-ticket sales.

Finally, the report suggests what may be coming:

- Demographic changes, most importantly around the aging population, increased levels of educational attainment, and the ethnic composition of the population. These changes will have profound impacts on participation, changing patterns of attendance, levels of attendance, and the demand for a greater variety of forms and styles. There is much uncertainty and anxiety about this trend, particularly as one generation of arts attendees is replaced by a younger generation whose participation has (to this point) been much lower than their parents'.
- Economic changes, such as rising incomes, are positive for arts participation, but there is also a trend toward viewing leisure time as a valuable commodity to be carefully allocated. This rising opportunity cost of time is likely to heighten the preference for flexible activities that can be tailored to individual preferences.
- The role of technology will continue to influence participation. On the positive side, new technologies will allow consumers to personalize their consumption, as well as increase participation through the media and by direct involvement in creating art. How technology ultimately affects participation in live events is uncertain, and may boil down to the importance of social interaction in the experience and the extent to which media participation is viewed as a substitute for attendance.
- The report suggests that there could be an overall increase in demand for the performing arts, but that increase will be uneven across forms of participation, sectors of the population, and disciplines. Several factors could increase consumption through the media, more direct involvement in the creative process, and the development of a variety of niche and specialized markets for consumers with the incentive and means to tailor consumption to their individual tastes.

Having established that the world of performing arts participation is changing and full of challenges for arts marketers, let's consider some of the particular issues and responses in the field.

Demographic Shifts in Performing Arts Audiences

The demographic composition of the United States is changing, with the population aging, educational attainment increasing, and the ethnic mix of the population diversifying. The challenge for performing arts marketers and facility managers is how to adapt to this changing world. Kelly Shanley of the Broward Center tells a great story about their work in adapting his marketing approach to demographic changes.

Fully aware of the sharp increase in the Hispanic population in Miami and Fort Lauderdale, Shanley and his team took a nontraditional approach to reaching new audiences. "Most people would have their programming director call New York and find some Hispanic-themed programs and hope people would come," says Shanley. "We started at the community affairs level, going out and contacting individual communities, and what we found out pretty quickly was that the Hispanic community can't all be painted with the same brush. There are many varied segments to the Hispanic community, and each of them feels a great sense of their own identity and doesn't necessarily want to be labeled 'Hispanic.'"

The Brazilian community provided an ideal test case for the Center's approach to audience development. "Brazilians speak Portuguese and do not consider themselves Hispanic, despite being such a large South American country," he says. "They get thrown into that group and they don't like it. We made contact with them early on because Brazilians are a substantial population down here, and they have great pride and connection in their own community."

The Broward Center's community affairs director started to move in Brazilian circles, talking to the leaders of that community, finding out what they knew about the Broward Center and their perceptions of the facility. "Three years ago we had our first 'Brazil Night' at the Center," says Shanley. "For that event, we had the Consul General of Brazil from Miami attend, complete with bunting on a box, receptions, business and political leaders, etc. That night, the Consul General stood on the stage and said, 'The Broward Center is the new home of the Brazilian community in South Florida.'"

That endorsement by the Brazilian Consul had a powerful impact. "If we hadn't made the grassroots connection to the opinion leaders of that community to acknowledge the Broward Center as a home for the Brazilian community, it wouldn't have worked," says Shanley. "There would not have been the same response if Kelly Shanley, an Irish white guy from Boston, stood up there and said the same things. But we have the endorsement of the Consul General, and we did our homework to find out what is important to the Brazilian community, what artists they'd like to see, what kinds of food and merchandise they would want at concession stands, stuff they are familiar with."

Shanley says that he and his community relations team are now building similar relationships and programs with the Venezuelan community, beginning again at the grassroots level, to show that the Broward Center is about much more than "dead Western European composers."

It's a great story. But what's important is the underlying approach, which might be summarized in the following steps:

1. Conduct research to understand the changing marketplace
2. Reach out to targeted segments of the market and build individualized relationships and partnerships with those communities
3. Identify programs that fit those communities
4. Promote those programs through the appropriate media
5. Create an environment that is comfortable and welcoming to that group

Competition

How we view competition in the performing arts is a very important issue. The challenge is in the definition of "competition." Are we competing only with facilities that do what we do, with organizations that produce work similar to what we present, with all other types of live events, or with any other use of leisure time and money? The answer seems to be different depending on where you are and whom you're targeting.

Teri Gorman, vice president for external affairs for the Broward Center in Florida, takes a very broad view of competition:

I think we compete with every business that takes disposable income. That would be sports and DVDs at home and movies and any number of things that show up in your weekly guide to entertainment, when people have X amount of dollars in their pockets and say, What should we do tonight? In that sense, we even compete with restaurants. In response, we follow the old expression, "find your niche, get rich." We ask ourselves: "What is it that is unique about this experience that doesn't occur in other places?" You have the engagement with the artist; you have the live experience; you have the pampering kind of experience at the performing arts center. It's an excuse to get dressed up, to bust out your nice clothes. So yes, it would be on all those bases that we compete, drawing the distinction between other experiences and our own.

The Tampa Bay Performing Arts Center coexists in a market with two other large performing arts centers in Clearwater and St. Petersburg. Here's vice president of marketing Michael Kilgore on competition and those relationships:

I don't worry too much about the other Centers, and I don't think they worry too much about us. We sort of all find our niches, and we all have things we are known for. We are known for Broadway, our cabaret series, and opera. We have our strengths, and there are things that people have come to expect from us—a certain level of quality and a certain type of experience, and that is what we push. I think about competition much more for smaller events, because our marketing budget is so limited. And there, it's more nontraditional competition like football or hockey games.

Kathleen O'Brien is chief operating officer of the Tennessee Performing Arts Center in Nashville. She considers competition more in terms of the "what" than the "who":

Our competition is the collective, very busy schedules of people. I know that I personally look forward to a night where I can go home and have nothing on my schedule. We are just so busy. I think getting both people's attention and their willingness to surrender their time are the most difficult barriers. Another is to show that subscribing is the better way to patronize the arts, that there truly are benefits for you in doing it as opposed to "cherry picking" as a single-ticket buyer.

Branding and Positioning

Branding and positioning are two words that tend to confuse, intimidate, or freeze up art administrators because of their association with the commercial sector and the pursuit of the almighty dollar. But branding and positioning need to be understood and embraced for what they are: ways for a nonprofit organization and facility to consider how they are perceived in the marketplace and how they should attempt to position themselves in the minds of their potential audiences and stakeholders. Let me present those ideas separately.

Branding

Branding is the external perception of the organization or facility. When people hear the name of your theater, what do they think of first: great shows, a historic building, or bad parking? A critical element of branding is understanding the differences between perceptions and reality, and working to bring those two into line. If a consumer believes that the parking around the theater is limited, then it is not enough for you to say that there are 800 spaces within half a mile. What you have to do is change the perception. That's the good news about branding. You have the ability to change external perceptions about your theater by virtue of what you program, how you promote it, and how you address those other elements of the theater-attending experience.

Byron Quann of the Whitaker Center for Arts and Science in Harrisburg, Pennsylvania, has this to say about branding:

> We use the word "branding" a lot. When I got here, I did something I've done every place I go: I grabbed up all the stuff that had our name on it, pinned it up on the wall, and looked at it to see whether I liked it, what it connoted, and whether there was any relationship from one piece to another. It is a specific thing you have to do, but it is an assessment of the continuity of what you are saying about yourself and what it means. You can do that in most any organization and be horrified. You do something to fix it, and then over time, you do it again and you get horrified again. I spend an awful lot of time making sure that every aspect of what we say and the way we look and do things is consistent, trying to maintain a certain level of quality.

But how do you brand the building and all of the different programs within? Peter Herrndorf at the National Arts Centre in Ottawa shares their approach:

> First of all, we brand each of the component organizations separately, so that the National Arts Centre Orchestra has a distinctive brand, the National Arts Centre English Theatre has a different brand, and so on. The season program, launches, and brochures are all separate. We market them around their artistic leadership, so that there are people here who are really only supporters and fans of the National Arts Centre Orchestra, some who are only supporters of the National Arts Centre French Theatre. The problem over the last few years was not how to brand the components, but how do you brand the whole? It was the reverse problem. We operate with the four main program areas and we market each program separately. We operate with our community stage; we operate a very clear brand with education. The National Arts Center itself is a kind of overriding brand.

Positioning

Positioning is a similar concept; it is about how you position your organization/facility in the mind of the consumer. Again, we are dealing with external perceptions, but now we must consider all of the other choices facing consumers. That might include another theater offering competing programs. But it also includes many other opportunities to view movies, art galleries, television, and so on. So, one must create an external perception of the organization/facility that is distinct and attractive in the minds of potential consumers.

Not long ago, I had the opportunity to hear a branding and positioning strategy presented to the senior staff of Proctors Theatre in Schenectady, New York. Patrick Reilly of Smith and Jones, an advertising agency based in Troy, New York, made the presentation.

The study sought to discover the Proctors brand, and the recommendations were based on meeting and talking with facility users, then analyzing those conversations. While the results were not quantifiable, their insights were valid.

The general public perception was that Proctors is about entertainment, not enrichment. Respondents associated Proctors with musicals, good seats, beautiful decor, a positive experience, and good parking. In thinking about brand, the Proctors staff decided to focus their ideas on the three segments of the brand audience: loyal patrons; nonloyal patrons; and staff, volunteers, and board.

Based on the desire to convert nonloyal patrons, Proctors came up with a new, more focused positioning statement: "To anyone within reach of the media buy, Proctors represents real, honest entertainment because it is the only landmark venue offering world-class programs in an atmosphere that respects each individual's relationship with the arts."

But a positioning strategy is only as good as the programs that support it. The Proctors' staff realized that risk, on the part of consumers, must be rewarded with good entertainment, and in order to mitigate the consumers' risk, an intensified education and outreach plan was called for. So, the next step was the development of a communications plan, with the following objectives and insights:

- Increased awareness will create familiarity on the part of consumers
- People will have opportunity to be curious with a broader media approach
- Clever communications will pique the interest of consumers
- Avoid the highbrow and stay populist
- Turn risk into opportunities to connect and have fun

The final step was the presentation of a media strategy, which directed the organization's expenditures toward more outdoor advertising; maintaining more focused print advertising (multishow, venue-oriented, specific, creative); limited television advertising; driving customers to the Web site; using direct mail to inform and entice potential customers; and using public relations to deliver a greater depth of information to potential audiences.

It is interesting how the presentation flowed from the abstract to the specific, from the strategic to the tactical. Finally, it was explicit in its suggestion that 75 percent of the organization's marketing resources should be targeted toward occasional arts attendees, with only 25 percent dedicated to aficionados and nothing invested in nonparticipants.

Subscription Marketing

National studies show that more and more consumers are shifting from subscriptions to single-ticket purchases. The New York City Opera's director of marketing, Claudia Keenan Hough, confirms that research. "Advanced sales just don't happen anywhere, and it's getting tougher and tougher," she says.

Doug Sheldon of Columbia Artists Management believes the shift in buying practices will increasingly influence the way arts presenters and marketing directors do business in the future. "We are now in a world where people don't decide in February or March that they are going to buy eighteen concerts of the New York Philharmonic beginning in September, some six months later, and send the check," says Sheldon. "They don't do that anymore. The old Danny Newman[3] 'Subscription Is Everything' philosophy, which was true for many years, simply isn't working anymore."

The problem, Sheldon says, is that "the audience has a last-minute mentality of when they are going to buy their tickets and to what, but orchestras still depend largely on a subscription base. Now they don't have the early large return of subscription income. That presents two challenges: one, you have a smaller pile of money coming in at the end of one season into the next season; two, you have many more single tickets to sell."

Sheldon believes this shift is partly responsible for the demise of many orchestras of late, including the Florida Philharmonic, which filed for bankruptcy, canceled all upcoming seasons, and laid off its musicians in 2003. "In effect, all income is down, whether gifts or earned, but no costs are down," says Sheldon. "Costs aren't going down—they aren't even staying flat. You can go to almost any organization and find a significant downsizing or a wage freeze—or, when positions become vacant, they just don't fill them. It has happened in artist management and orchestra management, and it has happened with presenters, opera houses, and orchestras, from the Chicago Symphony on down."

In order to meet these challenges, Sheldon believes that arts marketers must take a much more specific and timely approach to marketing. "They will have to target special-interest groups," he says. "If you bring the China Philharmonic with Lang Lang, you'd better know where your Chinese audience is and you better have a campaign for them, because the traditional campaign for white-collar white guys isn't going to sell those tickets. If you bring the

Kirov Opera, you can have any audience you want—all you have to do is find people who love opera. Send mailers to the Met list or advertise in every Russian newspaper, which is significantly less expensive than the *Times*."

Audience Research

Performing arts facilities can conduct significant and cost-effective research on audiences. We will focus here on primary research, meaning research designed and executed directly by the facility in pursuit of particular information.

Intercept Surveys

Theater managers have the opportunity to "intercept" customers on the way into or out of performances to ask very specific questions about the performance, how they heard about it, their experience getting to the theater, the quality of concessions, availability of parking, perceptions of safety in the neighborhood, and so on. It's a very effective way to collect precise information to support decision-making. It's also relatively inexpensive if house staff or others can run the surveys and then others can tabulate results internally. The keys are to train survey-takers and to keep the survey focused.

One variation on intercepts is to include a survey in the program and have pencils available to audience members, who fill out and return surveys as they leave. This can be effective, but there is an inherent bias in who chooses to fill out the survey—it's a bit like surveying the church choir about their favorite hymns. Thus, this approach is more appropriate for issues where precision and objectivity is less of an issue. So, for example, a facility might use these surveys to collect ideas for other shows that customers might like to see.

For Kathleen O'Brien, the key is knowing what you want out of the research. "We are most interested in buying habits, media preferences, how people respond to various media, programming choices, and reaction to specific products," she says. "We can track that information, as well as the sales, from our surveys, and in the process of asking people questions, we also let them know what programs and products exist."

Telephone and Mail Surveys

Telephone and mail surveys are two common and effective means to collect primary research from past, present, and potential customers. Telephone surveys are relatively expensive to execute, but they generate unbiased opinions that are statistically valid, and are thus strong tools for decision-making. There is some bias in the way individuals choose to participate, but most good research firms are able to assemble a pool of respondents who provide an accurate representation of the views of a much larger group. Mail surveys are cheaper to execute, but there is a much lower rate of response and a more significant bias in who chooses to take the time to fill out and return the survey. Nevertheless, both of these methods can provide valuable and relatively reliable information, particularly if gathered on a periodic basis that allows the facility to consider opinions on the same issues over time.

Focus Groups

Focus groups can be as simple as a group of customers chatting with the facility manager, or as formal as groups of different patron-types recruited on a random basis and led through a pre-approved script by a professional facilitator. That formality, though expensive, removes much of the potential bias from informal chats and focuses the discussion on benefiting the organization. The key to focus groups is using them to collect information and insights that are best communicated with a group of people around a table. For example, they are often used to test new programming or marketing ideas, where a concept is presented to them with words and pictures and feedback is then collected.

Cora Cahan of the New Victory Theater in New York sees audience research as an integral part of marketing and programming. "The marketing and public relations directors at New Victory are very intent on feedback from our audience," says Cahan. "We do a lot of market research. We use focus groups in the one-way mirror room, and we ask people to stay after performances to chat with us. This allows us to collect feedback on the programs, the theater, the concessions, the ushers, the bathroom, the toilet paper, you name it."

Database Management, Mining, and Marketing

Marketers of nonprofit facilities and programs have one great advantage that is becoming more important and easier to achieve: the wealth of information they are able to collect about their customers, principally through the sale of subscriptions and single tickets. This information exists in databases collected and maintained by the organization. It so happens that the world of database management and marketing has changed dramatically over the past ten years, driven by sectors as diverse as book clubs and catalog merchants.

A lot of performing arts organizations believe that they do data mining just by virtue of having an occasional look at their customer database. But "mining" data means much more than that. To start with, it is based on the idea that customers are different, that they behave differently, and that they respond to offerings differently. So, if marketers are going to approach customers in different ways with different choices, they need to understand who responds to what on an ongoing basis in order to drive marketing decisions.

Gordon Linoff is the president of Data-Miners, Inc. and is the author of *Data Mining Techniques for Marketing, Sales, and Customer Support.*[4] He provides the following advice to performing arts marketers just getting started:

> The first thing you have to do is gather the data you have on customers and determine what makes a good customer. Then, the question is, Do you want to develop your existing customers more, figure how to bring back the dormant ones in some particular way, or take what you know and expand your reach in the area around you?
>
> A good way to get started is by understanding demographic characteristics at the small neighborhood level. There is a lot of good data that is essentially free if you get it from the census bureau. Even buying lists from known list sources in small geographic areas is fairly inexpensive, but as you get into more sophisticated modeling, it does cost more money.
>
> For performing arts marketers, it is critical to do something called "house-holding" so that you can identify people over time. Then, when they give you a different name or a variation on their name or credit card, you can keep them connected with the organization.

The next step is predictive modeling, which is based on the idea that by looking at some past marketing effort, you can predict the outcome and find the customers and prospects who are most likely to respond to a future marketing effort. For example, what were the characteristics of the people who responded to a promotion for a particular performance, and what other people in your database might have been interested in that performance but didn't get that message?

The typical arts/nonprofit administrator can do data mining and marketing, but not without research, training, and the appropriate tools. Sometimes the best way to get started is to form a consortium with other groups that can learn and share information. But you need to be sure you are using it correctly. I see many examples of companies with expensive information systems, similar to ticketing systems, which don't use them correctly. The key is to know what you want and what you can know, so that you collect the right data that ultimately helps attract new customers.

Teri Gorman of the Broward Center is using data mining to build customers' profiles. She says:

> We are finding things out about our patrons like what their channel preferences are, do they prefer to buy over the phone or by the Internet, do they respond to direct mail or e-mail. We have that kind of information. We also know who the customers with high recency and frequency are, who bought X amount of tickets over the last few months. We can actually break that data out by strands, so we get the baby-boomer strand and we say, This group of patrons bought six or more tickets to past baby-boom concerts, maybe they deserve a personalized letter offering them group rates—things like that. We are getting to that detail. It's all about getting to "one-to-one marketing."

One-to-one marketing is every marketer's dream—the opportunity to customize the product and its packaging, and then promote it to one potential customer at a time.

Advertising and Promotional Choices

The branding presentation summarized earlier led to very specific recommendations on media choices, of which there are many. They each have their relative merits, and particular choices must be a function of the message to be delivered, the market to which it is being sent, and the relative cost and value of each medium, which varies tremendously by market. Let's work through each of these media, sharing insights on their use from our theater manager friends.

Direct Mail

Direct mail has been the advertising workhorse for performing arts facilities for a generation because presenters and facilities have large mailing lists of past, present, and potential customers who can be reached inexpensively on a regular basis.

Jeff Rosenstock, manager of the Queens Theatre in the Park, says that direct mail is by far the best method for marketing in a diverse community like Queens, situated so close to Manhattan. "Of course, there are several other media choices, including all of the major metropolitan area papers, radio, and television," says Rosenstock "But if I take out an ad in the *Times* or the *Daily News* or the *Post*, I'm paying a lot of money to reach a lot of people, most of whom would never come to Queens. So using direct mail is much more effective. I create my own database and then look at, rent, and exchange lists with legitimate brokers. If I do a play like *Master Class*, I might go to the Shubert Organization and see what lists they have of dramatic playgoers living in Queens and Long Island, rent that list, and mail it to them. And the key is building our own list. Even now, if I mail out 150,000 brochures with 30,000 going to addresses from my own list, I will still generate 70 to 80 percent of the income from my own 20 percent of the list."

Television and Radio

The effectiveness of television and radio advertising for the arts depends on the kinds of arts being advertised. For Broadway musicals, which draw the largest percentage of annual arts attendees, it is probably worth the expense. For an opera company whose audience makes up only 4 to 5 percent of the population, the costs may outweigh the benefits, unless the ad runs with television programs that target a demographic segment of the market that is similar to the opera company's (i.e., highly educated, older, and affluent).

Teri Gorman from Broward notes that, "with the advent of cable and satellite, really the concept of broadcast is being lost, and now it is narrow casting. You really have to pick the right show and the right network to make those decisions, because television is not an inexpensive medium to use. We try to be very careful about when we do television, to know where that information is going."

Radio advertising can be significantly less expensive, depending on the geographic reach and mission of the station. Many public radio stations will broadcast public service announcements of upcoming events free of charge, and the demographic profile of public radio listeners is usually a good fit for art forms like opera, ballet, jazz, and classical music. For more popular forms of entertainment, such as Broadway musicals, comedy acts, or popular music, it is logical to advertise on stations with a broader base.

Online Marketing

Online marketing has become particularly important for smaller institutions and facilities with limited marketing budgets. Let's dig a little deeper into what online marketing means and how performing arts facilities are engaged in this area.

E-mail

E-mail is a powerful marketing tool. Really, it's a marketing channel though which performing arts marketers can reach existing and potential audiences in a very cost-effective manner. Even more compelling is the fact that most people make an explicit choice to share their e-mail address with an arts organization. In marketing terms, they are "opting-in," choosing to receive information, and are thus less hostile to messages and much more likely to respond.

Cora Cahan of the New Victory Theater gives much credit to her theater's list of patron e-mail addresses. "We send out frequent e-mail blasts, reminding our patrons when the next show is, when we have workshops, etc." she says. "We can e-mail anyone who is registered with us as a member and uses e-mail, which is a large percentage."

But e-mail-based programs also have their limitations. According to Kathleen O'Brien, "e-mail addresses probably have a lifespan on the average of six months. That is the average. It is not like a home address that's good for a couple of years."

Web Sites

Most performing arts facilities have invested significantly in the development and maintenance of a Web site to describe who they are and what they do. And with the emergence of powerful search engines, consumers are more likely to find valuable information about facilities and programs. Fundamentally, Web sites can provide an incredible amount of information to consumers, artists, funders, and other constituents, in a very cost-effective manner.

A high-quality Web site is now a *sine qua non* of any successful arts facility. Carmen Pietri-Diaz of the Nuyorican Poets Café says, "Our most important marketing tool right now is the Web site. We're getting 150,000 hits a month, and a lot of those are from abroad. In one sense, 150,000 hits is not a lot. But it's not just audiences. There are artists, promoters, and students finding us through the Web. We get a lot of e-mail from school kids in advance of bringing them in for the spoken-word events, along with a steady flow of e-mail from countries like Italy, France, Germany, and Australia. Lots of those are from theater groups or poetry groups who are coming to New York and want to have a night at the Café."

New York City Opera has gone above and beyond the standard Web site to create a full-service experience for ticket buyers. "We do a lot on our Web site," says Claudia Keenan Hough. "So, for example, if you go to a page, it says all the other things you can do to enhance your experience. You can listen to music, and it tells you about the restaurant down the street and shopping and attending the lecture before the performance. We have found that people who know more about something aren't intimidated by it, but have a better overall experience if they know what they are going to see. So, before every opera, we have some synopses on the Web site, we play music on the Web site, we have in-depth articles from our souvenir program book. We do whatever we can do to make it a richer experience. If it is a rich experience, they won't be intimidated by it; instead, they'll know more and they will come back!"

Michael Kaiser, president of the Kennedy Center in Washington, also says the Internet is key to good marketing. "We have a system where you log on to our site and tailor it to your specific needs and interests. It also tailors our relationship to you," says Kaiser. "We have hundreds of thousands of sub-scribers, and we are as sophisticated users of the Web as any arts organiza-tion. Our biggest marketing challenge is that we do an average of seven or eight performances a night—it's so hard to prioritize. The reason we like this concept is that if you say your interests are anything from Indian to classical music, then the Web site is tailored to you, so that when you log on, you see information that relates to your interests, weeding out all the other stuff."

Online Ticketing

Finally, the greatest and most direct Web-based payoff to facilities and presen-ters is online ticketing. More consumers are buying tickets to events online. As Doug Sheldon pointed out, even the über-traditional New York Philharmonic sells one-third of its tickets online. The Kennedy Center also sells just less than one-third of all tickets online, but that stills brings in around $15 million in ticket revenue each year, according to Michael Kaiser. All of this is changing quickly. The Broward Center only started online ticketing in 2002. And after only one year, online ticketing had grown to 35 percent of ticket sales.

Finally, these three Internet-based tools should be interrelated. E-mail marketing is most effective when it can drive a potential consumer to the orga-nization's Web site, where, provided with a compelling opportunity, that con-sumer then makes the decision to purchase tickets and does so through a Web link. This is a new version of the affinity club, where a current or potential customer signs up for information and promotional material that suggests some level of exclusivity—the special offer.

Here's Michael Kilgore on electronic marketing in performing arts centers:

> Performing arts centers have come a little bit late to the Web, but are working to catch up very rapidly. Generally, I would say that Web sites are moving out of the tech department and over into marketing departments. That is useful because I think that the Web sites have to have urgency and timeliness to encourage repeat visitors, and the technology folks really just don't have the time to do that.
>
> We also have challenges with our ticketing systems. For e-mail blasts to

be the most effective, I think we need to be able to integrate it with our ticket-buying database. And not many centers have been able to do this. We're all catching up quickly, but there's a long way to go.

We have a list of 51,000 right now. We have three sources. We had an old listserv that people had signed up for, and they were getting text from us, so we incorporated them. We had a very active solicitation period during the campaign, a contest in which we gave away tickets to *The Lion King* and to the Broadway series. We have done very active solicitation to get people to sign up when we were starting our new series, and we also automatically moved people over from the ticket database. We sent them an e-mail telling them we were sending them over and they could opt out if they chose to. We make it very easy to unsubscribe. There are places that are much more difficult. At the bottom of our e-mail it says, "If you would like to unsubscribe, click here." That's on every e-mail we send because I feel very strongly that this can't be intrusive, and we want to make it as easy as possible for people not to subscribe. At the same time, we want to make it as advantageous for them to subscribe as possible.

Given all of this, our online ticketing is growing, though slower than I'd like. Broadway subscribers have been particularly receptive. They were able to subscribe online for the first time this year, and new subscriptions were up by 24 percent.

Publicity and Media Relations

Facility managers must develop strong relationships with local and regional media outlets. Often newspapers and television stations will work out partnerships with arts organizations and facilities, as is the case with the Capital Arts Alliance in Bowling Green, Kentucky. Carrie Barnett, until recently the executive director of the Capital Arts Alliance, says she invested a lot of time and energy into maintaining positive relations with local media. "Keeping those relationships alive is a big deal," she says, "and we have been very successful at forging partnerships with local media. For example, the NBC outlet here is our media partner. They use our facility and we mention them in programs, and in turn, we get benefits. Specifically, at NBC, we sponsor the 5:00 P.M. weather forecast every day, and we pay nothing for that. The benefit to NBC is that they originate the broadcast from our facility. The ABC affiliate is another partner—I wasn't sure we would be able to do more than one partnership because of their rivalry, but they mostly promote the IMAX and we get ad spots and other benefits from them. PBS partners with us on about ten shows a year in the theater, and we exchange mailing lists. We also have a partnership with the newspaper—the publishing side—and the publisher is on one of our committees. We have relationships with every media outlet in the community."

Telemarketing

Performing arts producing organizations, presenters, and facilities have been very successful at using the telephone to contact past subscribers, ticket buyers, and potential audiences. That may all be changing. Recent laws have been passed that limit the amount and kinds of phone calls that any organization can legally make. New York City Opera's telemarketing campaign has taken a direct hit from this new legislation.

"My understanding of the new law," says Claudia Keenan Hough, "is that if you have any kind of prior relationship with someone and you are a nonprofit, you can call, so that includes anyone who has asked for information or bought a single ticket or subscription. The problem is that I do big business with group sales. That business is basically cold-calling, and if it is taken away, I don't know what we'll do. But even without the law, caller ID is changing everything."

In the future, facility managers will have to be very careful when setting up telemarketing campaigns, finding ever more creative ways to reach potential audiences that have never bought tickets before. Michael Kilgore here expresses the view of many:

> I am not a big fan of telemarketing, only because of my experience and the experiences of people that I talk to in the industry. I don't answer my phone until I know who it is anymore. Between six and nine at night, I can't answer the phone without it being a telemarketer, and it is intrusive, so I don't know how long that industry is going to keep going the way it is. I would much rather lean on people who said they wanted my messages and try to concentrate on them, and try to give them a reason to sign up and do affinity marketing and reward them for staying part of it. We give them special offers,

and occasionally even a free ticket if a show comes up and we need to be able to do something last-minute. There is a lot we can do with the affinity clubs, and I fear that we might kill that goose too, but we are trying to be very careful in sending messages that are targeted.

Despite these challenges, some organizations are still able to use the telephone effectively. Teri Gorman of the Broward Center says:

> We have outbound calling, but it's not sales in a sense. Because of the way people live nowadays, 70 percent of the time you are going to get an answering machine. And our box office staff will call and say, This is the Broward Center, and this is a courtesy message to let you know that x-y-z show is going to be at such and such theater on this date, and if you'd like further information, please call us at the box office. And they leave a number. We have not received complaints about that; in fact, people have appreciated that service. And again, we are very careful, we are very targeted with what kinds of information about which shows are being left at what phone numbers.

Ticketing Systems and Pricing

Underlying many of these new research and marketing efforts is the rapid evolution of ticketing systems for performing arts facilities that allow managers and marketers to collect substantial information about consumers and migrate that information across marketing and fundraising functions. These new systems are also able to integrate online ticketing, allowing the marketer to better manage ticket inventories and to improve financial management practices.

Given the major changes now occurring in this world and the accelerating pace of innovation in this area, I am reluctant to dwell on today's state-of-the-art ticketing systems, as they will most certainly be considered obsolete in the near future. But what we can do is articulate a series of questions for managers to ask when considering an investment in these systems:

- Is there scalability to the system?
- Does the system allow for the integration of financial, marketing, and fundraising functions?
- Does the system include a relational database?

I can't resist introducing one possibility for the future. One of the continuing challenges for performing arts organizations and facilities is the relatively static nature of ticket prices in a world of dynamic pricing. Facilities have had only limited success in the delicate game of "yield management," to borrow the term from the airlines. It is also the case that the differential between the highest and lowest ticket price in most performing arts events has been more often shrinking than expanding. According to Claudia Keenan Hough, the Houston Grand Opera has achieved something of a breakthrough in this area due to the generosity of Continental Airlines, which donated a copy of their proprietary yield management software to the Opera. This is allowing them to aggressively manipulate ticket prices for different productions, days, performances, and seating locations, right up until curtain time. Hopefully, other organizations and facilities will gain access to this technology and thus benefit from the ability to manage ticket prices in a more precise fashion.

Customer Service and Experience Engineering

Customer service is a very important issue for performing arts facilities. But only recently have buildings begun to relate the customer service function to marketing. More often, they left the function, and the people in charge of it, in the operations department. But all of this is changing as people realize that selling the performing arts depends on selling a much broader experience than the simple act of sitting in the audience staring at the stage. The experience of the performing arts actually includes a set of connected experiences, including hearing about a performance, buying a ticket, getting to the theater, parking, eating/drinking/shopping around the facility, getting to one's seat, and seeing the show. Then there's all that comes after the performance, from getting out of the theater to any more opportunities for eating/drinking/shopping to getting home.

A recent buzzword to hit the field is "experience engineering," which suggests that those in the service industries have the opportunity to improve the experience of their customers with a bit of engineering. So, for facility managers, what are those elements of the theatergoing experience that might be engineered? Certainly there are lots of things that matter once the customer is inside the building, from the speed and quality of service in the box office to the state of the restrooms. Outside the building there is an additional set of experiences, but here, the question is how much the facility manager can engineer.

The traffic will be what it will be. Parking is controlled by separate contractors. And who knows if the chef around the corner will be on his/her game? So let's shift the effort from engineering to influencing. On this level, there is much work to do, from providing weather forecasts and traffic reports online to working out discounts with the parking operator to special pre-theater deals at all the neighborhood restaurants.

The work of promoting customer service inside the facility is a never-ending challenge. Here is John Haynes, executive director of the Marie P. DeBartolo Center for the Performing Arts at the University of Notre Dame:

> It has been a hard thing. And to tell you the truth, I think it's going to be forever a hard thing, first of all because customer service is a real tough business. The burnout in customer service is a significant factor. There is only a certain amount of abuse you can take. And the nasty truth is that there are many unreasonable people in the world. I don't care how nice you are or how good you are at it. A lot of people are going to give you a hard time, and that's difficult. There tends to be high turnover. The last couple of ticket offices I've had tended to attract people as employees that I used to describe as Druids, and I don't know why that is, but they tended to be resentful, black-wearing, body-piercing people. One-on-one they are lovely, but they tend not to make great customer service people for a variety of reasons. Teaching customer service in that environment is difficult.
>
> I learned an interesting lesson once. I went to an IBM training seminar once, and they said, "What business do you think we are in?" Everyone said, "Computers." They said, "No, we are a marketing company. We actually don't care what we sell. We happen to be in a business equipment company, but our business is marketing." I thought about that for a while and realized that in many ways, the business we are in is customer service. We are in the business of creating a seamlessly pleasant experience for people, from the moment they conceive of the possibility of coming to a live event until it's all over, and every aspect of it in between. Every way that they touch us, or that we touch them. Every part of it—they don't separate parking from the concert experience.
>
> One of the problems I encountered in California when I first got there was that all of my customer service staff and backstage people had a different attitude toward their work with events that we were presenting and events that were being presented by an outside organization. They tended to phone in the outside presenter events, and they were very proprietary and assiduous about

our own events. I noticed this and called them all together and said, "I have news for you—the public doesn't know what the deal is. They don't know what the contract looks like. All they know is that they are coming to our theater. They don't know that someone else is presenting it. They can't tell the difference, and they don't want to know. They come to our home, they are our guests, and we have to treat them as such, no matter what or who is on stage."

Successful Performing Arts Marketing in the Nonprofit World

So what makes a successful arts marketer? Claudia Keenan Hough says it is "someone who believes in the product and the mission of the company and is respected by the artistic staff, and therefore can tell the directors what the right thing to do is. It's an issue of trust. They have to understand that when I make a suggestion for programming, it is because I love the art, and I'm doing it for the organization."

Underlying that is an assumption that the marketer knows the business and understands numbers and research. "Marketing (and programming) choices must be based on information," says Keenan Hough. "Many organizations base all of their decisions on what they did last year, not on research, focus groups, or surveys. Every organization, no matter what its budget, can come up with some basic survey and have volunteers hand it out. It may not be the best research, but it gives you something to work from. But even if you don't have money or time for surveys or research studies, you can read the paper to find out what is happening in your community. You must understand why you are doing this and track every single effort to fully understand your return on investment."

NOTES

1. Brooks, Arthur, Julia Lowell, Kevin McCarthy and Laura Zakaras, "The Performing Arts in a New Era" (Washington, DC: The Rand Corporation, 2001).
2. Ibid., 25.
3. Danny Newman was the author of *Subscribe Now!*, published by the Theater Communications Group in 1977. The point of the book, expressed in its subtitle, is "Building Arts Audiences Through Dynamic Subscription Promotion." It was a seminal text for arts marketers for twenty years.
4. Linoff, Gordon, *Data Mining Techniques for Marketing, Sales and Customer Support*, Second Edition (New York: Wiley Publishers, 2003).

Chapter Five

The Financial Management of Performing Arts Facilities

The financial management of performing arts facilities is a complex undertaking, given the following:

- A very large investment of capital is required to build and sustain facilities
- Performing arts facilities require contributed income as well as earned income to balance the budget on an ongoing basis
- There are few productivity gains possible in the creation and presentation of the performing arts, which squeezes margins
- There is tremendous volatility around the financial performance of facilities

Let's address these challenges and see how successful facility managers respond.

The Economic Dilemma

In 1966, the economists William J. Baumol and William G. Bowen wrote a groundbreaking study on the state of the performing arts. Commissioned by the Twentieth Century Fund and titled "Performing Arts—The Economic Dilemma," the study discussed the performing arts' inability to improve labor productivity. Baumol and Bowen began their seminal study with the line, "In the performing arts, crisis is apparently a way of life." This study was the first (although certainly not the last) to use verifiable and accurate data to illustrate the difficulties the performing arts industry faces, both financially and socially. The conclusions surprised few in the performing arts industries, but resulted in an awakening in the public and business sectors. Or, perhaps more accurately, the study marked a turning point in the battle to educate the public and business sectors about the financial difficulties in the arts and the fact that those difficulties are not short-term or solvable, but are, in fact, chronic.

The study's most important conclusion was that the performing arts have a limited ability to improve their own productivity. Plays, operas, and concerts require the same number of performers and take the same length of time no matter where or when they are performed, through no fault of the managers, performers, or facilities. Haydn's *The Creation* still takes the same number of musicians and singers and the same amount of time when performed in 2004 by the New York Philharmonic as it did in 1798, on its opening night. However, the costs associated with performing artists (salaries) and the technical aspects (violin strings, space rental, point shoes, ticket printing, etc.) have grown exponentially. Compare that with the production of cars: How much time, labor, and cost did Ford's assembly line save? Those same cost-saving measures cannot be applied to Haydn—or Puccini, or Shakespeare, or Gilbert and Sullivan, or Balanchine. And so, Baumol and Bowen conclude, with costs constantly rising, and the inability to either raise ticket prices accordingly or find significant enough cost-saving efficiencies, the performing arts will always experience an income gap. And that gap, they hypothesize, will require greater and greater subsidy as the years go on. So this becomes the most fundamental challenge for financial managers in the performing arts—to manage the cost squeeze with some appropriate balance of earned and contributed income.

Financial Planning and Capital Structure

A key component of financial planning for performing arts facilities is understanding the capital structure of the enterprise. Here is a description of the elements of the capital structure of a typical performing arts center:

The Center for the Arts at George Mason University is a building with sophisticated technical equipment, staff paid on a regular basis, and significant operating expenses. There are receivables from those who rent the hall and donors fulfilling multi-year pledges. There has been debt to support cash flow requirements and pay off capital expenditures. There are reserves to support capital needs or operating shortfalls. And there is a small endowment to supplement operating expenses.[1]

All of these elements (assets and liabilities, income and expenses, reserves and endowment) make up the capital structure of the organization. What is important to remember is how all of these elements are interrelated, and why effective financial planning is important to maintain an appropriate capital structure. Consider the following scenario:

An operating historic theater receives a $1 million matching grant from a national foundation to expand their backstage area, thereby increasing the size of the stage, loading area, and related support spaces. They initiate a capital campaign to raise the additional $2 million required to complete the job and hire a design team to lead the effort.

The effort of raising additional funds and organizing the project puts a significant burden on staff. Other operating issues, like cash management and the collection of funds owed, suffer. In particular, the new capital campaign reduces the level of annual giving to the organization by 25 percent.

After one year of fundraising and design, the renovation project begins. Only $1 million of the required $2 million has been raised, so the Board authorizes a loan for the balance required. The eight-month interruption of operations significantly reduces income earned from rentals, presenting, and concessions.

Finally, when the theater reopens, the organization incurs higher operating expenses, given the additional staffing requirements and the larger space to occupy. Marketing budgets must also be increased to recapture audiences who stopped coming to the theater when it was closed.

All in all, a $1 million grant leads the organization into a situation where they have incurred over $1 million in operating losses since the project began and in addition now owe almost $1 million to a local bank. They are short of funds to pay their bills, lacking resources to raise the additional funds

> required to pay off the loan, and financially constrained from taking advantage of the programming opportunities created by the stage expansion.

This story highlights the unique and significant challenges for nonprofits in managing capital. In those challenges, we would include the following:

Restricted Funds

Performing arts facilities rely on contributions to sustain operations and fund improvements. But quite often these contributions come with strings attached—restrictions that stipulate how and when funds might be used for a particular project or period of time. The problem for the performing arts facility is that this lack of liquidity or flexibility limits the impact of capital and often compromises planning efforts.

The Relationship between Activity and Financial Performance

One of the great challenges in performing arts facilities is the relationship between activity and financial performance. We established in our discussion on presenting that this activity is often pursued with the financial goal that direct revenues (box office proceeds) should exceed direct expenses (including artist fees and promotion). But understanding the overall impact of additional bookings on the bottom line is more difficult. Because a large portion of facility operating costs is fixed, more activity should add more revenue than costs. But because most nonprofit renters can only afford a subsidized rental rate, new activity may actually increase the gap between earned income and operating expense. The danger is that some performing arts facilities have gotten to a point of believing that less activity leads to better financial performance, requiring less in the way of facility maintenance, promotional costs, or even personnel. But this leads inevitably to conflict with the mission of the facility, and a likely reduction in contributed income.

The Break-Even Mentality

There is a strong resistance in the nonprofit world to the concept of profit making within a nonprofit enterprise. This partly reflects a bias against those driven by profit, but also a concern that funders would be less supportive of an organization generating surpluses. But in fact, the generation of surpluses is the key way in which nonprofit facilities create and fund reserves to support programming, operations, and capital requirements.

Theaters as Assets

Another common problem is the sense that performing arts facilities are long-term assets with significant value to the owner. There are two problems with this argument. First of all, these assets do not generate operating profits. Thus, there is a negative return on investment (excluding the generous support of donors). Second, theaters have only limited asset value as anything other than a theater. They are not easily converted into other types of facilities, and thus, their value is limited by that lack of utility.

Programs and Core Business

There is an inherent tension in the nonprofit or public sector performing arts facility between the program and the core business of the facility. The core business is usually something like the presentation of arts and entertainment to the public on a sustainable basis in a safe and appealing physical space. The program, relating only to that which is offered to the public, is a more limited driver, but one that relates most closely to mission and the one that attracts both audience and financial support. Thus, the investment in program (whether related to presenting or the support of rental activity) tends to out-pace the investment in the physical structure or the administrative structure required to sustain it.

These points are well illustrated by the plight of the 1,100-seat Ellen Eccles Theater in Logan, Utah. In 1998 we were hired by the city of Logan to audit the operation and make recommendations on their need for continuing financial support from local government. What we discovered was that a strong and committed local leadership group was, with the best of intentions, squeezing the theater to death. They had come together some fifteen years earlier to save the theater, which was built in 1923 but not used from the late 1950s until it was renovated in 1991. They raised $6.5 million to restore and reactivate the facility with a combination of presented and rental activity managed by a professional staff. But after an initial period of success, they began to incur operating deficits. They responded with a series of changes over a period of years, increasing rental rates, reducing the number of presented events, and cutting staff. This led to less rental activity, reduced community participation, and less annual fundraising. And that then led to further deterioration of the operating budget and less money for capital maintenance of the facility.

By the time we came to Logan, the board was essentially running the theater with a staff of three, believing that they were acting as effective trustees of this community jewel. And funders—most importantly the city—were saying, "Why should we support an enterprise whose operating performance is declining and whose service to the community is shrinking?"

Of course, the answer was that the theater must invest in building the organization, increasing activity in the facility, and rebuilding community support (financial and otherwise). Even though their sense was that too much subsidized use of the theater hurt the bottom line, they were not accounting for the fact that funders were not likely to support a facility serving a shrinking cross-section of the community.

Building the Budget

The budgeting process for performing arts facilities is relatively straightforward, but there are many facilities that struggle to build an achievable budget, and fewer that are consistently able to hit their target. In interviewing a series of executive directors and their financial managers, we collected a number of best practices:

Anita Scism, director of the Walton Arts Center, says her staff begins with a vision for the year. "A lot of that vision comes from the programming that is beginning to be developed for the year. We start building the budget about six months before the year begins, and it's authorized probably about three months before. Throughout the process, the finance committee of the board is actively involved."

The budgeting process for James Brown at the Civic Center in Oklahoma City includes input from five people who develop the budget. "We start in December, it has to be presented in February, and it goes through the budget process and is approved in June, so the whole process usually takes six and a half to seven months."

Tony Stimac at the Helen Hayes Theater starts the budget in November that will finally be approved on July 1 of the next year. "But that November work is only the beginning," says Stimac. "It is submitted to the board in February, but I need to have some idea for the strategy session in January. We do a pretty good job of making our budget. On the earned portion, we have been within 1 to 2 percent for eight years. But for the unearned portion, we have been off by as much as 65 percent. It's a lot tougher to adjust that part of the budget as you go. You can cut shows, you can cut expenses—you can do all sorts of things—but you can't have another benefit on the spot or replace some big county grant that didn't come in."

Budget approval for a city-run facility can be a very complicated process. Rae Ackerman in Vancouver made a breakthrough when he convinced the city council to focus on his bottom line and not direct him to make changes in specific areas of the budget.

> This is the second budget we have done on a net basis, and it's much better. Before, the city took a lawn mower approach, directing us to cut everything by the same amount. And I admit that I was budgeting stuff just to be able to cut it.
>
> Now we look at things differently. They said, Look at your net number. And it makes sense. There are so many variables. And the main thing is that it's a smaller number to deal with. A 2-percent improvement in my bottom line, as opposed to a 2-percent improvement in expenses, means 2 percent of $200,000 instead of 2 percent of $5 million.

Overall, facility managers stress the following:

- Start early
- Engage lots of people in the effort, but don't lose control of the process
- Refer closely to past years' budgets
- Test assumptions
- Plan for uncertainty
- Encourage owners to mandate bottom-line performance, as opposed to managing specific elements of revenues and expenses

Balancing the Budget with Contributed Income

The need for contributed income to sustain performing arts facilities is a very sensitive topic. While it is generally understood that libraries, schools, and community recreation facilities require annual funding, there is often a reluctance to provide such support for performing arts facilities.

With our clients, the biggest problem is often separating the issues of annual funding and a deficit. Too often there is a belief that annual fundraising is required because the theater operates at a deficit, as if proper budgeting and fiscal discipline would balance the budget without annual funding. This simply isn't the case. Except for theaters like those in Branson, Missouri (commercial music in facilities best described as "cheap and cheerful"), and Broadway (where financial performance of the building, the show and the subsequent tour is intertwined), performing arts facilities require a combination of earned income and contributed income to balance the budget on an ongoing basis. Here is a chart that shows the size of budget and the annual funding requirement of a set of facilities of different sizes.

MAIN HALL CAPACITY	EVENT DAYS	PRESENTED EVENTS	OWNER	OPERATOR	OPERATING BUDGET	EARNED INCOME	% EARNED INCOME
Eisemann Center (Richardson, TX)							
1,563	175	6	City	City	$1,900,000	$1,000,000	53%
Flynn Performing Arts Center (Burlington, VT)							
1,453	280	60	Nonprofit	Nonprofit	$3,976,360	$2,680,138	67%
Garde Arts Center (New London, CT)							
1,500	120	55	Nonprofit	Nonprofit	$2,231,237	$1,111,227	50%
Great Falls Civic Center (Great Falls, MT)							
1,776	104	15	City	City	$456,597	$304,097	67%
Clemens Performing Arts Center (Elmira, NY)							
1,608	100	80	County	Nonprofit	$2,073,677	$1,184,209	57%
California Center for the Arts (Escondido, CA)							
1,535	80	70	City	Nonprofit	$6,900,000	$2,450,000	36%
Carlson Center @ JCCC (Overland Park, KS)							
1,300	250	200	College	Nonprofit	$5,500,000	$2,500,000	45%

How can it be that the sizes of budgets are so different among facilities and that the portion of the budget covered by earned revenue is so small for some facilities and so high for others? There are several reasons:

1. The primary reason that the scale of budgets is so different is the level of presenting undertaken by the facility. This is because we account for presenting by recording box office revenues and direct presenting expenses (artist fees, promotion, and so on) on the income statement. So, as opposed to a $500 rental fee from an outside presenter, we might record ticket sales of $15,000 and direct costs of $12,000 if we are the presenter.

2. The level of programming is probably the most important factor driving the earned-income component of the budget. But while marginal revenues might exceed marginal costs when tested in one facility, the same relationship does not readily apply from theater to theater. As often as not, busier theaters cover less of their budgets with earned income. Rental rates might be low, variable costs could be high, or perhaps fundraising is easier in a busy building.

3. A related issue is the nature of the programming. Here, what matters is whether programs are more culturally or commercially oriented. Culturally oriented programs tend to attract smaller audiences, but are still expensive to bring to the facility. Commercially oriented programs can draw larger audiences and sometimes command higher ticket prices to support high artist fees and promotional costs. What this means is that more commercially oriented programs tend to achieve a higher margin between direct revenues and direct expenses. The reason that facilities don't all abandon cultural programming in pursuit of better operating margins is that those with public and nonprofit sector owners and operators are guided first and foremost by a mission statement that mandates a series of goals beyond profitability.

4. Finally, there is often a problem with inconsistent and incomplete reporting. It's very difficult to get accurate representation of financial performance with facilities on a campus or facilities connected to local government. Funds and services are provided through different budgets that are not available or understood by facility managers. It's an endless struggle on our part to collect this information. A facility manager can say, "We operate with no direct subsidy," not accounting for the insurance provided through

the city's policy and the annual interest income from a fund established by the local Community Foundation.

We'll discuss annual fundraising to balance the budget in the next chapter.

Reserve Accounts

The final challenge outlined at the beginning of this chapter is the tremendous uncertainty around the financial performance of performing arts facilities. How is the facility to respond when a star cancels, a school budget for busing kids to performances is eliminated, or a blackout occurs?

One way to address these risks is with conservative budgeting, as mentioned earlier. But another important response is the creation of reserve accounts. We have already mentioned the need for a capital reserve. But we would add the need for an operating reserve and a programming reserve.

Here is Robyn Williams on the creation of reserves at the Portland Center for the Performing Arts:

> We established a capital reserve as part of our strategic planning process. We knew we needed adequate reserves so that if there was a big drop in lodging tax or a big drop in business or one of our major resident companies went out of business, we would still have adequate reserves to carry us through a two- to three-year period. That way we would have time to look at it as a long-term problem and find a long-term solution, or decide if it is just a one- or two-year problem that we just need to ride out.
>
> I was surprised in looking at other performing arts centers that so many of them didn't have any reserves set aside. We are trying to figure out what is an adequate reserve and no one had an answer for that question. I was asking all kinds of facility types, not just performing arts centers: "What kind of a reserve should we have?" I was unable to find anybody that was doing anything. We decided that we would set aside a six-month reserve (for us about $3.5 to $4 million) that would buy us time if there is a downturn in the market or whatever, so I wouldn't have to resort to the usual slash-and-burn tactics that the facilities had to do in the past to keep from just gobbling up a fund balance. We felt like that would be an adequate reserve.

We went through a process to determine how to build that reserve with the least amount of impact on our resident companies, and we decided to increase the user fee on our resident companies over a multi-year period. With the projections we had, this was part of a five-year strategic plan. Over the course of that plan, in those five years, that would get us the reserve, and then any extra would fall to capital. Our projections had us hitting that reserve amount in a two- to three-year period, depending on how our business was going.

This money was both an operating reserve and a capital reserve, and it was all very well and good until 9/11 and the economy busted before we had this reserve in place. So my lodging tax dropped off and I'm taking a $530,000 hit that is also tied to the lodging issue. I don't have that reserve built up yet, so now we are struggling with how to react to that. I felt like it was a good path for us to be going down. If things had stayed as they were, I think we would have been very successful. It may take two or three more years before it gets there, so our challenge is how to weather the difficulties over the next two or three years. How do we keep going until it gets back to full steam? We know that we will not be putting any extra money into capital, but fortunately we are working on some sponsorship and other things that will help.

Lance Olson of the Majestic Theater at Emerson College in Boston has developed a unique approach to reserves:

When we renovated the Majestic, we installed an excellent sound system. It was built for this 1903 theater, recognizing that there was never a sound system designed into the theater. We designed one that made sense in an acoustic environment.

We spent a lot of money on that sound system. I raised that money by going to foundations and explaining how rental groups pay immense amounts of money each year to rent good sound systems that don't really fit in the theater and sound lousy. I told them that those amazing sums of money every year were coming out of their pockets because they grant the money to pay for the rented sound systems. I suggested that we would all be better served if the foundations gave us the money to pay for the sound system. Then we would recover the cost by assessing a much smaller amount for rent, and we could build up a sinking fund so that when this sound system wears out, the next will be paid for internally and the foundations wouldn't have to see it.

We have now created sinking funds for a number of operations, capital items, and performance equipment. The marquee has a sinking fund. Every time you use the marquee, you put money into a sinking fund. Seven years from now, when it needs to be upgraded, I will have the money to do it without going back into general coffers.

NOTE

1. Adapted from Clara Miller's article "Hidden in Plain Sight: Understanding Nonprofit Capital Structure." Published in the *Nonprofit Quarterly*, Spring 2003.

Chapter Six

Fundraising for Performing Arts Facilities

For performing arts facilities, fundraising is a relentless part of the job. These facilities require significant ongoing capital to maintain the physical structure, to pursue improvements, and to balance the budget on an ongoing basis.

The development staff of a performing arts facility is relatively well paid (at least compared to others working in the performing arts field), reflecting the importance of their work to the organization, but also the extreme difficulty of raising funds from all sorts of different sources on an ongoing basis, no matter what the economic or political environment. On top of all of that, fundraising is very competitive, with performing arts facilities competing for funds with hospitals, schools, churches, and even the nonprofit organizations they serve. And finally, all of this is very dynamic—the sources of funds are changing, and funders are becoming more sophisticated.

Sources and Uses of Funding

When we speak of fundraising for performing arts facilities, we should first differentiate between different types of fundraising for three areas:

1. **Capital funding**. The pursuit of capital support for the development, expansion, or physical improvement of facilities.
2. **Operating funding**. The pursuit of funds for the ongoing support of facilities and their operation.
3. **Endowment funding**. The pursuit of funds with which to endow the building or organization with a perpetual income source to sustain operations or fund capital expenditures.

Halsey North and his wife Alice are fundraising consultants who specialize in performing arts facilities. They have built a successful practice helping organizations and buildings prepare for and execute all sorts of campaigns. We asked Halsey if there is a different skill set for people who are raising annual operating funds versus construction funds or endowment funds. He says:

> Not really. It gets back to the relationships and helping people understand how their gift will make a difference, how it will benefit themselves and their community. The best way to do this is through a planning process that gets key potential donors involved. As the saying goes: "Ask for money and you will get advice; ask for advice and you will get money." We are working with one organization now that has wonderful plans but fast-tracked them so quickly that they now have to give the rest of the community time to catch up and take ownership of the ideas. At our recommendation, they have slowed down and created a master plan task force of potential major funders to look at the plans, adjust them, evaluate them, tighten them, and buy into them. This group may come out with basically the same set of plans, but the plans will have been filtered through the prism of those who will eventually pay for it. This process of involving potential donors in the planning process is absolutely crucial to a successful capital campaign. It also helps strengthen annual program planning.
>
> We are working with one client now that has a 1903 theater that hasn't been operational since the 1950s, so it has no constituency. They are using the process of asking for advice to build a constituency. They are systematically identifying potential donors and asking them what they want the theater to be and who else might be interested in supporting it. The very process of asking for advice in an organized way has helped them develop active and committed potential donors. It has taken us a year and a half of

questions and asking for advice, but we are finally ready to begin asking these advisors for money.

Now consider the potential sources of funds. From the public sector, there are grants and donations from different levels of government. One would think first of traditional arts funding through local arts councils and cultural affairs offices, or state support from state councils or appropriations. And then there is federal funding, historically coming from the National Endowment for the Arts. With all levels of government, there is traditional arts funding from programs set up to support the arts. And then there is funding secured for arts facilities and organizations designed to serve broader community goals—like education money that can serve a facility's education program, juvenile justice funding that supports the development of after-school programs in theaters, or economic development funding that supports theater development as a part of a downtown revitalization effort. We'll come back to these trends later in the chapter.

From the private sector, there are funds from individuals, corporations, and foundations. (The latter may in fact represent the generosity of individuals or corporations.) Funds are disbursed through grants, donations, sponsorship of programs, participation in special events, and planned giving.

The Importance of Endowments

Raising money for an endowment is increasingly seen as an essential means to stabilize an organization and address future needs. The inclusion of an endowment component in a capital campaign to build or improve facilities is ideal, but not often practical. Often it takes some years for a performing arts facility to build credibility, skills, and resources for such an effort. Here is John Richard, executive vice president and chief operating officer of the New Jersey Performing Arts Center (NJPAC), which opened in downtown Newark in 1998:

> We started in a quiet phase of an endowment campaign some five years after we opened. We received lead gifts that were not big so much as they were symbolically important, coming from the Ford and Duke Foundations. That helped to lay the groundwork with our board members, who soon made a commitment to the effort of building the endowment. We now have $50 million in

commitments, and are looking at probably doubling that goal over the next ten years.

Siobhan McDermott is a partner in Strategic Management Consultants, another successful fundraising practice specializing in the performing arts. Here she speaks to the practical challenges of putting an endowment in place:

> Endowment campaigns are much harder to sell because they are not putting anything in the ground and they are not bringing in three thousand school kids this year. It's a more difficult argument to make, but it's a cornerstone in every project we become involved with. Attaching an endowment component to a capital campaign is very important because it ensures the capital donors that their investment will be taken care of for the long run. It's like insurance. It makes them feel as if you have done the right homework—you've done the right planning.
>
> The great thing about an endowment at the beginning of an institution's life is that you don't need it right away, in the sense that you don't need your repair and replacement funds to replace the HVAC system or carpet right away. You need an operating endowment, but you don't necessarily need a capital endowment until a few years down the road, which opens up your door to the quest for planned giving. That leverages money that you wouldn't be able to get otherwise for a capital campaign because somebody doesn't have the resources now, but will after his or her death.

Planned and Deferred Giving

Probably the area of greatest growth and change in the industry is planned or deferred giving. Financial advisors, foundations, and other experts are designing more complex products that allow donors to reduce income and estate tax, defer capital gains tax, and earn a lifelong income from assets that go to a qualified charity upon the death of the donor. Here's an analogy for this approach: Donate the tree, but keep the fruit.

There are many deferred giving vehicles, but changes in the tax code make it difficult and unwise to pick favorites. Here are a few of the broad types:

- **Charitable Remainder Trusts**: Donors create a trust with a gift and then collect income based on the fair market value of the assets until they die, when the trust goes to the charitable beneficiary.
- **Charitable Gifts Annuity**: A donor transfers cash or property to a charity, and the charity pays the donor a specific amount each year for the donor's life.
- **Pooled Income Fund**: The charity sponsors and manages a pool of assets that distributes earnings to noncharitable beneficiaries.
- **IRA or 401K Account**: Retirement accounts can become deferred giving tools when assets are left to the charity.
- **Will**: A will is a deferred giving tool when the assets are left to charity.
- **Life Insurance**: A term or whole life policy's death benefit can be assigned to charity.

Performing arts centers have gone so far as to promote deferred giving opportunities on their Web sites. Examples include the Kennedy Center, which describes how to make a variety of deferred gifts (*www.kennedy-center.org/support/plannedgiving/estate_planning_options.html*) and the Strand-Capitol Performing Arts Center (*www.wpg.cc/stl/CDA/homepage/1,1006,438,00.html*).

The Role of the Executive Director in Fundraising

Managers of performing arts facilities come into the job with varying levels of fundraising experience, which tends to affect their interest and inclination to get involved. According to Halsey North:

> Theater managers tend to try to do fundraising on top of everything else, and they don't carve out the time to do it in a methodical, planned way. Fundraising is one of those things that an organization must incorporate into everything they do. If theater managers were to stop and think about fundraising as an ongoing program—not something they do to make other things happen—and integrate it into their ongoing operations, they would be more effective.

Executive directors who are the most effective at fundraising take the time to build relationships. We recommend, especially for capital campaigns, that executive directors spend basically 50 percent of their time on fundraising, working to build relationships with individuals, businesses, foundations, and government agencies. It is the relationship building that makes the fundraising possible. I am reminded of the Maui Arts & Cultural Center and Chris Cowan, president and CEO, who has done a remarkable job in building relationships. Previously, she was director of education and, when she became president, she created a network of support among community leaders—engaging them, involving them, and giving them a sense of "ownership" in the success of the Center. She built on that network to implement a very successful fund drive to expand and endow the Center.

The Role of the Board in Fundraising

There are different schools of thought on the role of the board in fundraising. It depends on the maturity of the organization, the quality of the board, the funding requirements faced by the organization, and so on. But generally speaking, there is a significant board role. Here's Siobhan McDermott on the role of boards:

The product is the most critical element to fundraising success. But the board is the second-most critical element. And it really starts at the top. If your chairperson is engaged, then there is also a challenge to the other volunteers to be engaged, and a challenge to the staff to do their very best. In an institution where that doesn't take place, the other volunteers are less accountable, and therefore, very little fundraising is done at the volunteer level.

The best fundraising is done between a partnership of top senior management and volunteers, because the volunteer can speak to the vision and the necessity of a project or an ongoing annual fund, and the staff person can explain why this works and what the financial numbers are. If the board isn't engaged, there is a tremendous ripple effect all the way down.

With one of my clients, there was a group of cultural institutions within a district, and three of those institutions had very powerful boards and very engaged boards that raised a tremendous amount of money and recruited new people with regularity. They recruited new donors and board members, had active special events, and were able to expand facilities and programs. The other institution that we were working for had a community board, and while the community board rightly represented the people that used that facility, because it was more of a community based institution, they had no capacity to fundraise and very little capacity to give themselves. They have struggled constantly because they weren't perceived as the place to be seen, or the board to be associated with.

Corporate Partnerships

Twenty years ago, corporations provided some support to performing arts organizations and facilities, mostly as an act of philanthropy. Those gifts often reflected the interests and preferences of senior management, with little regard for the relationship between giving and broader corporate goals. Two things have happened:

1. Corporations are now very careful and deliberate in the ways that they give money and the effort of making sure that the world knows of their acts of charity.
2. Corporate support of the performing arts has shifted from philanthropic to marketing departments, as businesses view sponsorship of events as an opportunity to reach their customers.

This is old news for most in the performing arts world. But I would contend that the way that corporations give and what they want back is still evolving. Simply put, more and more corporations are less satisfied with writing a check to get their name on a production poster. They wish to be more active and more involved in the effort of delivering a positive message to their customers. Here, Teri Gorman of the Broward Center talks about a recent success:

For the Brazil Night presentations, we have struck up a partnership with TAM-Brazilian airlines. This was obviously so we can get airline flights out of Brazil to get the artists here and so forth, so it was a cost-saving measure on our part. On the part of TAM-Brazilian airlines, they got access to an audience that was likely to travel to Brazil, and that would also include Americans who were attracted to Brazilian culture. So we had a very upscale, mixed audience here at the Broward Center that TAM-Brazil was quite interested in. But interestingly enough, TAM is also involved in a number of other community initiatives and working with the Brazilian-American Chamber of Commerce. They also support other Brazilian cultural entities, particularly in Miami, but because TAM was so pleased with their relationship with the Broward Center, they said they want to be our partner forever on anything Brazilian. That has been nice. We can count on TAM to be a supporter of any kind of Brazilian activity that is going on here, and we have been able to work with them in planning events.

Gorman is part of a growing group of facility marketers who see more change coming. As she says:

I attended a marketing conference in Sydney in 1997, and the futurist Faith Popcorn was there by satellite. She was talking about sponsorships and where they were going, and damn if she wasn't right. She said the day of mass marketing was over and that we would be doing mass individualized marketing. Then she explained mass individualized marketing and essentially the one-to-one marketing theory. She said that sponsors in the future would be sponsoring you in order to get access to your relationships; it was all about relationship marketing. Those relationships will become your most valuable asset.

She also said the days of "put my logo on the brochure" are coming to an end, because it's really going to be that access to the relationships that you have developed, the ability to communicate with those people, that those sponsors are going to be seeking. So as a result, we have developed a lot of our sponsorship proposals with that in mind, and it has been quite successful.

So the challenge for the facility-based marketer is to consider what they have to offer potential sponsors in a number of areas, including:

- Value and meaning of association with a particular presented event or series
- Opportunities to use the performing arts facility and spaces therein for

product promotion and the design of customized special events for the sponsor

- Sharing of mailing and online lists
- Cultivation of public relations for the benefit of the corporate sponsor

But the most fundamental goal of the business is to use sponsorship as a marketing channel—a means to reach a particular group of people and deliver a compelling message. So the key for the performing arts facility is to be able to describe their audience and match them to the target markets of potential sponsors. Thus, they become an effective way to reach prospects and convert them into customers.

Keys to Fundraising Success

Finally, Halsey North lays out his keys to success in fundraising:

> To be successful in fundraising across the board, organizations have to start with strengthening their annual operating support and membership campaigns. We recommend establishing strong membership campaigns that give sequentially more compelling benefits the more members give. Donors want to feel special. They want access to the best seats, good seats at the last minute, and good parking, for example. People want a chance to meet artists and other important people in the community. So, if you take the mix of things people want and create benefit packages, people will pay more money to have a richer experience and, in some communities, a more privileged experience. As you increase those experiences and become more and more important in terms of donors' lives, they will get more involved, and the more they will give. Once you build those relationships, annual donors will be more willing to give capital gifts, and once they have given capital gifts, they are more willing to give endowment gifts as well.

Chapter Seven

Facility Development

ost theater managers, at some point in their careers, face the question of whether to expand, renovate, or adapt their facilities—a complicated issue with major implications for any organization. In this chapter, we consider why it happens and how an organization should approach the facility development process. Then we will review some of the best and worst advice given to facility planners.

Why Develop, Expand, or Improve Facilities?

Facility development or redevelopment projects occur for a number of reasons, including:

Expanding Needs

When facility users outgrow a space, managers are encouraged to explore facility development. Consider a building with a resident producing theater or dance company. Over time, production values increase, creative aspirations change, and audiences grow. Thus, producing organizations need bigger, more technologically advanced facilities, or perhaps spaces that reflect a new creative direction.

We recently completed a project in Schenectady, New York, for the historic Proctors Theatre. There, a small stage and constrained backstage space limited the size of shows coming to the space. In addition, the facility saw the need in the community for smaller performance spaces, as well as for this grand old building to become the anchor of a cultural district at the heart of a downtown redevelopment effort. That idea has become a $25 million project with significant public and private-sector support. The organization and its supporters have moved outward from their own very practical needs to recognize the opportunity to do a lot more that will benefit the arts, the downtown, and the community as a whole.

Declining Facilities

Theaters, like all community facilities, are heavily used, and thus subject to rapid physical decline. Heavy usage wears them out, from public spaces (lobbies, auditorium, and restrooms) to production space (stage, backstage, shops, support space, and storage areas). Some theater managers mitigate the deterioration process through regular maintenance. More often, they only address problems after the facility has deteriorated to the point that repairs are mandatory, and more disruptive.

A case in point is the Capitol Theater in Bowling Green, Kentucky. The theater was built in 1925, closed in 1970, and reopened after a $6 million renovation in 1985. The theater's managers made some periodic inspections but invested very little capital on physical improvements. Then, in 2001, part of the ceiling collapsed, raining large chunks of rotted plaster into the auditorium. The organization was in no way negligent—all inspections were up to date—but a more proactive capital improvement plan would have forced earlier roof repairs. Carrie Barnett was the executive director of the Capital Arts Alliance at the time. She says:

> It was November 28, 2001; I'll never forget it. About thirty minutes after a sold-out performance in the house, a twenty-by-twelve-foot section of ceiling fell forty-five feet onto about six rows of chairs. Then it butterflied, cracked in

the middle, and two sections broke off toward the walls and came down, which damaged about seventy-five seats with the impact. It would have been disastrous if people had been in the building. We were extremely blessed that the performance had ended and the people were away from the damage.

Over the years there had been some minor leaks in the roof that had not been repaired and some moisture had built up in the joists, and over time, those joists became swollen and compromised. That night, there was an extremely loud concert in the house. It was raining outside at the time and there was weight on the roof. Then, there was one big clap of thunder and it fell.

Compliance with Codes and Laws

Given that theaters are places of public assembly and industrial work areas, they are subject to stringent codes and laws as to how they are built and maintained. This includes fire and life safety codes, and laws that guarantee access to facilities for the handicapped. As these codes and laws evolve, facility managers are obliged to make sure that their facilities are in compliance. There are two big issues in the field today. One is the amalgamation of a series of regionally administered codes into a national building code, now referred to as the International Building Code. Second, the Americans with Disabilities Act of 1990 is a set of laws on accessibility that are having a profound impact on the design and operation of theaters. We'll come back to ADA and its impact later in the chapter.

New theaters are designed to comply with current codes. Old theaters are not, and are not generally required to meet all current codes unless they are in the process of making substantial changes or improvements. Naturally, groups are often reluctant to undertake capital repairs for fear that it will trigger the need to comply with newer codes and laws. This has a major impact on the planning process, and is another reason why older theaters tend to delay capital improvements.

"The Opportunity"

The final reason to invest in facility improvement usually begins with an approach from someone outside the organization who presents a new possibility. For example, someone may ask, "Why don't you take over that store next door that's about to close down?" Or, "Perhaps you should become the operator of the Paramount Theater downtown!" Or even, "We could get some big federal grants if you could renovate and operate those apartments next door as space for artists to live and work."

These situations present exciting opportunities, but because there is usually a short period of time in which to decide to proceed, many organizations get into a real pickle. They make rushed decisions based on imposed deadlines, often ignoring their long-term goals and fundamental mission in order to make a deal.

Carmen Pietri-Diaz, managing director of the Nuyorican Theater, speaks of the frenzy that erupted in her organization when a nonprofit developer came along:

> They said they wanted to build an apartment complex across the street from our theater, and that it would be a stronger project if there were some cultural uses for the ground floor. Suddenly we were planning a new theater that was twice the size of our current space, plus a gallery and café! It was just so enticing for us as an organization. Never mind that we were struggling to pay our bills in our existing facilities and had no idea how we might activate larger facilities.

For all of these reasons, and especially for "The Opportunity," it is critically important that organizations understand why they should invest in facilities and that they can rationally approach that decision in a way that engages all key constituents.

I would add one small complication: It is rarely only one of the four situations just described that drives the decision. More often, a combination of issues moves an organization toward a project. For example, an old building needs improvement, the operator needs more space than it has, and there is a great new site down the road. There are many decisions to be made and many competitive options to evaluate. This is not a bad situation, but it's complicated, and what matters is how to respond to that complexity.

The Process of Facility Development

We are management consultants to people who build and operate theaters. A lot of our work focuses on helping government, educational institutions, and arts organizations make decisions about whether to build, expand, or renovate performing arts facilities, and then (if appropriate) moving them toward that goal. A few differences exist when building a new facility without an operating organization already in place, but the process is generally the same. We see that process as a series of steps, which we'll now work through.

The Needs Assessment

This is the critical first step in the process, designed to help the manager make the fundamental decision of what to do. Together with our clients, we examine six important issues:

Audiences

Additional facilities presume additional audiences, so we must understand the regional market and its potential to support the programs and events made possible by the facility project. This is easier said than done. In fact, it is one of the more vexing problems we face. Arts audiences are a fickle bunch, and it is not easy to predict their behavior. We generally work through the following questions:

- What is the geographic reach of current audiences?
- Has that market area grown over recent years, and will that growth continue?
- Has the demographic composition of the population changed, and will it continue to change (the most important issue being the level of educational attainment)?
- Has the organization managed to expand its audiences over time, and do they have the skills and resources to develop new audiences?
- Is there more competition for audiences, and is the organization well positioned to compete for those audiences?

The challenge in assessing potential audiences is that there is no way to demonstrate a market for new facilities—only for the programs that will be presented in new facilities. Thus, it is critical to assess the organization's ability to create and promote new programs, and then consider how likely it is that the market will respond.

A case in point: Some years ago a Latino theater group in Chicago wanted to build a new theater downtown. At that time, the Latino population in Chicago was growing rapidly, and we felt confident that the increased population would translate into expanded audiences for the theater's programs. But we also discovered that Latino audiences in Chicago kept to their own neighborhoods and were unlikely to venture downtown. Thus, we concluded that the market would not initially support a downtown facility for that market, despite the group's specialized appeal to a growing Latino population.

Facility Uses

The critical issue with new, expanded, or improved facilities is how they will be used. So we must get a strong fix on the level of demand from local and touring programs and on how they will activate new or improved facilities. Management, boards, and funders need to know that new facilities will be busy. To me, this is the most important test. New facilities need to be busy in order to justify all of the money it will take to build and sustain them; otherwise, why do it?

There is a catch. New facilities might not exist for three or more years, so we cannot definitively predict how they will be activated. Arts organizations are very fragile. Not many can engage in meaningful planning, and some will likely not exist when new facilities are in place. All we can do is make reasonable assumptions about how facilities respond to user demand and suggest which of those users are likely to be around when new facilities open.

Other Facilities

We must also confirm that new facilities will differ from existing ones. We develop an inventory of current facilities, measuring them in terms of their components, shape, capacity, condition, flexibility, and accessibility to potential users. There are important reasons to do this. It is difficult to make the case for new facilities if current ones adequately meet the demands of arts groups—that is, unless the facility is meant for only one user (which is rarely the case).

Proposed arts facilities should never compete with existing arts facilities. In other words, new theaters should not put existing theaters out of business. This is always a touchy matter with theater managers. In 2003, the city of Durham, North Carolina, was considering a plan for a hall that could convert from 4,000 seats down to 2,000 seats. The principal existing theater in town is the Carolina Theatre, which has just over 1,000 seats, a small stage, and limited backstage space. Their response to recommendations for a new theater was predictable: They were scared to death that a new, larger theater would put them out of business. The city could do a lot to appease them, but it would be an uphill battle to convince them that the presence of an adequate 1,000-seat theater does not negate the need for a larger, better facility.

Benefits and Impacts

The next question to ask is whether new, expanded, or renovated facilities will in any way contribute to the broader goals of the community. Will they contribute to economic development efforts? To the residents' quality of life? To the sense of pride that people feel about their community? To cultural tourism? Or to the effort of attracting businesses and employees to relocate to the community? All of these are important issues, and new performing arts facilities can contribute significantly to each one.

Establishing the benefits and impacts of new facilities helps to build broad support for facility development efforts. Only a minority of adults attends performing arts events each year, but almost everyone cares about community development. If we can frame these projects in terms of broader impacts, we are likely to build a broad base of support, with the endorsement of even the least non-arts-oriented civic leaders.

Comparable Facilities

Another valuable part of a needs assessment is research on comparable facilities in similar communities. There is nothing more compelling than the experience of other communities that have succeeded with similar plans. Stories from other places can play a significant role in informing the organization about particular challenges and issues. They can also give an organization or community the confidence to proceed. It empowers the group with the sense that "If they can do it, so can we!"

Relationship to Mission

The final test for facility development is assessing its relationship to the mission of the sponsoring organization. Will the addition, expansion, or improvement of facilities help the organization achieve its mission? It sounds simple, but too often an organization will pursue a facility development project with little or no regard for the mission and vision that they worked so hard to craft. Their mission may be repeated in grant applications, but its relevance to actual activities is marginal.

The needs assessment can be completed internally without the use of outside consultants. It is cheaper and faster, and may yield the desired results. However, the use of consultants is beneficial when:

- An outside and objective perspective is needed to bring credibility to the project
- There are multiple opinions about the right answer for the organization and community, and thus the need for consensus-building around one idea
- Outside funders are being asked to provide financial support for the effort
- The right decision made early in the process can save the client/community from spending substantial funds on the wrong project

Business Planning

Once the basic viability of the project is determined and if there is a strong consensus, the next step is to consider the implications of new facilities on an organization, to measure the financial implications of new/improved/renovated facilities, and then to engage in planning that will help the organization to prepare for new facilities.

As with the needs assessment, the steps and results of the business plan vary tremendously depending on the situation. However, there is a process for business planning that generally includes the following steps:

Activity Profile

An activity profile is an effort to get a more precise view of who will use new facilities and how, then thinking about the operating impacts of that additional activity. We often hold an event where all potential users of new or improved facilities come together. We talk about their current experiences as facility renters and users, and how those arrangements inhibit or support their efforts. It's amazing how that exercise is very therapeutic for most groups. They don't realize that they share many frustrations, and they relish the opportunity to vent about their current situation. Then we discuss how new or improved facilities might be operated, considering such issues as rent, booking horizons, booking priorities, presenting, scheduling policy, and so on.

The most important step is that we put some blank calendars up on the wall and pretend that new facilities are ready for booking. Then we work through the process of deciding who gets to book first, who gets their dates, and how we are able to fill up the calendar. This is a helpful way to validate demand, to test operating policy, and to get facility users on the same page.

Governance and Operations

For new facilities with no sponsoring organization, we must determine what form of organization to create and how it should be operated. But for projects with a sponsoring organization, it's a different exercise. Here we must consider what additional resources are necessary to operate new or expanded facilities, and then how those resources align with the rest of the organization. Some of these additions are self-evident, but some are not. Specifically:

- *Production staff:* To support the creation of work in new facilities
- *Technical staff:* To manage the operation of the physical space
- *Ticketing staff:* To sell more tickets to more customers
- *Marketing staff:* To promote additional programs in new facilities
- *Development staff:* To fundraise for more programs in new facilities
- *Administrative staff:* To support the building and organizational functions

Pro Forma Operating Budgets

The key to a good business plan is producing pro forma operating budgets that estimate the impact of new or improved facilities on the organization. Our theory for these budgets is that activity is the key driver of earned revenues, which provides the basis for estimating additional expenses. Given this approach, a good budget starts with detailed and defendable estimates of activity (hence our emphasis on the activity profile and the scheduling session). With these inputs, we can fairly estimate how additional facilities will be activated.

With an organization behind the plan for new facilities, the other key is building an operating budget that shows impacts on the larger organizational budget. Through the magic of spreadsheets, we can develop a forecast that starts with several years of actual results, then forecasts the impact of the construction project on an organization, and then, finally, the impact of new facilities. We recently developed an operating pro forma for Proctors Theatre in Schenectady, New York, based on their plans to expand the backstage of a 2,500-seat auditorium and add a new 450-seat theater for community programs. This is an eight-column forecast, showing three years of actual performance, this year's budget, two years of renovation and construction, and finally, two years of operation in expanded facilities. While it might seem like overkill to include so many years in the forecast, we find that historical performance provides the basis for many of the elements of the new forecast, and that the emergence of reasonable and recognizable trends can only occur with those extra years' worth of data.

Funding for Operations

While we are not fundraising consultants, it is inevitable that the issue of fundraising comes up during the business planning exercise. Our pro formas estimate earned revenues and operating expenses with some precision, leading to an estimate of contributed income requirements to balance the budget. In this area, we have observed several general trends:

- New facilities often increase the annual need for contributed income. This is a great surprise for some, but it is an economic reality in this industry. As we've already discussed, the increment depends on the operating costs of new facilities and the nature of the programming they support.
- Capital fundraising can put a strain on annual giving if funders are less inclined to give money on an annual basis as they make contributions to a capital campaign.
- At the same time, if the capital project succeeds, annual giving is more likely to increase. That is to say, a successful project that supports good work will attract additional giving, either from new or existing patrons.
- As discussed in the previous chapter, annual campaigns succeed when integrated into comprehensive fundraising strategies, addressing the role of the board, staff, and other constituents in supporting the organization.

To complete the business plan, it is important to suggest how new facilities affect the total operating budget, including contributed income. Here again, historical trends are helpful, as are stories from comparable projects and a sense of the capacity of the market to fund additional activity.

Economic Impact Analysis

The public sector often plays a role in providing financial support for the construction, renovation, or operation of new facilities. But unless those funders are made up exclusively of arts aficionados, they will need to know what impacts their investment might have on the community. As we said before, a politician who has never set foot in a theater could be your best friend if you can prove benefits and impacts.

Economic impacts are some of the easiest to prove. Americans for the Arts and a number of state and local agencies have published studies that demonstrate how a relatively small investment in this industry has yielded substantial and positive impacts on local and regional economies. We can bring this down to specific projects, forecasting the impacts of the construction or renovation project, the impacts of expanded operations, and the impacts on ancillary spending. This final category is very important, as arts consumers generally spend significant amounts on food, drink, merchandise, accommodation, and transportation as a part of their experience of going to a show.

There are several different models used to measure economic impacts. We favor the RIMS II model developed by the Bureau of Economic Analysis in Washington. For a reasonable fee, one can purchase multipliers for a defined geography and then estimate how expenditures on construction, expanded operations, and related purchase lead to increases in final demand, additional earnings, and new employment.

The question of economic impact, and particularly of ancillary spending, raises one more important issue, which is the trend towards the development of cultural districts. Ever since the 1960s and projects like New York's Lincoln Center and Cleveland's Playhouse Square, communities have recognized that the concentration of cultural activity and facilities can have a major economic impact on a community, attracting a critical mass of activity that acts as a catalyst and anchor for major commercial development. What is new is that communities now recognize that you don't need a facility on the scale of Lincoln Center to achieve these benefits. The Proctors Theatre expansion and addition will receive significant funding from a state agency because of its future role in anchoring a new cultural district in downtown Schenectady.

Physical Planning

We often encourage our clients to begin the physical planning for new or expanded facilities in conjunction with the business planning exercise, because of the relationship between physical, operating, and financial issues. At the end of the needs assessment, we made broad recommendations about the right facilities. So, the task is to flesh out these broad recommendations to the extent that people understand what they are getting and what these new or improved facilities are likely to cost.

There are several different ways to achieve this planning. There are architects, acousticians, theater consultants, and cost consultants who are most interested in providing these up-front services for a very reasonable cost. Part of their motivation to provide those up-front services is that if they do a good job and establish a good relationship with the client, they are in a stronger position to secure a planning and design contract if the project proceeds. Some say that these specialists will do or say anything to get a client into design and construction, but this has not been my experience. Most of these specialists are reputable and will not recommend a project unless it makes good sense. These service providers are highly motivated to work on studies, but they're not going to sacrifice their professional reputation for a questionable contract. The following are key services to be provided at this stage in the process.

Space Programming

A theater consultant and/or architect begins by developing a list of all the spaces and rooms needed in the proposed building. This is a complex exercise, and the team must identify and estimate the net square footage for each needed space, then translate the sum of the net square footage into an overall gross floor area. The difference comes from the adding of mechanical spaces, walls, corridors, and other unprogrammed areas. To be conservative, many consultants recommend adding 50 percent to get the total net area up to the gross floor area. This exercise is appropriate whether the project involves new construction or the renovation of existing space. The key is identifying all of the space needed to fulfill the objectives of new or improved facilities, and then seeing how those spaces fit together.

Robert Long, principal of Theatre Consultants Collaborative, has been writing space programs for more than twenty years. He says:

Some architects and designers don't like the restrictions and bother of creating a space program. I see them as the fundamental expression of what the building wants to be, so I am very pro-program. I like to see at points in design how close we are or far away we are from the program. That tells me if we're being efficient, sloppy, or selfish.

Steve Friedlander is a partner in the theater-consulting firm Auerbach Pollock Friedlander. He sees the programming phase as an opportunity:

Throw your mind forward twenty years to imagine what you are going to do in the building. Now, of course that probably yields a fairly big program, because when you dream, you dream big, and then the realities of budget start to impact the process. But no matter what happens, you can go back to that original program and say, "Okay let's test this. Are we just being hopelessly optimistic, or is this something we want to do?" And the key to any decision is having the space do what you need to do. And if you don't build that in to begin with, you rarely build it in later. You can always add ten more line sets or a new lighting console or new dimmers or some new wiring. But adding another twenty feet to your stage is going to be a tough thing to do when everything else is built up around it. So use the programming effort to define those long-term needs.

Conceptual Design

The space program is valuable as a means to estimate the total footprint required for recommended facilities. It is often valuable to have an architect or theater consultant do a preliminary design to show how key components fit together. This is not any kind of true design, but it does help to see to the overall building in plan form, if only to consider how it fits on a particular site.

Site Planning

Issues around site planning for new or improved performing arts facilities are often very controversial. Sometimes people don't want them at a particular location. More often they do want them in a specific place, generally because of the positive impacts facilities can have on an area. The real challenge with site planning is coming up with a process that allows a group to evaluate potential sites and draw reasonable conclusions. Critical to that exercise is the development of site criteria: The local group must decide and agree on what is most important to them about sites. It is valuable to have this debate before introducing specific opportunities, and interesting to see how these criteria change from community to community. Generally, we see the following near the top of the list: cost of acquisition; proximity to amenities; local and regional access; relationship to other projects, economic development potential and architectural fit.

Capital Budgeting

With a space program, conceptual design, and site plan, specialist consultants are in a position to develop a project budget, including hard costs (for construction), soft costs (permits, fees, and site development), and other project costs (opening events, bridge financing costs, public relations fees, and so on).

Perhaps the worst thing that can happen in a facility development process is that someone throws out a number that represents his or her best guess as to what it will cost to build or renovate at the beginning of the process. Inevitably, the number is less than it should be. Often, it's less than half of what it should be. So, when the architect, theater consultant, or cost consultant finally comes out with a real number, there is some combination of shock, dismay, and political fallout to deal with. Sometimes, particularly when that original number was shared with the local media, the real number can halt, or even kill, a project. And, along the way, the messenger usually gets shot.

Fundraising Feasibility

The next step calls for a very different set of skills. Once the business and programming plans are complete, fundraising experts are often retained to help determine whether the capital resources are available to support the proposed plan. Sometimes, people in a community can figure this out for themselves. Other times, they need outside experts in fundraising and cultural building projects who can provide an objective opinion combined with real skills to help a community to determine if and how funds can be raised.

The process of determining fundraising feasibility is somewhat mysterious. The basic idea is to go out into the community to test an idea with potential funders, determining if some group of supporters is likely to donate significant

funds to the project. The key is to determine how large the single largest donation might be. Fundraisers think of these campaigns as having a pyramid
form, with one single large donation at the top and then lots of small donations at the bottom. If the amount of the largest single donation is known, it
becomes possible to estimate all of the other, smaller donations in order to get
to a total level of funding. If that total estimate does not approach what is
required for the project, it is back to the drawing board for the project sponsors as they try to determine if there are other sources of funding not yet identified, or if there is some way to reduce the project budget to match the available resources.

If the fundraisers suggest that the project is feasible (i.e., that the funds
are likely available to support the project), then you're off and running. But
sometimes there's a catch, as some fundraisers will say, "Yes, the money is
there in the community to support this project, but you're more likely to reach
that target if you hire us to develop and execute the capital campaign." As
they say, caveat emptor.

Design and Construction

Armed with an assessment of needs, some preliminary physical plans, a business plan, and a fundraising feasibility analysis, the organization is finally
ready to proceed with design and construction. This is the most visible and
intensive phase of the effort as the organization proceeds through several
steps.

Selecting Designers

It is an amazing and wonderful thing that there are architects and other specialist consultants who are generally willing and able to compete ferociously
for design and construction projects. The most important first step for the
client is to write a request for proposal (RFP) that invites all of the disciplines
to bid on the project. These proposals can be done separately for each discipline, or by encouraging the formation of teams. Writing a good RFP is in
itself an important step, as it ensures that the client is clear about the project
and the skills it needs to make it happen.

A well-written RFP distributed through proper channels should yield a
large number of submissions. And if that RFP is clear about the criteria with

which architects and consultants would be hired, it is a relatively straightforward effort to take that list of submissions down to a short list. Too many RFPs include unnecessary requirements that can cause responders to lose interest or to see the project as poorly managed.

With a short-list in hand, the client is in a strong position to evaluate prospective design team members who will come and make a presentation of their qualifications, skills, and experience. And it is often amazing to see the extent to which these professionals will go to present themselves.

I would only add one small reminder. No matter how dazzled one might be with one or more groups, don't forget to check their references. In fact, go beyond the references provided and have discussions with lots of previous clients. This will help you make an informed choice and be a smarter client.

The Concept of the Design Team

Perhaps the most challenging aspect of theater development projects is that they must be taken on by a team of specialists, not just an architect. Depending on the size and complexity of the project, one generally needs the following:

- **An architect** to be the designer of the project and often the primary contractor with the client. On larger projects there are often two architects—one engaged to lead the design effort, and one for the production of drawings and local management of the project.
- **An acoustician** to address sound and noise issues, such as the need to keep noise out of the performance space and the critical need to design an acoustical environment in which audience members and performers hear what they are meant to hear.
- **A theater consultant** to help design the auditorium and the relationship with the stage; to create a functionally efficient building around the performance space; and to design, specify, and commission all of the performance equipment systems needed to bring the space to life.

According to Steve Friedlander:

The theater consultant is both a leader and a partner in the planning and design process. I am leading the team in understanding the whys and wherefores of the building. But I'm also collaborating because the buildings are so expensive and complicated that the stakes are very high. Fundamentally, I am a big proponent of form following function, so I'll spend a lot of my time focusing on those functional requirements.

- **Structural, mechanical, and electrical engineers** to design and specify structures and systems that make the building work and meet code requirements.
- **Cost consultants** to estimate project costs on a periodic basis through the planning and design process.

Stewart Donnell is president of Donnell Consulting Inc., one of the pre-eminent theater cost consultants in the world. He describes his practice as follows:

> Our firm is involved in project and cost management of theaters, opera houses, concert halls, and museums in North America and abroad. We feel that our fundamental importance in the development of planning of these complex centers is to establish realistic and comprehensive construction and capital budgets with the owners prior to, or concomitant with, the engagement of the theater planner and the architect. Then, once that is established with suitable provisions made for schedule, for acoustic quality, and for internal and external architectural qualities, and with due regard for the intended site and location of the building, our role is to monitor the project design—from schematics all the way through to completion of construction documents in all the design disciplines. That's the core of our input.

- **General contractors, project managers, construction managers, and owner's representatives** in some combination to get the project completed on time and on budget.

The task of hiring the right team and getting them working toward a common vision is very complicated. And within that is the key dynamic between architect, acoustician, and theater consultant. Richard Pilbrow is the founder of Theatre Projects Consultants and a pioneer in the field of theater consulting. He has worked on hundreds of projects, searching for that balance:

Good theaters are exceptionally complex buildings, serving as a vessel in which art can be created. For better or for worse, they are highly technologically serviced; they must be intimate, which complicates their construction; and they've got to be soundproof. All that together makes the complexity. We've seen, time and time again, that if we let an architect go and do it on his own, it's usually a disaster. An architect with the best intentions in the world cannot have spent his life working on the stage or behind the scenes. Similarly, acoustics is a highly sophisticated craft, and these three disciplines have to come together. And if they don't come together, work as a team, and achieve balance between them, the project is usually in trouble.

Design Steps

With the team in place, a number of months are generally devoted to designing the building, first in schematic design and then in design development. That first round of design is more rudimentary in nature, and allows the client and design team to make fundamental decisions. It is also important because a much more precise cost estimate comes at the end of the schematic design phase. That allows for basic changes in the design without having to redo a detailed design.

Construction Documents

In this phase, members of the design team write construction (or contract) documents, which form the basis for contractors and equipment providers to bid on the right to provide materials, services, or products for the project. The quality of these documents, and the extent to which they are integrated, are very important.

Bid Period

This is the period of time in which potential bidders submit questions and ultimately bids on all of the elements of the project. Successful bidders are contracted to provide materials, products, or services according to the specifications provided.

Construction

Finally, the project goes into construction. In this phase, it is very important that the interests of the client are appropriately represented. Depending on the size and complexity of the project, it may be appropriate to hire a project manager or owners' representative to be on site and help to manage the process.

Commissioning, Training, and Other Preparations

As the project nears completion, significant efforts go toward commissioning new equipment, training personnel to use new facilities, and other preparations. Most important of these is the planning of special performances and events around the opening or new or improved facilities. It is an important opportunity for publicity, a means to build community support, and an important opportunity to recognize those who have contributed to the project.

Managing Costs

The cost to build, renovate, and expand facilities has grown exponentially over the past twenty years. Joshua Dachs is the principal for Fisher Dachs, another world-class theater consulting practice. He sees the escalation of costs this way:

> People are aspiring to a higher level of quality than they did a hundred years ago. Back then, vaudeville houses were thrown up as a commercial enterprise. I think it's generally true that a commercial enterprise is more interested in producing the minimum level needed to produce a profitable result, whereas a performing arts company creating a home for itself is interested in perhaps something more than that.
>
> A city producing a building for itself is interested in something more than just an economic engine—they want to create the postcard image for the town that will appear on the phone book and the post cards. They want to create an important building in the community that will be attractive to large segments; they want to create lobbies that you can throw parties in and that will glorify the donors or the taxpayers of the community. There are a whole range of objectives, some of them having to do with producing for an impressive result, and others having to do with the newer economic and market realities of performing arts centers, which seem to demand higher levels of income-generating space. It's not enough to have four to five square feet per person of entry vestibule and then a bunch of seats.
>
> Today, one looks for a café or restaurant and the donor lounge and the grand foyer that you can rent out for parties and on and on and on, and that

drives the size of projects up beyond what they strictly need for people to come up and sit down and watch whatever is on stage. The other thing that has contributed enormous sums of money to the cost of projects is the idea of "world class" acoustics, where people now commonly aspire to rooms that maintain absolute silence when nuclear bombs are going off across the street; nothing less than that is deemed acceptable. That drives the cost of projects enormously.

Stewart Donnell suggests that the escalation is not inconsistent with other building types:

I could name three office buildings that, if one wishes to express the costs in the old square-foot basis, exceed anything that we've seen coast to coast in performing arts centers. Having said that, it is certainly the case that the ordinary office building, factory, or school is less expensive than a performing arts center. At the same time, a performing arts center is doing a lot more than your conventional building. Costs increase because of the complexity factor, the acoustic value of the theater, equipment values, etc., and what is involved in back of house. And architectural quality externally and internally plays a big part in that.

There's another important aspect around so-called soft costs, and that is the length of time it takes to prepare drawings, the number of meetings that the design team has to have with each other and with the client, and then the time it takes to construct these buildings. When you add it all up, a typical reasonably sized performing arts center could easily take five or six years to do. Often it's more. The same monetary value on an office building will be done in half the time. And then the choice of architect can influence the cost of the building. These days, a lot of prominent clients are engaging offshore architects for their design expertise, which can increase both fees and the time it takes.

Richard Pilbrow has also observed this escalation, which he turns around as a challenge to the industry:

They are very complicated buildings. They are hard to design and hard to build. Whether that should always be the rule is an interesting question. I think the parallel with the growth of sophistication in theater buildings ought to be a quest to make them lighter, more flexible, and cheaper. There is also a complete dichotomy between the arts rapidly changing and it taking seven years to design a building. Theater architects of the nineteenth century would design, build, and open a space in twelve months. So I think that is something we all have to address in the industry.

The high costs in general and the rapidly increasing costs of facilities suggest that it is almost inevitable that there will be at least one point during the design process that the cost estimate will come in well above the budget. The challenge is not to panic but to understand why it has happened (generally some combination of the passage of time, construction cost escalations, and a larger program), and then determine how to move forward. And to move forward, it is important to understand the variables in play. I find it useful to think in terms of the following diagram:

The program is the size of the building and what's included. Quality is much more broadly defined, including the level of architecture, materials, finishes, acoustical quality, theatrical functionality, etc. The cost is self-evident.

The thing to bear in mind is that only two of these variables can move at a time. If the cost must come down but a certain level of quality must be achieved, the only answer is to reduce the program. If the program must remain and there is no more money to be raised, then quality must be sacrificed. And so it goes until there is consensus on the likely cost of the project and what one gets back in terms of physical space and its quality.

Affect of ADA on Theater Design and Construction

In 1990, President George H.W. Bush signed the Americans with Disabilities Act (ADA), declaring it "the world's first comprehensive declaration of the equality of people with disabilities, and evidence of America's leadership internationally in the cause of human rights. With today's signing of the landmark

Americans with Disabilities Act, every man, woman, and child with a disability can now pass through once-closed doors, into a bright new era of equality, independence, and freedom."[1]

Though fairly recently passed, the ADA has deep roots in the Civil Rights era of the 1960s and reinforces the Fair Housing Amendments Act of 1988. The law is a windfall to the more than 53 million estimated Americans (a number that is growing with the "graying of society") who have one or more disabilities, and who, until the 1990s, could not participate equally with the rest of America in many cultural events.

However, the requirements of the ADA have also significantly increased the cost of building and designing theaters. Robert Long believes the ADA is about 90 percent useful and 10 percent not. "The ADA is a well-intentioned legislation, but the implementation of it has been a real mess," he says. "It is quite a cost-driver. Some of it is wonderfully appropriate, but some of it is problematic because of the lack of guidelines. It has been interpreted in some cases to demand wheelchair access to technical catwalks and grids, which is impractical and potentially unsafe. So in the name of equal access, we are encouraging unsafe practices to happen that would not otherwise have happened."

Richard Pilbrow agrees, "ADA has had an enormous impact on the entire country, and of course an extremely expensive impact. Everyone supports access for people with every form of disability to theaters. However, because the law is interpreted locally, there are areas of the country where the principles are carried to an extreme, and that makes buildings very difficult and expensive to design and build, which is unfortunate."

The Role of the Client in Planning and Design

Throughout the planning process, the role of staff and board is critical. Nonprofit arts organizations tend to be overworked even without a construction project to deal with, so it is very important that additional resources are brought to bear on the facility development effort. Josh Dachs has seen the good, the bad, and the ugly. Here's what he looks for in a client:

> No project succeeds without leadership, and woe to that community where the architect provides that leadership. The leadership needs to come from within the community and within the organization that is going to be operating the

facility. That leadership needs to have the will and the political acumen and the business intelligence to move the project forward through a vast forest of obstacles and challenges on fundraising fronts, on political fronts, in every way. We out-of-towners can certainly help educate, inform, prepare, and advise, but we are not the ones who are going to go to lunch with the mayor and have a serious chat that is going to result in the city changing its mind about some key issue.

The other thing is that they need to take the time to understand the project in all of its infinite details, and be prepared to make decisions about hundreds of issues. And in this, I think the clients that are the best off are the ones who have local leadership in place and who have hired a skilled facilities manager during the planning process, or even at the outset of the planning process. So when it comes down to making tough choices—because there is never enough money to afford everything you might like—those choices are made in the context of an overview of the business plan. This ensures that things are not traded away that might otherwise have produced key elements of revenue, or reduced contract cleaning service costs in some way, or whatever.

It has to be somebody like Paul Beard coming on during the programming and schematic design effort in Fort Worth and fighting as he did for his catering pantry and his refrigerated storage, which we normally wouldn't have included to that extent. Yet his feeling was that this was going to be an important component in making that building's business plan work. And if you talk to him today, I'm sure he'll say that that was needed.

Lessons Learned

Finally, I would offer some advice after fifteen years in the field of advising others on performing arts facility development. I have organized that advice under a series of truths and falsehoods that often play a huge role in our work.

"It Takes a Long Time for Something to Happen Suddenly"

This is from Louis Fleming, a director of Theatre Projects Consultants and the man who taught me to do this work. What it suggests is that facility development projects often have a long and painful gestation period. A project is often an idea that floats around the organization and the community for months and often years before anything happens, which tends to drive people away from the project. Then, when things finally come together, the project takes off, moving at high speed through planning, design, and construction.

"We May Work in the Arts, But It's All about Politics and Economics"

This is Fleming's second truism, and it's closely related to the first statement. The reason that many projects take so long to get off the ground is that their progress depends heavily on political and economic issues. We might be able to make a strong case for the project to serve the needs of an organization or the cultural community, but we must also line up the political and economic forces necessary to make it happen. This includes our work on economic impacts and the funding plan.

"A Bigger or Better Theater Is a Good Idea, as Long as It's Financially Self-Supporting"

Too many clients of ours come into these projects insisting that it can't be a "money-loser." That statement is misleading to begin with. Cultural facilities don't make money. They survive by balancing their operating expenses with a combination of earned revenues and contributed income. That contributed income is not just there because the facility can't make it on earned income. It is there because it is a worthy investment in the organization and also, hopefully, the community.

"I Never Met a Partner I Didn't Like"

This is not Mae West speaking, but it does reflect one of the new realities of facility development—that they rarely proceed without the presence of partnerships. These projects are so expensive and so challenging, and take so long to achieve, that project sponsors need all the help they can get. There are many kinds of partnerships, including the following:

- A school partner provides operating funds and facility management expertise in return for daytime access to facilities.

- A commercial developer provides capital funding and construction skills in return for the right to develop residential space above new cultural facilities.
- A corporate partner gives equipment, capital funding, and ongoing support in return for its name on the theater and special programs directed toward its employees.

"Bigger Is Better"

This is one of the great frustrations in these projects. It seems to be a very difficult thing for people to separate quality from quantity. I remember sitting in a politician's office a couple of years ago, trying to convince him to support a plan for a wonderful 1,200-seat hall. His opinion, expressed with a fist thumping on the table, was: "Paducah's got a 1,800-seat hall, Owensboro's got a 2,000-seat hall, and I want a 2,200-seat hall!"

I don't mean to make light of this issue, because it's very important. In many communities, the issue of capacity becomes the debate. And given that resources are scarce, it often boils down to a choice between bigger or better. We often (but not always) end up arguing for better, because smaller facilities tend to be more responsive to the needs of local arts groups, and because better facilities create opportunities for the presentation of great work. I would also suggest that this issue will become even more important over the next ten years. The performing arts face extreme and growing competition from other forms of live and electronic media. And the only way to compete for audiences is by offering wonderful aesthetics, great acoustics, and a sense of intimacy, all contributing to an unforgettable experience.

"Keep Your Eyes on the Road"

Building projects have a nasty way of diverting the attention and focus of an organization away from their core activities of producing or presenting. Perhaps it's just less success with fundraising and marketing. But it can also lead to major problems with programming, staff, and volunteer leadership. I remember working with a ballet some years ago that was so focused on getting new facilities that they completely neglected their dancers, audiences, and school. When facilities finally opened, they were in a deep hole in terms of talent, money, and energy. And it took them years to climb out.

"Give Us a New Theater, and We'll Be Great"

This is a falsehood—that organizations will automatically perform better in new facilities, as if the lack of new facilities is the only thing holding them back. This is rarely the case, and that there are too many instances of organizations failing once they arrived in bigger and better spaces. To be positive about the whole thing, consider the case of the Dallas Symphony, which worked long and hard to prepare for the new Myerson Concert Hall. And when that facility opened, the Symphony was absolutely prepared to take full advantage of the new hall. Their board was stronger, their staff was expanded, the quality of their program was better, and their audience development skills and resources were enhanced.

"It's All about Teamwork"

Robert Long here summarizes the collaborative nature of theater development:

> The process of designing a performing arts building is parallel to the dynamic of creating a performing arts production, in that the most successful ones are the ones where there is the best collaboration of talent. I'm very comfortable with the nature of collaboration between the theater consultant, acoustical consultant, architect, construction manager, and engineers, which envelops various aspects of the development: structural, mechanical, electrical, civil, landscape, graphics, food service, safety, traffic, parking. The way that all of these collaborate to achieve the final outcome is very much like a production, where you have a director and a costume designer, lighting designer, set designer, technical director, production manager, performers, make-up director, sound designer—all of those things come together to create the most effective production.

NOTE

1. *www.adata.org/whatsada-history.html*

Chapter Eight

Strategic Planning for Performing Arts Facilities

I n this chapter we explore the development, use, and execution of strategic planning in performing arts facilities. By "planning," we mean the effort engaged in moving the facility and organization toward the achievement of mission. This does not include the capital planning that we discussed in chapter 4, though it is often motivated by the need to improve, expand, or replace facilities.

Though I've been largely avoiding comparisons between facility management in North America and other parts of the world, I can't resist this anecdote from Teri Gorman, the vice president of external affairs at the Broward Center in Fort Lauderdale, but previously the marketing director for the Aotea Center in Auckland, New Zealand:

> New Zealanders are quite good with strategic planning. Not only do they do a strategic plan, they do a backup plan, and a backup plan to the backup plan. These people plan like planning is what it's all about, and to a certain extent they have an edge over Americans.
>
> I was at a meeting one time in Auckland, and in my typical American way, I enthusiastically proposed an idea. They said, "Well, where's your plan?" I said, "You don't need a plan—it would just be great!" And they said, "You know, one of these days, you Americans are going to learn that your

enthusiasm doesn't always overcome your lack of planning." That was kind of an eye-opening cultural difference for me. We are the ultimate optimists here. "It will be great! If we just work hard enough it can go!" But sometimes it just doesn't work that way.

Strategic Planning and Mission

"Strategic planning" is simply and best defined as "planning with a goal." And in the case of nonprofit or public-sector arts organizations and facilities, that goal is all about the mission of the building and organization that runs it. In fact, to be strategic, planning must move the building/organization toward the achievement of mission. Here are a few fairly typical mission statements for performing arts facilities:

The mission of the *Arts Center and Theatre of Schenectady* is to provide a diverse program with excellent performances, to restore and preserve the beautiful Proctors Theatre, to serve as a cultural center for the Capital Region, and, to the extent that resources permit, support activities that contribute to the quality of life of the region.

The mission of *Lubbock Regional Arts Center* is to build and maintain a community arts center that is available and affordable to local artists to facilitate their art through education, performance, and exhibition for the citizens of the South Plains.

Maryland Hall for the Creative Arts serves the Anne Arundel County community by providing a broad range of creative experiences through quality arts education and culturally diverse programs in the performing and visual arts.

As the focal point of performing arts activity in South Florida, the *Performing Arts Center of Greater Miami* will serve as a showcase for the finest in established and developing cultural programs. The Center will be the foundation on which resident organizations build their programs and extend their reach. The Center will serve as both a showcase and laboratory, providing first-class, accessible facilities for smaller, emerging, and developing organizations as well as resident companies. It will provide audiences with opportunities to share South Florida's many cultures, offering insights and understanding. As an educational resource, the Center will broaden the horizons of our children and enhance our quality of life by offering a full range of cultural and learning experiences.

So what characterizes a good mission statement?

1. **It is a big idea**: Fundamentally, the mission must be a based on big idea, one that motivates people inside the organization and is worthy of support from outside the organization. A mission that is based simply on filling a niche or serving a particular group might be seen as uninspiring and unworthy.
2. **It is understood**: In order for the mission to inspire and invite support, it must be understood. It cannot be too complicated or obtuse.
3. **It is inclusive without being vague**: Too many mission statements suggest service to too many groups in too many ways, such that it sounds either watered down or impossible.
4. **It should be theoretically achievable**: Some mission statements bite off much more than a nonprofit organization can chew, creating a sense of unreality around the enterprise. On the other hand, the mission can't be seen as being too easy to achieve.

One of my favorite facility mission statements is that of the Nuyorican Poets Café. Their mission is:

To furnish the information and the vision to empower the underclass to join the mainstream and reinvigorate the American temper.

It is an ambitious, compelling, and inspiring mission statement. It provides a lot of flexibility to the organization as it considers how to accomplish its goals.

It is not likely to change. And if that mission is achieved, it will be time for a large celebration, followed by a plan to close the whole thing down. Or, as one former client used to say: "It will be time to declare victory and move on."

I also admire the mission of the Arts Center Foundation in Dayton, Ohio, which manages the historic Victoria Theater and the new Benjamin and Marion Shuster Performing Arts Center. President Mark Light says it well:

> Our mission statement is a very brief seven words: Celebrating life by making our customer the star. That's it. But it allows us to do a lot. It is a reminder that you don't celebrate life with a dark building, and it also reminds us that our focus is on making our customer the star. We have a real customer focus, and that idea flows down into all of our lines of business.

Changing the Mission

One of the great debates about mission statements is how often they should change. At one extreme, there are some who believe that the mission should be something figuratively carved in stone, meant to remain unchanged over the life of the organization, if not the building. At the other extreme are those who take the position that the mission should always be evolving, based on changes in the organization and the environment around it. Rod Rubbo, president and CEO of the Cultural Center for the Arts in Canton, Ohio, says:

> I don't have a problem with changing mission. I think changing times and changing situations almost require you to re-look at your mission statement. I think any mission statement, even a brand new one, will retain the essence of that organization, although it may have been reformed or restated in another way. We are a classic example—we are in effect reinventing ourselves because we have to if we are going to grow, not only to increase our funding, but to strengthen our role in the community. This has caused a total review and restatement of the mission statement and operational plan.

On the other side of the argument is Christopher Beach, director of the Performing Arts Center at Purchase College, part of the State University of New York system:

I like that our mission statement has a certain permanence, like the Constitution. Certainly there are pressures to changes the mission, usually when artistic direction changes. If they sack me here and hire someone else, they are going to end up with someone else's vision. But I think the mission statement is written broadly enough to encompass different artistic visions.

So let's accept that an occasional change to the mission might be appropriate. And we'll do that partly because it turns out that the process of rewriting the mission statement is as valuable as the result of that effort. This is because the effort is usually undertaken by a group of people within the organization. It gives them an opportunity to think through and share ideas about the organization, leading (usually) to a more unified and cohesive leadership. This same comment may be made in reference to strategic planning as a whole, when a focused leadership group assembles to set or reset the course for the organization.

Mission, Vision, and Values

In addition to mission statements, many nonprofit arts organizations develop vision statements and express a set of core values that drive their behavior. These are important steps for some organizations, if they feel that the best way to think of the future is in terms of what they might look like as an organization when they get there, or what shared values will send them in that direction. These are valid tools and exercises to help organizational leadership express and agree on where they are going, how they are going to get there, and what they will look like when they arrive. But these additional exercises do not replace or diminish the importance of mission, which is required for all nonprofit organizations and is critical to their formation and operation.

The Strategic Planning Process

Most performing arts facilities follow some sort of strategic planning process. Here, Kelley Shanley talks about strategic planning at the Broward Center for the Performing Arts:

We have an ongoing strategic planning process here and a plan that is as inte-grated into the daily operation as we can make it. It is understood by as many people in the organization as possible, and it is revised annually to adjust for changes in conditions in the performing arts. The amount of time we spend looking at future trends and planning is perhaps a bit of a luxury to an organization that is just trying to get through today. But for us, it has been worth the five years it has taken to get to a point where if you asked any employee whether they knew anything about the strategic plan at the Broward Center, they would probably be able to tell you a little bit about it. Hopefully they could even tell you about the piece of it that specifically relates to them! And when you congratulate people on a job well done, you can relate it to the greater organizational goals.

But changing the mission is also incredibly important for moving into the future, because what we do now is not going to work in ten years. Most businesses tend to develop a business plan based on a certain growth curve. Over time, that growth will level off, so a lot of our work must go into extending that curve to be viable for the long term. Our planning focus right now is how to extend this curve. How are we going to get higher per-capita concessions? Should we raise the price on parking? Should we do more prof-itable programming?

Colin Jackson, CEO of the Epcor Centre for the Performing Arts in Calgary, takes a very active role in the development of a strategic plan:

I'd like to think it was a consensual process the last time around. It went back and forth—it was board visioning, and staff visioning, and then back into smaller groups and back to me, and then back out into smaller groups and then back to the full board. An inflating and deflating process of back and forth. The current plan ended in 2003, so we prepared another four-year plan.

I am driving the development of the new plan. The board is expecting it, but I am driving it. We have been able to move them to a more of a gover-nance role. That's one of the blessings of having some fairly serious corporate people on the board—they do get it. So the process is valuable, but it's also painful. That's partly my fault, because I think too laterally and confuse people by not being clear. But it's also because these organizations are so diversified. If you were building a business from scratch, you wouldn't put together property management, customer service products, entertainment, education, research, and advocacy into one business—you would realize that is a really stupid idea.

Approaches to Strategic Planning

There are as many approaches to strategic planning as there are strategic planners. But there are some common threads. I would suggest that planning breaks down into four sections:

1. Planning to Plan
2. Internal and External Environment Research and Analysis
3. The Development of Strategy
4. The Execution of Strategy

Let's consider each of these elements in turn.

Planning to Plan

Planning to plan, the first step of strategic planning, is often ignored and too often diminished as a critical step in the process. Planning doesn't start by itself. Someone has to get the ball rolling. Sometimes it's a staff member who sees that the last plan has expired. Sometimes it's a board member who believes that changing circumstances necessitate a new plan. Or sometimes an outside force (i.e., government or a private funder) dictates the need for a new plan as a condition of support.

However it happens, there is then some impetus for a plan that requires someone to develop a planning proposal. That proposal should include a definition of the objectives of the plan, the process by which a plan will be developed and implemented, a description of the resources required (human and otherwise) to complete the plan, and a schedule for the effort.

The next step is building support and consensus within the organization on the need for a plan and how it will work. Senior management and leadership must sign on in order to formalize their commitment to the effort, and also to make sure that all are coming into the process with the same objectives.

That might sound like a small point, but it often happens that key personnel can come into a planning effort with different goals and varying degrees of commitment to the process.

Ultimately, the planning proposal should become a planning contract wherein key parties agree on what they're trying to achieve, how they'll do it, what effort it will take on everyone's part, and when they'll have it completed.

One of the big challenges at this stage is setting the timeframe for the plan. Is it a two-year, three-year, five-year, or even ten-year plan? The farther out the horizon, the more visionary one can be, but the value of the effort drops quickly with the decreasing reliability of the forecasting.

We've done planning work for a couple of performing arts organizations whose long-term planning efforts had been largely stopped because they'd lost faith in the value of planning. And the principal reason they'd lost faith was that soon after they'd finish a plan, circumstances would change, invalidating many of the planning assumptions. So, were they making bad assumptions, not building enough flexibility into the plan, or attempting to plan too far out into the future?

Internal and External Environment Research and Analysis

The research and analysis are the grunt work of strategic planning—the effort of collecting all of the information required to assess the position and prospects of the organization/facility. On the internal side, there is much information to collect:

Mission

A review of the past and present mission statements, and an assessment of how the organization is moving toward the achievement of the mission.

Mandates

Mandates are externally dictated things that an organization must do. For example, a 501(c)(3) organization must have an educational element to its mission in order to qualify for tax-exempt status. Here again, the task is to identify mandates and assess how well the organization is working to achieve them.

Resources

There must be an audit of the current skills and resources of the organization, including its personnel, programs, volunteer leadership, and supporters.

Present Strategy

Whether or not current strategy is explicit, there must be some review of what it is and how it has been followed.

Performance

Analyzing performance tends to start with financial analysis, but it should also extend to other indicators, such as media reviews, how the market is being served, the development of artists and/or programs, the role of the organization/facility in the development of the community, and so on.

Then, on the external side, there are several areas to explore:

Forces and Trends

This covers all sorts of things going around the organization that can influence its pursuit of mission. John Bryson, in his book *Strategic Planning for Government and Nonprofit Organizations*,[1] suggests that there are eight major forces at work that will have particular importance in the nonprofit sector:

1. Increasing social and organizational complexity
2. More privatization and increased interaction between public, private, and nonprofit sectors
3. Continuing technological innovation and change
4. Limited public-sector resources and growth
5. Diversity of the workforce, customer base, and citizenry
6. A shift toward individualism, personal responsibility, and civic republicanism
7. Increasing concern for quality of life and environmentalist
8. Societal changes that are incremental and continuing, not revolutionary

Each of these is fascinating in its own right. The real challenge for the performing arts facility is determining which ones are more or less relevant to the future of the organization.

Resource Controllers

Resource controllers are things/people/programs that can affect the assets and value of the organization. Good planning depends on understanding each of these groups and how they are changing. For performing arts facilities, resource controllers tend to include:

- **Customers:** those who attend events
- **Clients:** the arts organizations and promoters who activate facilities
- **Funders:** those who provide financial support, from both the public and private sectors
- **Regulators:** local, state, and federal government through laws and guidelines for nonprofit, tax-exempt, and educational institutions

Competitors and Collaborators

Finally, there must be extensive analysis of the organization/facility's collaborators and competition. Collaborators might include other facilities with whom shows are booked, organizations whose programs are presented, and schools where programs are delivered.

Competition is a difficult concept within the nonprofit performing arts industry. The first challenge is deciding who and what a performing arts facility competes with. The easy answer, and one that often ends the analysis, is that we compete with all other uses of leisure time—from television to naptime. And who can compete with that?

As we discussed in chapter 5, the challenge is to limit the analysis first to direct competition and then to those other activities that keep people out of a theater. This way, you can work on how to best position the choice to attend a live event at your facility as you compete for the time and resources of the potential consumer.

It also helps to think of competition in terms of what one is competing for. In the case of performing arts facilities, that usually includes audiences (where else our current and potential audience might go), programs (who will be the presenter of a particular event), and funding (the increasingly intense competition for capital and operating support from the public and private sectors).

SWOT Analysis

The final step in research and analysis is defining the strengths (the *S*) and weaknesses (the *W*) of the organization, as well as the opportunities (the *O*) and threats (the *T*) it faces. Note that strengths and weaknesses are about what's going on inside the organization today, whereas opportunities and threats are more about what's going on outside the organization today and looking into the future.

This is a good group exercise, taking all of the facts and insights from the review of internal and external environments in order to present an assessment of where the organization is today and what future it faces.

There are a couple of keys to the research and analysis:

1. One simple rule is that the more you put into this, the more you get out of it. If all you're going to do is download reams of information developed somewhere else, then you won't get much back. It is very important to do good research that is current, relevant, and actionable—meaning that it gives you something to work with.
2. The most important thing, in terms of external analysis, is that the organization takes a position on the future. You can't just present all sorts of data in all of its complexity and uncertainty. You have to go further to say what you think will happen going forward based on the information you have at hand. This does not mean wild guesses, but rather informed conclusions. For example:
   a. "We believe that the local economy will continue to expand for at least three more years, adding prosperity and stability to the community."
   b. "Technological advancements, and the local adoption of new technologies, are likely to make online ticketing more feasible to the extent that significant capital investments in ticketing systems are soon appropriate."
   c. "Regional competition for touring product will likely intensify over the next five years as the supply of shows and number of promoters shrinks."

The Development of Strategy

The most difficult and least linear part of planning is the somewhat magical process by which ideas and insights about the organization and facility turn into strategy. In my experience, the best way for this to happen is to assemble the planning group in a room, looking at the results of the SWOT analysis (which they have hopefully informed), and then to collectively look for themes, links, and ideas based on that summary.

The core strategy for a performing arts facility, as for other organizations, may be one simple idea, such as, "Become the preeminent home for the performing arts in the county," or, "Create opportunities for the entire community to participate in the performing arts."[2]

But at the same time, that strategy must be:

- Technically workable and philosophically acceptable to key stakeholders
- Ethical, moral, legal, and in pursuit of the organization's mission
- Connected to the strategic issues it is intended to address

That final requirement is often the most difficult, reflecting the challenge of connecting a big idea with the preceding research and analysis that led to the identification of issues and themes. Michael Kaiser describes a very focused approach to strategic planning:

> I believe in using a strategic framework that is logical and flexible. It allows one not just to come up with a strategy, but also to modify strategy as the environment changes. And so I use a very simple framework for developing strategies. I teach it and I use it, every day. I don't believe that strategic planning is about committees and meetings and filling out charts. It is about finding a creative way to solve problems, using what you have, and working through environmental constraints to achieve your mission.

The Execution of Strategy

The execution of strategy is often a greater challenge than the development of strategy, and the failure of strategic planning is often the result of poor execution. Too many organizations invest significant time and energy into writing a strategic plan, then push it aside as other priorities emerge. This is not just a problem for performing arts facilities, nor simply for the nonprofit sector as a whole. It is a problem for all who undertake planning.

Much thinking and writing has been done over the past ten years on the problem of strategy execution. Out of this research have come a number of new tools and approaches that help organizations stay focused and disciplined as they move from planning to the execution of plans. One of the more successful tools is called the Balanced Scorecard. It was developed by Robert Kaplan, an accounting professor at Harvard University, and David Norton, a Boston-area consultant, on the basis of a research study they conducted on performance measurement in a set of companies.[3] The study suggested that a reliance on financial measures of performance was affecting the ability of these companies to create value.

Over the last decade, the Balanced Scorecard has become a popular and well-used strategic planning tool for corporations. But only recently has the tool been adapted to and then adopted by the public and nonprofit sectors. We learned of the Balanced Scorecard at the 2003 Opera America conference, where the Lyric Opera of Boston conducted a session on their use of the Balanced Scorecard. We see it as a powerful tool for nonprofit arts organizations because:

- It is a well-established approach that has worked in the public and commercial sectors
- It connects mission, vision, values, and strategy to everyday practices and efforts within the organization
- It focuses the organization on the execution of strategy by establishing objectives, measures, targets, and initiatives that go beyond financial performance in pursuit of mission
- It is an inclusive process that engages all levels of staff and volunteer leadership in the achievement of strategy

As with other good planning tools, the Balanced Scorecard depends on the following:

- High-level engagement and support of the planning effort.
- A clear understanding of mission and, if appropriate, the vision and the core values of the organization.
- The development of core strategy per the above sections.

The Balanced Scorecard really kicks in once core strategy is set. It is therefore a tool to move from strategy to implementation. The first step is the development of a strategy map that demonstrates how the organization can achieve its mission using a core strategy in terms of four different perspectives. Those perspectives are:

1. **The Customer**: Whom do we serve as an organization, and how do we serve them?
2. **Internal Processes**: What are the things we must do well in order to serve our customers and achieve our mission?
3. **Learning and Growth**: In which areas must we learn and grow at the individual and organizational levels?
4. **Financial**: What results must we achieve in order to survive and prosper?

The Balanced Scorecard becomes most powerful when the organization can connect these perspectives—expressing strategy through cause-and-effect linkages. For example, additional fundraising (financial) will allow the organization to increase marketing training (learning and growth), which leads to a more effective segmented marketing strategy (customer), which in turn leads to greater community support.

Once a strategy map is completed, the next step is to identify measures to track progress in the achievement of various objectives. There are both leading and lagging measures. Lagging measures tell you if you have met your objectives after the fact. Leading measures tell you how you are doing along the way, allowing you to adjust performance and be more successful in achieving that particular goal.

Following are a series of possible leading and lagging measures for a performing arts facility, considered in terms of potential objectives for the organization:

OBJECTIVE	LEADING MEASURE	LAGGING MEASURE
Enlarge volunteer base	New volunteers sign up	Impact on customer service
More corporate partnerships	Number of pitches to potentials	Level of corporate funding
Increase board giving	Accepted give or get policy	Level of board giving
Increase earned revenue	Marketing plan adoption	Ticket sales

The leading measures, though often harder to identify and quantify, are very important as a means to see how the organization is doing while it's still early enough in the process to change course and consider other options.

The next and final step in the development of the Balanced Scorecard is the effort of translating objectives and measures into specific initiatives with budget allocations. Here again are several examples for a nonspecific performing arts facility.

OBJECTIVE	MEASURE	INITIATIVE	ALLOWANCE	TIMING
HR Policy	Annual Evaluations	Hire HR Director	$50,000	FY2006
More Research	Annual Surveys	Staff Training	$10,000	FY2005
Diversity	Audience Breakdown	Ad Campaign	$20,000	FY2004

There is no magic to these ideas, but the specific plans and budgets help the organization to be disciplined and focused on their realization. That is the value of the Balanced Scorecard and similar tools. They provide an effective means to translate strategy into specific tasks and budgets. But they only work if they are:

- Embraced by leadership (both staff and volunteers)
- Understood and adopted throughout the organization
- Supported with human and financial resources

Here is Judith Allen on the execution of strategy:

As soon as everybody on staff and board agrees, I develop an implementation plan with every single thing that is listed. I go back to my staff and/or board and I say, "This is the timeframe I've put down. Is it realistic? If it is, you need to meet that. If you cannot meet it, you need to tell me as soon as you can. If it's a stupid idea, we are going to take it off the table, or let it evolve into something else." In truth, it's a discipline. And if you stick to it, it works.

NOTES

1. Bryson, John, *Strategic Planning for Public and Nonprofit Organizations* (San Francisco: Jossey Bass Publishers, 1995), 88.
2. Ibid.
3. Niven, Paul R., *Balanced Scorecard Step-by-Step for Government and Nonprofit Agencies* (New Jersey: John Wiley & Sons, 2003).

Chapter Nine

Staff and Volunteer Management

Performing arts facility managers are fortunate in that most of the people who work in these buildings are pursuing this work as a career, and they want to be there. It's an attractive place to volunteer and/or work for many reasons. For some, it's the chance to see and hear great performances. For others, it's the opportunity to work near artists, entertainers, and celebrities. And for others, it's the societal value and benefit of the arts and culture. So the staffing challenge for the facility manager is matching the expectations of those who seek this work, providing the support, training, and opportunities for advancement that will keep people in the business, and advancing the next generation of facility managers. And the volunteer challenge is to create opportunities for community members to add value to the operation of the facility while still allowing those individuals to take something positive out of the experience.

But here's the problem: In most nongovernmental performing arts facility organizations, there is little in the way of structure and systems relating to employee and volunteer management and development. And facility managers are often spending more time than they would like dealing with human resource issues, nervously hoping that their improvisational approach won't land the organization in hot water.

Brenda Carter, the director of human resources for the Cincinnati Arts Association, which runs the Aronoff Center and other facilities, talks about how the HR function evolved:

> Twenty years ago, HR in the arts meant maintaining a personnel file. Then, people started to recognize that it's a bigger deal. They were partly motivated by fear and anxiety about litigation, as well as the more proactive part of taking care of their people. So the field has evolved a lot since then.

The other broad issue is that those who work in the arts are sometimes not as disciplined or effective at the dirty work of managing a large group of people. Tanya Collier is the human resources director for a series of public facilities in Portland, including the Portland Center for the Performing Arts:

> Performing arts centers are generally run by arts people, and they tend to be a little more informal with their rules and regulations. And they can be pretty bad at disciplining and firing folks, so you kind of need somebody to do that, and that goes without even mentioning the labor contracts.
>
> To begin with, I offer to do almost all the writing for managers who are working with people. If they have to discipline someone or have to fire someone or whatever, I'll do those letters for them. I first approached it saying I would train everybody to do it themselves, but there are so many legal ramifications of not doing it correctly, and folks hate doing it so much that they don't do it, and then we get into more trouble in the long run. So I've adopted more of an attitude of, "I would love to help you out by doing this. How about if I draft a letter and you edit it, instead of you drafting it and me editing it?"

So let's work through some of those structural needs and see how some facility managers have put those in place. Then, we'll consider how a range of management styles is used to develop effective and committed staffs.

Human Resource Management Structure and Systems

Only the largest performing arts centers have distinct human resource departments, and even in those cases it's a relatively new phenomenon. Historically, many performing arts centers have managed to avoid the expense and hassle of an HR function, or were able to take advantage of HR systems and structures in place within local government. This is changing as facility managers bring these issues front and center. According to Judith Allen in Charlotte:

> Only ten years ago, performing arts centers were not appreciating the importance of HR. They didn't see it as money well spent and they didn't make the connection between training and low turnover. When you have a training person instead of your supervisors training everyone, it helps people maximize their knowledge of things like computers. And then you have leadership training and supervisory training, and it reduces the threat of litigation. I believe that HR is like a library at a university—it affects everyone. Now everyone seems to be getting an HR director. Everyone's looking at employee handbooks, training programs, and programs that provide information on details like who gets cell phones or how to limit personal use of computers, in addition to programs on training and employee relations.

Here is a quick review of the principal elements of a human resources function relevant to a performing arts facility:

Labor Law

The first and most important responsibility of the human resource function is to ensure that the law is being observed and obeyed with regards to the employment of paid and volunteer staff. Labor law in the United States is based on complicated and ever-changing legislation designed to protect the rights of employees, employers, and labor organizations. Those rights include freedom of speech and assembly, equal rights, and the right to sue.[1] It is a significant task and responsibility to translate these rights and laws into operating practices and policy.

Recruiting and Hiring Policy

There are very specific ways that facilities can and should recruit new employees, including laws on how jobs are advertised, guidelines for the selection of candidates, and good practices in the way that employees are invited to join the organization. Kelley Shanley hits the mark with this comment on teaching supervisors how to interview:

> Supervisors tend to hire who they like, who they got along with in the interview, and who they had a couple of drinks with. And while a good attitude is an important element, it's certainly not the only element that you want to scrutinize during an interview process. But then they get nervous about what they can and can't ask in the interview. So it's very important that they're trained by a human resources specialist.

Job Descriptions

It is very important that all incoming employees and volunteers have a written job description that lays out the responsibilities of the job, reporting relationships, and the expectations of employers. It is also important that these descriptions are revised and updated periodically.

Basic Employment Practices and Guidelines

All employees and volunteers should be aware of basic operating practices and principals guiding the organization, including standards of conduct and such specific areas as how purchases are made, travel policy, use of telephones and equipment, liability for personal property, guidelines on outside work, and policies on working hours and conditions.[2]

Training Programs

Staff and volunteers both need training to do their jobs better and to create opportunities for advancement within the organization. Human resource personnel design or approve training programs, then ensure that benefits accrue to both employee and employer.

Employee Benefits

The selection and provision of employee benefits is a huge effort for the organization, given the ever-changing world of healthcare, shifting tax laws, and the proliferation of benefits and services offered to and/or desired by employees.

Arbitration and Conflict Resolution

Organizations must prepare for the prospect of conflicts with employees, often regarding compensation. This motivates the development of mechanisms for arbitration and conflict resolution that must be fair and explicit well before conflicts arise.

Annual Evaluations

Employees and employers are both aided by a formal performance appraisal policy, at least once but often twice a year. This is an opportunity for both employee and employer to give positive and negative feedback on performance. It is also a critical opportunity to improve communications between staff and management, and to set goals and expectations for the period to come.

Employee Handbooks

Many performing arts facilities set down policies and procedures in an employee handbook that provides all of this much-needed information. The great challenge for many organizations is updating the handbook as policies and circumstances change.

Litigation and Other Legal Issues

The great anxiety within larger organizations is that an unhappy staff member or volunteer will ultimately lead the organization into litigation, whether due to dismissal, punishment, or lack of advancement in the organization. A large part of the human resource function is avoiding a situation where litigation is required with better policy, clearer definitions of expectations, formal procedures for conflict resolution, and clear guidelines for management on how employees are to be managed and, if necessary, terminated.

Brenda Carter, human resources director for the Cincinnati Arts Association, says that HR managers can't do their jobs without expert legal counsel. It is a frequent and necessary part of the job:

> I was on the phone today with counsel, speaking with one of our attorneys
> about an issue that I have going on that involves the Equal Opportunity

Employment Commission. I have to consult legal counsel because these issues move quickly beyond the language and understanding of staff. Yes, it's expensive, but I'm not going to risk making a mistake by attempting this myself.

The good news is that the field of human resource management is large and well developed. There is no shortage of individuals and organizations ready and willing to add HR capabilities to performing arts center organizations. The bad news is that selling these skills and resources into the organization is very difficult, basically because it's so hard to justify the time and expense of activities that seem so far removed from taking care of and programming a building. Certainly there are some legitimate concerns about building bureaucracy, but there are also many compelling arguments for the investment in HR, including:

- Staff morale, productivity, and retention are improved with structure and systems supporting their work life
- Litigation and related costs are reduced
- Employees have a sense that there is a person in senior management more likely to be informed on and to advocate for workplace issues
- One is better able to manage the distribution of effort between full-time staff, contract staff, and volunteers
- A customer service orientation is easier to achieve within a human resource–sensitive organization
- Human resources are more effectively deployed and supervised
- Funds are more efficiently spent on benefits and their administration

Brenda Carter believes that what's coming next in the world of HR for the performing arts is more strategic planning and a greater investment:

Training and development is an underutilized, underfinanced, and undersupported area. But if we don't take the time to train and develop our employees, we are not growing as an organization. Typically, in the nonprofit area, there are lots of budgetary constraints, and one of the areas always under pressure is training and development. But it seriously impacts our productivity as an organization and will be my next major focus.

Organized Labor Relations

Some performing arts centers do not employ any unionized labor. Others support workers from a number of unions. For example, the Aronoff Center in Cincinnati has seven different labor contracts. When there is a labor union present in the building, it is the responsibility of building management to organize collective bargaining to coincide with the expiration and renewal of labor contracts. Here, the ability to negotiate is critical to avoiding labor disruption while maintaining the financial integrity of the organization.

Judith Daykin, the just-retired head of City Center, takes a healthy view of unions and relations with organized labor:

> We are in midtown New York with a theater that seats 2,800 people. There is no way we would be under the radar of theatrical unions, and my policy is, if they are a true partner with you in planning, you will get a much better response to your needs. Our heads are the heads on the production crew, so they have a strong sense of ownership in that program. They are loyal to the companies that play here all the time, and less loyal to those who come in from the outside, but they are the best possible crew.
>
> Our approach is to be very proactive. We don't exclude the unions from any aspect of what we're doing, so if we are planning something for the future, they are at the table. They are not in the shop, being left out of the discussions. And we now have good relations with all of the theatrical unions. I think it's difficult to play an adversarial game, because finally union leadership is going to say, "We are not as interested in this institution as we are in that one." The reality is, you are not going to get rid of them, not if you have a large venue. It's just not possible or practical. At my first negotiation with the Local One of IATSE, the business agent said, "Well, what happens if we don't agree to all these changes that you want to make?" I said, "Well, we'll probably close." And he said, "That's fine, because someone else will come in to run it and we'll still be here." So instead of facing off with those guys, we worked it out.

As to the future of organized labor in performing arts facilities, I am not willing or able to hazard a guess. But I can suggest that unions can do a lot with management to brighten their own prospects. Tanya Collier speaks of this challenge in Portland:

> I don't think unions are as strong as they were. And our biggest problem is that stagehands have not done a good job of replacing themselves, having training programs where some person can say, "I think I want to be a stage-hand" and go learn how to do it. We don't do that, and consequently, we've got a bunch of old stagehands. We are going to go into bargaining again with the stagehands next year. They only had a one-year contract instead of their usual three. And every year we raise the issue of apprentice programs, and they say yah, yah, yah. But nobody really grabs the idea and runs with it. I guess an alternative would be for us to do it, but we are not necessarily the biggest user of stagehands. It's certainly in the union's interest to do that.

Volunteer Management

Volunteers are often active in performing arts centers, mostly as ushers and ticket-takers, but also assisting in the offices, stuffing envelopes, or manning the phones. And then there is all of the volunteer work of committees and boards, which we will review in the next chapter. For now, we will focus on some of the benefits and challenges of volunteers and their management.

The benefits of having volunteers are substantial, starting with the simple fact that someone is prepared to work for the organization for free. Most performing arts organizations attempt to maximize the value of volunteers by considering where they are able to get the most and best free labor. But of course, the equation is not so simple. A disheveled usher who is poorly trained has the potential to cause great damage to the organization in the way he or she delivers a service on behalf of the facility.

Then the equation becomes a question of how much should be invested in the recruitment and training of volunteers to maximize their value to the organization? In some facilities, management has made the choice to switch from volunteer to paid ushers because of their importance to the experience of customers, or the need to have trained and dependable staff in place in case of emergency. Or, they sprinkle paid staff into a volunteer corps to motivate a higher level of performance.

Now let's add another dimension to this, which is that a large part of the value of volunteers is the opportunity to build awareness, interest, and support for the facility in the community, creating boosters and stronger connections. Volunteers who are given appropriate tasks, with good training and recognition from the organization, are likely to be strong supporters of the facility, acting as goodwill ambassadors and word-of-mouth marketers within their families and social circles. So, it matters less what service they deliver and more that they have a positive experience as volunteers, which transforms them from free labor into a marketing channel. According to Carrie Barnett of the Capital Theater in Bowling Green:

> People support what they know about. So by having our group of volunteers, we are developing a word-of-mouth marketing campaign that is better than gold, because they tell people, "We just sent these newsletters out last week and it talked about this great show . . ." Having people in the building and working becomes an invaluable marketing tool. It's important to invest some time and money into taking care of the volunteers so that they have positive things to say about us.
>
> It's also important because this organization was created by volunteers who saved the building and attracted programming. We've proven that people invest in what they see is valuable, and they express that value by helping out. So by providing those volunteer opportunities, we are also creating donors and future supporters for the organization, which is imperative for our success.

Bill Reeder, who runs the Center for the Arts at George Mason University, tells this great story about the impact of volunteers:

> Our problem used to be that not many people in the community had been to the Center. Now, as we work harder to get them here, we see a much greater impact on the organization. We had an elderly woman from Long Island whose granddaughter was taking a piano lesson here from a student. She brought her other grandchildren to her student recital and was appalled that there were so few people in the audience. So she called me up, came over, and said, "My son's an important lawyer. He is really good at fundraising, so we are going to put him in charge and we will get an audience." Turns out, her

son was going to be the head of the County Legal Aid Society, and he said, "Let's pick a recital, and I'll make it the fundraiser for my group."

So we picked the jazz concert and called it "Jazz for Justice." Last year we had 200 lawyers show up for this great event. This year we had 1,400 lawyers show up—on a Tuesday night, no less. And they raised $12,000 for the Legal Aid Society and gave a $3,000 scholarship to the music department. But the bigger point is that that nearly 1,200 people who had never been here before now feel a strong connection to the Center and the University. That's what volunteers can do.

But the management of volunteers requires more than creating opportunities and recognizing contributions. Tanya Collier just went through this in Portland:

A couple of months ago, our volunteer coordinator at the performing arts center had a volunteer that really needed to be let go. Our coordinator spends all of her time holding volunteers' hands, and she is a wonder at it, but when she had one that she had to let go, she called me, and we ended up handling it like we would an employee. We coached the volunteer and the supervisor through the process, and eventually we helped the individual find a volunteer position somewhere else. But it only worked when we treated the situation as if the person were an employee, not a volunteer.

Professional Viewpoint: Management Styles

Finally, let's spend a moment on management style, meaning the approaches and techniques used by facility managers to get the most out of their paid and volunteer workforces. Rather than describe and critique various management theories, here are several performing arts facility managers speaking on their styles and how they manage.

Bruce Macpherson, managing director of Charles W. Eisenmann Center for Performing Arts and Corporate Presentations:

I am very patient—I have an ability to wait the game out and let things happen in the proper order and not try to force things to happen before they should. That goes for all things, including how staff does its job, how client groups use the building, and how the public at large appreciates the facility.

I think I've learned through my career to give credit where it is due. When I'm working with my staff or anyone else, if it is not my idea, if I didn't come up with the concept, and if we implement it and it works on all fronts, I am not going to take the credit for it. It will be passed on to those individuals who made it happen. I think it is extremely important for people to comfortably and consistently give their best opinions on things, and not to feel that those opinions won't be rewarded or recognized if they come to fruition.

Linda Shelton, executive director and a trustee of the Joyce Theater Foundation:

A big part of motivating staff for me is getting them out of this place to see what goes on in other theaters. They need to be encouraged to do that, and I have to find the money to do it, whether that means bringing five people to a DanceUSA conference or pushing them toward professional development workshops. Because if you don't do it, you're living in a vacuum.

Victor Gotesman, president of the Center for Creative Resources in New York City, and former manager of the Cerritos Performing Arts Center:

You have to allow people to do their jobs without getting in the way, by delegating responsibility and authority in the execution of their jobs, not being heavy-handed, not being in control of every aspect, letting the department heads run their departments, and creating a work environment that is supportive and appreciative.

I had little control over pay increases in Cerritos—that was all part of the City process—but we didn't lose many staff. I fought for them and supported them when the City came and said we have to do this or that. I would fight for the staff, and they knew that. That's the kind of atmosphere you have to create.

Judith Daykin, former executive director of the City Center in New York City:

I arrived at City Center in 1993 and immediately interviewed the whole staff and board individually to try to find out what the problems were. Then we made a series of changes. Now I'm retiring, so my advice to my successor is to let the dust settle, keep your vision and mission in the front of your mind and find out who responds to that mission. Within four to six months you will have a good idea of who is pulling the cart in the right direction and who is sitting down in the mud. And then you know what you need to do.

Kelley Shanley, executive vice president and general manager of the Broward Center for the Performing Arts in Fort Lauderdale, Florida:

My desired management style is hands-off. And I think it's my most natural, my default management style. Actually, everyone needs to be managed differently, and sometimes I need to manage one person in a way that is not completely comfortable for me, but works best for them. It takes an enormous amount of effort, and I'm not saying I'm really great at it, but sometimes I'll need to remind myself—wait, this person responds better to command and control. They want to know exactly what I want them to do; they don't want to be left with ambiguity, so I need to get more involved.

Michael Kaiser, president of the Kennedy Center for the Performing Arts:

To the public I'm this genial guy, but to my staff, I am extremely focused and extremely demanding—not demanding in terms of yelling a lot, but in terms of saying, "Here's what we are trying to accomplish, here is what we are not trying to accomplish." And I stay laser-focused on what I am trying to do.

Most of that comes from my background in turnarounds, because when you are turning around an organization, you have no margin for error. You have to be truly focused on the things that really make a difference and separate the wheat from the chaff so quickly. This is going to work; this isn't going to work. This idea is dumb; this idea is great. You have to be able to do that so fast in a turnaround because you have no time.

NOTES

1. Langley, Stephen, *Theatre Management and Production in America* (New York: Drama Publishers, 1990).
2. Wolf, Thomas, *Managing a Nonprofit Organization* (New York: Simon & Schuster, 1990).

Chapter Ten

Board Development

Not all performing arts facility managers have to deal with a board of directors or trustees, but many do. For those administrators, there is often shock and surprise at how much time and effort it takes to manage a board. And the skills it takes to work with a board are not commonly taught at any school. In this chapter, we will review how boards work (or don't work) and how facility managers get the most out of volunteer leadership.

Board Development

I used to subscribe to the old pyramid model that suggests how an arts organization pulls people into the organization and then up through levels of involvement. Here is how that might look:

Board Member
Committee Member
Volunteer
Member
Subscriber
Single Ticket Buyer
Free Event Attendee

The idea is that you start at the bottom in building participation and then, from that initial pool of attendees, you recruit subscribers, members, volunteers, and so on. There is a logic to the process because you start with a large pool of potential supporters from whom you seek those who are willing and able to contribute more to the organization, whether that means time (as, say, a volunteer usher), skills (planning and advice as a committee member), or money (as a board member). And the size of the pool gets smaller as you go higher up the pyramid.

I've seen this work well in all sorts of organizations. And it often works best as a reminder to managers that they should look first within their family of supporters for potential leaders. My favorite example is of the music festival organization that discovered that the recently retired chair of United Technologies was toiling in volunteer obscurity as an usher. They quickly pulled him up the pyramid, and two years later, he was chair of the organization's campaign to develop new facilities.

The problem with the pyramid is that many potential leaders don't have the time, patience, or inclination to work their way up. Great potential leaders are often discovered outside the organization, and it is often the case that they could/should serve immediately at the board level. This creates a series of challenges for the manager. One has to quickly educate new leadership on the mission and culture of the organization. Though love of the organization's creative output is a great thing to have in all board members, it should not be a prerequisite.

We recently surveyed a number of opera companies on the nature of their boards. We specifically asked what percentage of their board members were opera lovers when they come onto the board. Of the six organizations surveyed, only one of them had a stipulation that one had to be an opera fan in order to come onto the board. And most of them observed that only one-fourth to one-third of those coming onto the board came on as opera fans.

Roles of the Board

Thomas Wolf, in his guide to nonprofit management, lays out six principal areas of responsibility for trustees or directors:[1]

1. Determine the organization's mission and set policies for its operation
2. Set the program from year to year and engage in long-range planning
3. Establish fiscal policy and boundaries with budgets and financial controls
4. Provide resources for the organization through direct financial contributions and support of fundraising efforts
5. Select, evaluate, and, if required, terminate the chief executive
6. Develop and maintain a communications link with the community

Wolf then suggests that trustees of a nonprofit organization should not do the following:

1. Engage in the day-to-day operation of the organization
2. Hire staff other than the chief executive
3. Make detailed programmatic decisions without consulting staff

Some years ago, we were working for a complex of two historic theaters in Pennsylvania, helping them consider the operational and financial implications of various physical improvements. Along the way, we did an audit of the organization, including a review of the board and its work. Here we discovered that over a period of time, leadership had allowed the board to stray from its core responsibilities and become much too involved in operations, most importantly in programming. In fact, an appointment to the programming committee had become the plum assignment for board members, as they were given the opportunities to pick the shows to be presented in the two theaters. So, someone might stand up at the committee meeting and announce that he'd seen this great entertainer on a cruise last month and, "Wouldn't she be great in our own little theater?" Thus, bad shows were picked, there was no overall programming plan or strategy connecting these choices, and board members were allowed to believe their service to the organization had something to do with picking shows.

Even though the determination of what the board should and shouldn't do is relatively straightforward in the abstract, it is important to recognize how the role of the board should evolve with the organization through different levels of corporate maturity. For nonprofit arts organizations, one generally sees three distinct levels.

The Emerging Organization

The emerging nonprofit is often a creatively driven organization, lacking structure and systems, but having a high level of passion, purpose, and entrepreneurial energy. The board is formed to fulfill regulatory requirements, and is
not particularly active. Members of the board are asked to provide administrative skills lacking at the staff level. They have been recruited mostly through
some personal connection to the organization and its founders.

Chris Ball inherited a board when he took over operation of the Astor
Theatre. With no other full-time staff, he saw their role as essential. Here he
talks about how he got them reengaged:

> Before I came on, the Astor was owned as a private business for a very short
> time, until the owners found that you can't operate a theater in Nova Scotia
> as a private business and actually make money. So they decided to form the
> Astor Theater Society to operate the theater, and kept the previous owners on
> as management. The previous owners and managers still wanted to run and
> own it as a private business, without the interference of the board. And that's
> what they did, keeping secrets and not getting the board involved. Naturally,
> the board lost interest in what was going on.
>
> So, when the managers left (I replaced one and then the other left) I didn't
> want anybody pointing a finger at me, saying, Why did you book that show?
> I wanted that finger pointed at several of us. So I started to get the board
> involved again. I found they had the interest, but were never given the oppor-
> tunity to do anything. So I gave them the opportunity to form a programming
> committee, which looks at the programming policy and how a season takes
> shape. Then they started creating additional committees as people stepped for-
> ward. For instance, someone would say, "I'd like to head a committee that looks
> after the maintenance of the building," and we'd set that up.
>
> Originally you had to fight to get people to join the board under the old
> management, but as they became more involved and as the audience grew, we
> found it easier to find people to get on the board, because they wanted to have
> a say as to what goes on here and to share in our success. So, by changing the
> way things were done, we created an interest in being on the board, and also
> in coming back and being a customer again.

The Adolescent Organization

The adolescent nonprofit is a larger, staff-driven organization that has acquired significant administrative and creative skills. The board is larger and more active, supporting policy development and fundraising, but also providing skills and services required by the organization. More members are recruited on the basis of skills and resources, though it is unlikely that the organization has the credibility or community standing that would attract anyone not well informed or supportive of the work of the organization.

The Mature Organization

The mature nonprofit is a still larger, leadership-driven organization, with a strong and active board playing those roles suggested by Tom Wolf and avoiding most operational issues. Members are recruited from the community on the basis of their ability to "give or get" funds, their connections into the community, and their ability to think and plan strategically. At this level, the organization has the ability to attract the best and brightest from the community, even if they are not active attendees/participants. That's because, at this level, they recognize the worth and value of the organization to the community. There is also a strong social dimension to board membership at this level. Some people are attracted because of the cachet associated with that particular board, and they enjoy all of the opportunities to see and be seen with this group. In addition, representatives of corporate supporters are often on these boards, there to promote the role of the corporation in the organization and to effectively gain some return on their investment.

For existing performing arts facilities, we tend to see organizations and boards at or in between the adolescent and mature stages. Clearly, the board at the mature stage is capable of having profound and positive impacts on the organization, as follows:

- It can attract potential members from a much larger talent pool of community leadership, rather than relying on friends and supporters.
- The board has the financial resources and focus to add significant contributed income to the organization, which then leverages growth in operating expenses and earned income.

- Their connections into the community are much more likely to support the facility's role in improving quality of life, cultural development, and other broad elements of the mission.

There is a healthy Darwinian process by which many organizations disappear before they leave the emerging phase, and another group that does not make the progression from adolescent to mature. Funds and skills are scarce. The laws of demand and supply work. Mistakes are made. But it is also interesting that many organizations that might well have all of the ingredients to make it to a mature level choose not to, opting to stay as they are. Certainly there is no practical reason not to pursue the mature stage and the board that goes with it. So why don't they? Several reasons come to mind:

- Founding staff and board members become too attached to the way things are, resisting change and evolution as something that might hurt their role and position with the organization.
- They are also leery about bringing corporate and community leaders into their group. They are perhaps insecure about their lack of skills and sophistication. Or they perceive those leaders as being philistines who will compromise the artistic direction and choices of the organization.
- There is a reluctance to go through the whole process of recruiting and training a bigger, broader board, and also a sense that there are neither time nor funds in place to support that effort.

Of these reasons, the most valid one is the threat that a group of community leaders will come in and change the mission and artistic direction of the organization. And certainly, there are examples of facility organizations that have gone through such a change. Here, Tony Stimac describes a board that he inherited when he arrived at the Helen Hayes Theater in Nyack:

> When I got here, the board was mostly made up of local shopkeepers. They had been doing all the work in the place prior to my arrival. When I came, they greeted me and my expertise with enormous enthusiasm; then they wanted to continue their routine by telling me what to do and designing the brochures, so we clashed.
>
> The board president had spent two years trying to explain that we had a

staff that would do that stuff, and that the board should start to do board work. He got a brochure entitled "Boards That Make a Difference" and made them all read it. That was our first retreat. Half of them embraced it, while the other half elected to leave the board because they couldn't tell me what color the season brochure should be and what play I was to do. That caused a bit of bad blood in the community because they had been there for seventeen years and it was their theater. And it could have continued to be their theater, but we needed the board to be a governance board.

Despite these risks, the pursuit of the mature stage and the mature board is a worthy one. It brings financial stability, connection to the community, and much-improved odds of achieving mission.

Perhaps the most interesting discussion about the role, value, and impact of the board is around the question of who works for whom. Does the board serve the executive director, or is it the other way around?

Michael Kaiser has risen to the top of the performing arts facility management profession as a great manager and leader. I first heard him talk about the relationship between the board and the executive director when he was at American Ballet Theatre. Strong working relationships served him well at successive institutions, including London's Royal Opera House at Covent Garden and the Kennedy Center. He takes the position that running a performing arts facility is a very difficult job that requires a very specific set of skills. The manager knows what he's doing, so let him do it. And if he's not doing a good job, the option is not taking over or directing that person's work, but simply replacing him. At the same time, there are things that the board can do that staff can't, in the areas of fundraising, connecting to the community, and acting as objective trustees of the mission. So it's less about reporting relationships and more about the different roles and responsibilities that lead to the achievement of mission. Here's Kaiser in his own words:

I take the position that the board should work for the executive director. That tends to make people nervous. When I say that, it's not about arrogance, it's not about saying that I run the board—because I respect my board. What I mean is that, because I am at this job seven days a week, I have a level of knowledge that the board members don't have, and I have to be a leader for the board and help direct their focus so that they stay on track and helpful to the organization.

When board members run off by themselves without enough information, they oftentimes make a decision that is not based on enough data to be a good decision. I guide my board, and they appreciate it as long as things are going well. I think there are moments when they resent me for that, but I've never been fired yet. I believe my knowledge of my organization surpasses that of my board's. That doesn't mean my judgment is better, and it doesn't mean they shouldn't give me input, but I have to guide the conversation to those issues that need to be discussed. The fact that you can run a successful investment bank does not mean you can run a successful arts organization, unless you learn how to do it. So when boards come in and take over because they feel the staff is incompetent, you have decisions being made by amateurs. That's not good.

I think of my board as a group of donors. I don't think of them as my friends. I market to them. I try to make them feel as good about the organization as possible. I try to get them as involved as possible so that they can (a) take the time to learn and make the best decisions, and (b) be as generous with their own money or their friends' money as possible. I take a very positive attitude towards my board. I spend very little time with them as a group, as we have only three board meetings a year, and those last an hour and a half. But I spend a lot of time with many of the individual members. Some of them are presidential appointees, some are members of Congress, and some are ex-officio members because of a major position they held in life. And I'll spend time with them on a range of issues, from fundraising to getting help in Congress.

Judith Allen of the North Carolina Blumenthal Center for the Performing Arts takes a similar position:

Generally speaking, I would say that the board works for the CEO as leader of the organization. Volunteer boards are exactly that—they are volunteers, they mean well. They need to hire the right individual as the CEO, someone who has the expertise so that the day-to-day business and operations meet the mission that is stated and all agreed upon. But the board can't run the business.

When a business gets in trouble, I don't care if it's a symphony or a theater company, the board fires the director and then they try to run it. That has happened over and over here. A local museum let its director go, and the board tried to run it. Well, guess what? They had no idea what they were doing, and the result was disastrous. So it's a balance. In this situation, I am hired for my expertise. If I do a good job, great! If I don't, then fire me.

Now, there are other instances where it is the other way around. I work for them when it comes to the broad policies of the organization or a major capital development. I really see it as a balance, as a conversation. I have lots of conversations with my board folks. My job is to listen to them and their job is to listen to me, and then we try to get the best ideas. We both learn because we are open to being educated—me to their position, understanding, their knowledge of the community; them to my knowledge of the business. And I've never had a fight with my board.

And finally, here's Joseph Golden, author and former managing director of the Civic Center of Onondaga County, who describes a fluid situation:

The relationship between the board and senior management changes from situation to situation. The board members are generally reputable and well-placed citizens, influential people in many cases, professional people in all cases. And they always have intuitions, insights, knowledge, experience about how to get things done in a community, about what will sell and what won't sell, and they give good reasons for it. They will be in a position to alert us to certain socio-political situations that I may not be aware of.

A good board is an invaluable tool, and because I am the director, they have much influence over what I do. If they say, "Joe, don't do this, I'll tell you why you shouldn't do this. At least don't do this now," and those opinions are backed up by good reasoning, I say, "Okay, there are always lots of options." If we didn't do A, we would do B. So it's give and take.

Board Development and Composition

There are very few nonprofit boards, and almost no successful ones, made up of people who are all alike. Good boards are diverse in many ways—in terms of demographic characteristics, resources, views of the world, and patterns of participation in the arts. That's a good thing because the board should represent all constituencies who might be affected by the organization, help the organization reach and make connections to those groups, and raise funds from as many different sources as possible. Here is Michael Kaiser on structuring and restructuring boards:

> I am looking for people who can make a financial contribution or solicit financial contributions from others and then participate in a healthy and contributing way to the organization. I don't believe in the need to have a lawyer and a marketer and a builder on your board. The specific expertise required to market an arts organization is so different from marketing steel that I don't believe that there is necessarily great help available. That does not mean people don't come on with great expertise and can't be immensely helpful. But I can't count on it.
>
> When I got to Alvin Ailey, we had thirty-six board members; within the first year, we replaced eighteen of the thirty-six. To do that, we completed a strategic plan, and part of the strategic plan was to set a board giving level. And we set it at a level that the board approved of—they approved the plan, and created the plan with us—but half the board could not meet that level or chose not to meet that level and left of their own volition. That was an organization with a budget of close to $6 million, but the board in total was giving less than $100,000 a year. It was just not feasible. I am absolutely convinced that the health of the organization in the last thirteen years has come from building that new board, many of whom have since left. But the process of changing the way the board functioned from a community group to a participating group was essential.
>
> Also, I'm generally not in favor of term limits. If someone's great, I want him there forever. And if someone's awful, I get him off right away. I do believe boards need to change over time, but I'm not sure that setting term limits is the way to do it. It is the accepted way to do it, but it is not necessarily something that I would suggest.

One way to view the composition of the board is as you would view the roster of a baseball team—as a group of individuals with very different skills, backgrounds, and training, who are all needed to make the team succeed. If we carry that analogy forward, it provides a board development tool. When reviewing the composition of the board and the need for additional resources, think in terms of who currently plays what position, where there is relative depth, and where additional help is needed. There is also the issue of team chemistry, the intangibles about a group of people and the way that they interact that affects the performance of the organization. Here, Judith Daykin describes the constant challenge she faced of structuring the board at the City Center in New York City:

> I inherited a board that had been brought on by the chairman who was in place when I was hired. It was comprised of people who were on the boards of those companies that used City Center. It was completely untenable because they didn't care about City Center—they only cared about their own company, and they were basically coming to board meetings to spy on what the financial situation was so that they could go back and tell the boards of their respective companies.
>
> So we made a very big effort to ease those people off and bring on people who were really interested in City Center as an entity. That is what it is now, although some of them are interested in dance, some in theater, some in musical theater, and some in architecture and the city relationship. It's very hard because we are in a city where there is enormous competition for board prospects, and a lot of institutions with a lot more panache and style and history than we have.
>
> We are constantly meeting with the executive committee and asking, "What are we missing? We've got too many lawyers and too many investment bankers, and we need some CEOs and some others who can influence corporate giving and so on." That's a never-ending process.

One of the key considerations in board development is making sure that the board is reflective of the community. Judith Allen went through this when building her board for the North Carolina Blumenthal Center for the Arts in Charlotte:

> This used to be basically a white institution that did not reflect the community, which is 26 percent African American and probably 8 percent Latino. As we shifted from the board that built the Center to the operating board, I asked them, "How do we represent the community on an operating board, which is different from the founding board?" So we went looking for people from these other communities, people with expertise, people who were well

connected, people who understood and appreciated our mission. And that search led us to people from different cultures who fit the organization and then gave us a representative board.

Committees of the Board

The pyramid at the beginning of this chapter suggests that committees play a vital role in the leadership development process, a step that allows an organization to recruit volunteers to work in specific leadership areas, and then, based on that experience, determining who might graduate to the board. As rational as it sounds, it is often not the way that committees work, if they work at all. Michael Kaiser suggests:

> I find that the best people who you really want on your board don't want to serve on a committee to test themselves out. They want to be on the board, so you just put them on the board. Many committees of many boards discuss things, but they aren't very potent, so I'd rather just find great people and put them on the board right away.

Some boards choose to recruit board members who have not worked their way up the pyramid. Others populate their committees exclusively with board members. And then, many other boards have no committee structure whatsoever. Here's Tony Stimac of the Helen Hayes Theater on a functioning committee structure:

> You do not have to be a board member to be on one of our committees, and they do help recruit people onto the board. But because we have a $5,000 give or get policy, there are many people who just go so far as committee work. We have a finance committee that meets before each board meeting, and we also have a very effective executive committee that doesn't make more work for staff. We really brainstorm, we work as colleagues, sitting around and trying to face and solve our biggest challenges.

Committees can have a significant and positive impact on a performing arts facility organization. They bring skills and energy to the organization that add value and pushes them down the road toward mission. They are a leadership development tool, though not the exclusive means by which board members need be recruited and tested. And they build the network of supporters and word-of-mouth marketers that sell tickets and build support for the organization in the community. Following are committees often formed to support the board for a performing arts facility.

Executive Committee

The executive committee is a leadership group taken from the board that meets frequently to wrestle with major decisions and move the organization forward. It often includes the officers of the board.

Nominating Committee

The nominating committee is charged with identifying and recruiting candidates for the board and other committees. It is a critically important group because of the challenge of bringing new talent to the organization, but also because their choice of who comes on the board and their officer nominations are so important to the direction of the organization. As Rod Rubbo in Canton says:

> The most important committee on my board is the nominating committee, because that's where it starts. It starts with that group—with its breadth and depth—acknowledging that they will bring their resources to that task is the first major step. You make that one step; the rest of it becomes pretty easy, because then the board's executive committee trusts that information.

Fundraising Committee

The fundraising committee drives the ongoing annual fundraising, mostly focused on donations from individuals, corporations, and foundations through solicitations, grant proposals, and special events.

Campaign Committee

A capital campaign committee is formed to organize and execute a capital campaign as and when needed, with some connection and overlap to the fundraising committee.

Building Committee

The building committee oversees the care and condition of the building, particularly focused on the planning and execution of capital projects.

Finance Committee

The finance committee supervises the financial condition and performance of the organization, with a particular effort surrounding the preparation and approval of annual operating budgets and capital budgets.

Planning Committee

The planning committee develops and implements long-range plans. See the discussion in chapter 8.

Marketing Committee

The marketing committee oversees the marketing effort of the organization, including the message, media, and promotions, and use of research to drive marketing decisions.

Programming Committee

Despite the cautionary tale about the two historic theaters in Pennsylvania—where the board began choosing what shows to present—a programming committee can play a beneficial role. It can oversee programming choices, providing advice about potentially controversial selections and ensuring that programming decisions are consistent with an overall programming plan, which must also be monitored in terms of the mission of the organization.

Challenging Boards

Let's finish this examination of boards by looking at several of problems that occur on boards that make them unwieldy and difficult groups to manage.

The Operational Board

An operational board is one like the board in our Pennsylvania story, which becomes too active and involved in operational issues. It becomes a burden to staff and organization by virtue of the needless work that it creates and its inattention to things that members should be paying attention to, like fundraising.

The Board of Stewards

At the other end of the scale is the board of stewards; they see themselves as protectors of a performing arts facility, inclined to resist any ideas that bring new or different programs to the facility. They focus inward to the point that they lose connection to the community they serve and marginalize the organization.

The Board of Friends

Some boards are dominated by friends of management, either because they started that way or because it's a very social organization where strong friend-ships have developed. This is a tempting scenario for management because these boards are easier to manage and direct, but it is a situation to avoid because the objectivity of the board is usually lost, and it becomes very diffi-cult to recruit others to join a group that has become so tightly connected with management.

The Board of Intrigue

Boards made up of powerful people with time on their hands can become a hornet's nest of intrigue, with all of the energy of board management wrapped up in gossip, politicking, and gamesmanship. Senior management ends up spending an inordinate amount of time putting out fires on the board and separating combatants.

The Eccentric Funder's Board

Finally, there is the board controlled by one or two eccentric funders, whose increasingly bizarre whims and fancies must be followed by management and the rest of the group in order to keep their money coming, at least in the opinion of management. This generally leads to a blowup, when senior management finally declares "enough is enough," throws that person off the board, and gives up the funding source that has become the organization's crutch.

None of these are happy situations, but many organizations pass through them. That's also the good news—that boards and their dynamics are as fluid as any other set of people sitting around a table. Boards can go wrong, but they can also be fixed, and return to a position where they are providing significant and ongoing value to the organization.

<hr>

NOTE

1. Wolf, Thomas, *Managing a Nonprofit Organization* (New York: Simon & Schuster, 1990), 29.

Chapter Eleven

Education and Performing Arts Facilities

These days, we tend to take for granted the close relationship between education and performing arts facilities. But where did that come from, what does it mean, and where is it going?

To answer those questions, I will continue to refer to the views and stories of the facility managers and staff we've interviewed. But given my relative inexperience in this area and the complexity of the issues, I will refer extensively to another terrific source: *Acts of Achievement: The Role of Performing Arts Centers in Education*, published in 2003 by the Dana Foundation.[1]

I would also encourage those interested in this topic to obtain a copy of the report, information on which can be found at the Dana Foundation Web site (*www.dana.org*).

The Dana Foundation is a private philanthropic organization with particular interests in science, health, and education. In 2000, the foundation started a program to fund innovative professional development programs leading to improved teaching of the performing arts in schools. The response to the program was very positive, leading to a symposium on options, resources, and best practices available to planners of K–12 schools with an arts focus. That symposium and the resulting publication (*Planning an Arts-Centered School: A Handbook*) then spurred a second national conference, held in Washington, D.C., in April 2003.

The focus on education programs in performing arts facilities was a response to foundation grantees, who were most interested in learning how to engage school leadership in arts education, bringing together the teaching artist and the classroom teacher, and building community support for education in performing arts facilities. As we proceed through this chapter, I will refer to the findings of the Dana Foundation study, as well as to some of the best practices uncovered in their work.

The Rationale for Education in Performing Arts Facilities

The philosophical basis for education programs in performing arts facilities is very strong. Facilities that are incorporated as 501(c)(3) corporations gain their tax-exempt status on the basis of having a mission with an educational component. With that fundamental beginning, facilities are obliged to deliver "education," however it is defined.

There are also important practical reasons for the strong connection between performing arts facilities and education. First of all, fundraisers generally have had great success raising money for arts facilities when they stress education and opportunities for families and children. Many people who would not set foot in a theater are prepared to support any institution that improves the lives and prospects of their children.

The development of educational programs in performing arts centers is also a response to the loss of arts education in school systems nationally. A generation ago, the U.S. Department of Education issued *A Nation at Risk*,[2] which declared a crisis in public education and, in particular, arts education. Ever since that time, performing arts facilities have joined with school reformers to improve K–12 public education.

In addition, performing arts facilities have come to approach education programs as an audience development strategy. According to *The Capacity of Performing Arts Presenting Organizations*,[3] 77 percent of these organizations are using programs and performances for K–12 as an audience development strategy. Even for smaller presenting organizations, 69 percent are using this strategy. Christine Sheehan, education director of Proctors Theatre, confirms that approach:

> Performing arts centers should have education programs to ensure the sustainability of the live performing arts. That's what our mission here at

Proctors is all about—the viability of live performing arts and cultivating the audience of the future. If we are going to expand, we have to cultivate our audience, starting with the younger generations.

Arts Education Programs

The *Acts of Achievement* initiative documents the size and scope of K–12 education programs at performing arts facilities. After issuing an open call to facilities, the Dana Foundation received 138 completed profile submissions from thirty-seven states. Seventy-four of those submissions were selected for inclusion in the *Acts of Achievement* report. What is most interesting about these profiles of arts educations programs is that half of them were instituted after 1990, with only twenty predating 1983. The rapid development of these programs is fascinating, and must be attributed to a new commitment on the part of facilities, together with the appearance of financial support for these activities.

Going through the profiles in the *Acts of Achievement* study, one is struck mostly by how many different programs are offered by each of the facilities. There are no facilities with fewer than six different education programs, and some have as many as eighteen different programs. Clearly, facilities have gone beyond busing kids in to watch a matinee performance, moving on to all sorts of wonderful things, from teacher training and residencies to summer institutes and after-school programs. How did that happen?

Linda Shelton talks about the evolution of education programs at the Joyce:

When the Joyce first started an education program, it was about exposure— just sending the kids in to see a show was fine for us. But now I think it has to go beyond that to be a bigger engagement for kids and adults. You have to offer them other ways to get them to understand. So, we hired a consultant to come in to look at our program, and she gave us some options for what a program could be. Then we interviewed a number of people to get them to fill a full-time director spot. Now we're able to deliver programs that really help the kids understand what's going on and engage them. And they now get a lot more out of the experience.

Fred Johnson is senior vice president for education and the humanities at the Tampa Bay Performing Arts Center. His history with the TBPAC began in

1987, when the it first opened, as he was the first performer to ever perform on stage there. He eventually joined the education department in 1991. Here, he describes the development of the department:

> A gentleman named Norbert Bukowski put together the education department here. He was an educator, having taught kindergarten and the primary grades. He developed our first programs, which were to bring kids in from the schools to see shows. That program, now called "On School Time," presents a year's worth of programming to bused-in kids.
>
> Two other programs were established initially. One was called "The KidTime Series," a family series that happens on Sundays where the whole family can come, and another program called "Wee Folk," for pre-K and kindergarteners. That is done in our rehearsal hall, and is an up-close first-time experience for kids with artists. Now, we're up to twenty-one different programs currently happening in the center.

Virtually all of the facilities profiled in *Acts of Achievement*, from Symphony Space to the Yerba Buena Center, include programs outside of their facilities. Naturally, the first question is, But why? According to Chris Sheehan of Proctors Theatre:

> It's a tricky question. It revolves around our programming, obviously. But it's part of our mission to promote academic, behavioral, and social achievement in students. We create programs that link learning standards to our productions, whether they are dance, Broadway, etc., and we create a program for the schools that can deliver that using teaching artists.
>
> In many cases, we are delivering arts into schools because the schools aren't doing it themselves. The schools are absolutely thirsty for this kind of programming, and in our case, we are seeking private dollars to do that in school districts, so of course they are going to want it, because they are not paying for it in many instances.

Like many larger facilities, the Tampa Bay Performing Arts Center made the leap to programs outside the building long ago. According to Fred Johnson:

> The leap for me was easy, as I grew up in one of those neighborhoods where not a lot of art came to us, and where there were a lot of things you could do

wrong, and art was a real lifesaver for me. So I've always worked from a community perspective.

One of my roles when I first came here was to connect folk in the community who had not walked through the doors of the performing arts center, to create an understanding that this is a place for everybody. For a lot of the people that come by that building often, the presumption is, I can't afford those shows, I've seen some of those prices. And I really believe that a major component in the success of developing a viable performing arts education initiative is that you have to go to the people. A number of people on my staff are members of a chamber of commerce or a community group, because we want to be perceived as a viable participant in the community, not just somewhere you go to see a show.

It would seem that where one delivers the program is much less important than what is delivered. Here is John Richard, chief operating officer of the New Jersey Performing Arts Center in downtown Newark:

We deliver education programs in the Performing Arts Center by virtue of having special performances for kids. We deliver some programs directly to schools because it's easier to get one instructor to the school than to get thirty kids to the arts center. And we also have a dedicated facility for arts education, which has a black-box theater, a rehearsal hall, and a dance space, right behind the performing arts center.

I would venture to say that some education programs are better than others. Each one must be conceived based on a need and the presence of resources with which to execute. And those programs must be evaluated and reassessed on a periodic basis. According to Fred Johnson, the programs in Tampa Bay change frequently, based on external mandates and the evolution of the community:

The look of our school programming has changed drastically because of this comprehensive aptitude test that the state of Florida has made a requirement. Many of our programs have changed and are now geared more towards curriculum connectors. We work very hard to stay at the cutting edge of communication with the educational systems, to see what their trends are.

We also try to stay up with the pulse of what is happening in the community. We try to diversify our programs. I have an outreach coordinator. I will send her out and say, I want you to go to an area of this city that you have not been to before, where we have not done any outreach. I want you to find the elementary and high school and see if there is a theater in that community, if there is a movie house in that community, if there is an art gallery in that community. Get a sense of what is happening there, get to know the people to get an idea of what it is that they would like to see happen, get a sense of the demographic.

The more you know about your community, the more you get a sense of the people in your community. As a writer, it helps you to be a better writer, and as an educator, it helps you to provide opportunities to folks that they want, which attracts them.

Funding Education Programs

The growth of education programs in performing arts centers would not have happened if not for the emergence of funders and funding programs supporting those efforts. Those people and programs have responded energetically in many communities. Carrie Barnett describes the situation in Bowling Green:

There is a set of donors in this community that specifically wants to do things that are helping children, but we have such a limited group of nonprofits that are children-based that the donors want to spread their money out. They don't want to spend it all on the Boys Club or Big Sisters. So we had a specific group of corporate donors in the range of $20,000 to $30,000 who want to do something that is kid-friendly, and so the school-day program was created.

We have done some things with the family side of it so that it is marketable. They see their name out there and know that there is more to it than just helping kids come in during the day, but the program lets the community know the donors are doing it. It has continued to be successful because we were able to adjust based on the growing needs of the sponsors in order to justify how they spend their money.

On the other hand, it is a significant effort to get that funding in place. According to Chris Sheehan:

The search for money is constant. We did not want to tap into funding sources from our annual campaigns. Our balance of funding comes from corporate, foundation, and legislative monies. So the education department right now writes our own grants, and our target is about $150,000 in grant support.

It's a pain, but we're in a better position to identify funding opportunities than the development department. We do a lot of research on it. I have an assistant now, and a great deal of her job is focused on that research. We are advocates for those kids and we are advocates for those programs, so who better to write the grant applications?

Building an Education Department

Many facilities start education programs before the facility is even opened. Here is John Richard from the New Jersey Performing Arts Center:

We actually started our arts education program before we opened. We did this with a series of different residencies at schools. Actually, our first arts education program was a program we called "Mural Magic." Over one hundred schools participated in creating murals around the site during construction.

What was really important about that signal was that over the period of time of construction in an urban center, there was not one mark of graffiti on any of the murals. We hired a vice president of arts education about three or four years before we opened, and he created a ten-year plan, which is now ending. We are now looking at the next five-year plan for arts education. The last plan included a full compliment of residency programs and focused on different age categories of kids in New Jersey who were seemingly lacking in arts education offerings.

For those who have not yet put a program in place, or who are considering a new approach, I would relate Christine Sheehan's story on the genesis of an education department at Proctors Theatre in Schenectady:

It's sort of embarrassing when we tell people that we didn't have an education program until 2002, but we took a very deliberate approach to creating one. We did focus groups; we interviewed people. We studied compendiums and studies, and did focus groups with administrators and superintendents and parents and community members, to learn what Proctors needed to do for this community. We knew that above everything else, we needed to have a program that was relevant to this region.

So, after all of that work, we came up with a three-pronged strategy. It's about product, money, and relevance to this region, all under the umbrella of sustainability. If we are going to sustain the performing arts, we need to sustain our education program. We did a lot of experimenting in the first year, quite frankly. Some things worked and some things didn't. Product was not a problem. We already had a children's program that had been very successful for twelve years, and we had our Broadway programming.

The first big change was to make our school-day program more diverse. We had booked a lot of really fluffy, white-bread sorts of performances, because the mission of the school-day program up until that point was to make dollars, unfortunately. We decided to change that to provide more educational programming, so instead of *Sleeping Beauty*, we have Alvin Ailey and Diabolo and those sorts of things.

We also decided to offer workshops in association with those very basic sorts of things that we thought teachers might bite on. One of the great things we did was we built partnerships with entire school districts so that we could leverage additional funding through these arts and education co-service agreements in the state aid ratios. We built partnerships with youth service organizations strategically. And of course, we built partnerships with superintendents and teachers.

Peter Herrndorf is promoting education within the National Arts Centre in Ottawa:

In 2001, we made the public declaration that education was now going to operate on par with music, theater, and dance. So it was going to become a core piece of business for us, and that meant dramatic changes here.

I'll give you a couple examples: When the orchestra toured last year, they did a seventeen-day tour of Mexico and the U.S. We played ten concerts in ten major cities, and we did seventy-three educational events over the seventeen days. As part of that tour, we distributed a teacher's study guide on Mozart to 17,500 elementary schools in Mexico, the U.S., and Canada.

We have created in the last few years a summer music institute here led by Pinkas Zuckerman. We have a summer music institute. One part is for instrumentalists from around the world. The second part is for young conductors, and the third part is for young composers. Each summer, we have about sixty-five young people ranging from twelve to twenty-nine years old from all over the world. This is all a new initiative, and there are many more like it. So education suddenly became a growth stock at the national arts center. What surprised people was that when we announced our strategic direction, there were four main planks, and the third of those four planks was education in all of its manifestations. So when an organization puts education that front and center, you begin to see the ripple effect very quickly.

future Trends

Clearly, education programs are growing in size, scope, and importance to performing arts facilities. They are providing new and different opportunities for people of all ages to participate inside a facility, in their schools, and in their communities. There are other interesting trends, a couple of which can be seen at the Tampa Bay Performing Arts Center. As noted, Fred Johnson's title is senior vice president for education and the humanities there. As he explains:

> The suggestion was made to expand our scope to an education and humanities department, because it gives us a greater opportunity to collaborate with colleges, universities, and scholars. We now do festivals that include live performance, but also lectures that involve a performing artist, a visual artist, and an historian. For our American Music Festival, we did a retrospective on the Harlem Renaissance, so we looked at the music, we looked at poetry, and we looked at what was happening culturally during that period of time. So we've really begun to broaden our sense of how creative expression connects to other parts of the community.

Tampa Bay is also one of the larger centers in the country, adding facilities specifically for education, including the Dr. Palavi Patel Conservatory, a 45,000-square-foot addition that includes classrooms, a small theater, rehearsal hall, multimedia space, sound and lighting booth, tech theater space, costume, and a library with books devoted to the performing arts. It's a $7 million project funded mostly by the private sector that opened in the fall of 2004.

Advice from the Dana Foundation

Following are the paraphrased recommendations from *Acts of Achievement* on how to raise the quality and quantity of education programs in performing arts facilities:

- Examine the state of arts education in your community and set measurable objectives for improving available programs.
- Establish relationships with university-based schools, the primary source of teaching artists and teachers.
- Learn from the experiences of others in the field, looking to national resources such as the Arts Education Partnership and the Kennedy Center, as well as discipline-based service organizations.
- Engage the entire community in the development of programs.
- Launch internships and residencies for teachers and other educators within performing arts centers.
- Document the learning for the benefit of artists, teachers, and coordinators, and their colleagues elsewhere.
- Sustain program support through targeted advocacy efforts.

In closing this chapter, I would like to quote Joseph Golden on his motivation for strong education programs as he helped to open new performing arts facilities in Syracuse:

> Performing arts facilities should not be allowed to open if they don't have strong education programs. We always viewed our facility as one part roadhouse, one part production house, and one part schoolhouse. And thousands and thousands of kids came there thinking they were going to a schoolhouse, but it happened to be a theater.

NOTES

1. The Dana Foundation, *Acts of Achievement: The Role of Performing Arts Centers in Education* (New York: Dana Press, 2003).
2. U.S. Department of Education, "A Nation at Risk" (Washington, D.C.: U.S. Department of Education, 1983).
3. The Urban Institute, "The Capacity of Performing Arts Organizations" (Washington, D.C.: The Urban Institute, 2000).

Chapter Twelve

Performing Arts Facilities and Community Development

One of the most interesting and positive trends in the development and operation of performing arts facilities is their increasing sense that they are a vital tool for community development. This has not always been the case. We can point to a series of buildings and communities where the performing arts and performing arts facilities have been viewed as elitist enclaves, large palaces of the arts for the rich and famous. Interestingly, this is more the exception than the rule. Through history, theaters have served a broad cross-section of communities. Think back to the early Greek and Roman theaters and their appeal to the broad populace. Or think to the Globe Theater in London, with a teeming mass of audience members crammed (standing) in front of the stage. Or, more recently, to theaters built 150 years ago on the North American frontier, which served as community gathering places for all who lived there.

The Community Development Argument

In the last thirty years there has been an evolution in the way that we think of the role of performing arts facilities in their communities. Generally speaking, the arguments have evolved as follows.

Cultural Development

"Let's build performing arts facilities to develop the cultural life of the community, advancing the cultural organizations based here and creating new opportunities for arts audiences by virtue of having high-quality facilities."

This is a relatively straightforward argument. As we described in chapter 7, new or renovated facilities support the development of local arts organizations by physically accommodating the needs of production and their audiences. In addition, new or improved facilities make the market more attractive to touring programs, bringing more and better shows to the community for the benefit of local or visiting audiences.

Economic Development

"Let's build performing arts facilities in recognition of the fact they can play a significant role in the economic development of our community—whether that means creating a center or focal point for the community or acting as the catalyst for downtown redevelopment."

This is an argument that really took off in the 1960s with projects like the Lincoln Center for the Performing Arts, which played a key role in the development of the Upper West Side of New York City, or Playhouse Square, which was a catalyst for the revitalization of downtown Cleveland. Then there are more recent projects that include cultural facility development within larger commercial development projects. A recent example is the North Carolina Blumenthal Center for the Performing Arts in Charlotte, built within a mixed-use development and under the sixty-story Bank of America tower.

Americans for the Arts recently completed national research on what people do and what they spend in association with their attendance at events. Entitled *Arts & Economic Prosperity*,[1] it is the most comprehensive study of its kind ever conducted. Ninety-one communities across thirty-four states participated. Detailed expenditure data were collected from 3,000 arts organizations and 40,000 arts attendees. Project economists customized input/output models for each of the ninety-one communities to provide specific and reliable data about each community's impact.

The study found that the nonprofit arts, unlike most industries, leverage significant amounts of event-related spending by their audiences. Attendance at arts events generates related commerce for local businesses such as hotels, restaurants, and retail stores. For example, when patrons attend a performing arts event, they may park their car in a toll garage, purchase dinner at a restaurant, eat dessert after the show, and return home and pay the baby-sitter. This spending generated an estimated $80.8 billion of revenue for local merchants and their communities in 2000—an average of $22.87 per person per event, not including the price of admission.

In addition to spending data, survey respondents were asked to provide their home zip codes, enabling researchers to determine which attendees were local (i.e., reside within the county in which the event occurred) and which were non-local (reside outside the county). Local attendees spent an average of $21.75 per event, while non-local attendees spent $38.05 per event (74.9 percent more). As would be expected, travelers spend significantly more in the categories of lodging, meals, retail, and transportation.

A lot of the economic impact of performing arts facilities relates to this phenomenon—that performing arts patrons spend money before and after the show, and that the placement of performing arts facilities in the right area can capture significant traffic, which supports local businesses and leads to significant ancillary development.

Community Development

In the third phase of this progression, performing arts facilities are valued not just in terms of cultural and economic impacts, but also in terms of broader community impacts, such as:

- **Tolerance**: What impact might facilities and their programs have on racial tolerance in our community? This is, of course, a very complicated issue, but we have seen a series of instances where arts projects have been viewed as an opportunity to get people of different races and ethnicities together to build a better community, working together to create places where different cultures are expressed and shared for the benefit of all.
- **Educational Opportunities**: As discussed in chapter 11, arts facilities create new educational opportunities for all in the community.
- **Corporate Recruitment**: Cultural facilities and programs play a key role in attracting corporations and their employees to relocate to a given city.

Think of all those brochures published by local Chambers of Commerce that have a ballet dancer or symphony orchestra on the cover.

- **Quality of Life**: In the broadest sense, arts facilities and programs can be seen as improving the overall quality of life in a community. Through all of those magazines ranking cities according to quality of life, the presence of cultural facilities is always an important consideration.

All of this means that performing arts facilities can and should play an important role in the life of the community, not just serving artists and their audiences, but also contributing to the achievement of broad community goals.

One of the great development projects of the last twenty years is the New Jersey Performing Arts Center (NJPAC), which opened in downtown Newark in 1998. John Richard is chief operating officer of the organization, and has been there since 1992. Here he talks about the conception of the project as a community development tool:

> A statewide study recommended a world-class performing arts center for northern New Jersey that would impact the urban community and maximize opportunities to attract a large and diverse audience. The city of Newark then became a champion for the project and lobbied very hard to be designated as the right geographical location for the center. So the city and the private sector formed an affinity group called the Mayor's Performing Arts Center Task Force, which built support for the arts center long before the professional staff was hired.
>
> The project was a success for the city of Newark the day it opened. And we continue to work with the city to make sure that goals are achieved in a variety of different ways. We are a significant employer of a diverse workforce. We have an ambitious arts education program that includes children and families, not only in programming, but also in the development of residency programs for kids in public and private schools that connect to the life of the arts center. And we have a very large site that is two-thirds undeveloped, for which a master plan is evolving.

That is the philosophical argument that urges facility managers and leaders to get involved and stay connected to all sorts of other community development initiatives. But there is also a practical argument—in any given community, there is only limited support for funding an organization and facility that serves the arts. Less than one-half of the adult population will attend a performance this year,[2] and the participation rates for specific disciplines are surprisingly low. Yet if a performing arts facility is viewed not as a playpen for the cultural elites but as a tool for economic and community development, there is a much greater chance to secure financial support from both the public and private sectors. Those funders need not be concerned that their constituents (or even they themselves) wouldn't be caught dead at a ballet performance, as long as they see that support of a performing arts facility supports their broader goals for the community.

We asked fundraiser Halsey North to comment on efforts to raise money for performing arts facilities for the sake of community development:

> Civic leaders and corporations can be motivated to give because of the enhanced quality of life that performing arts centers and theaters provide their current and prospective employees. Often, they give to historic downtown theaters due to the added impact on economic development and downtown revitalization. Another important motivation for giving is kids. People will give money to make sure that kids have opportunities that they didn't have growing up. Access to the performing arts at performing arts centers for young people is really one of the most compelling reasons.
>
> When promoting annual memberships, a theater can say, "You can get better seats and you will be helping kids come to the theater through your gift." That combination works very well. It's a combination of both the emotional need to have better services and the intellectual need of wanting to do something for the community. Fundraising is both emotional and intellectual, and you need to speak to both sides of the brain at the same time.

Here is John Richard from NJPAC on fundraising on the basis of the community development potential of the facility:

> For us, the number-one message we delivered from the beginning was the potential impact of the building on the community. Funding for the arts came second, followed by a message about arts education. Even now that we're raising operating support and an endowment, we lead with the arts center being

a centerpiece of a renaissance here in New Jersey and for Newark. And it's a much more sophisticated appeal now, particularly with foundations and corporations who are sophisticated donors that are looking to link their own mission to what we offer here.

Professional Viewpoint: Delivering the Message of Community Development

Having established that there is community development impact to performing arts facilities and having discussed the philosophical and practical reasons to pursue those impacts, let's now discuss the challenge for facility managers and volunteer leadership in making it happen. We'll hear in their own words how they connect their facilities to the community.

Victor Gotesman, former manager of the Cerritos Performing Arts Center:

> I invested a lot in the idea of community relations and connecting to the broader community when I arrived in Cerritos, California, to manage the new performing arts center. I had to go to the Optimist Club meetings, which I had never heard of before I got to California. It was worth it because you make these contacts, and these are the people who not only give money, but also attend performances. I would go to all the openings of playgrounds and parks and libraries and senior centers. I had to do all of that—network and schmooze and be seen. I went to virtually every performance—stood in the lobby for every performance, greeting people and talking with people who were central to the center.

Robyn Williams, executive director for the Portland Center for the Performing Arts:

> Community relations are a big part of my job because we're trying to make our facilities important to the community. People like the old facilities and have warm fuzzies about your building. If you lose your funding, you want the community going to the political powers that be and asking them to take care of these buildings. It's so critical that you be an important part of the community fabric. Plus, you know it is easy for politicians to say the arts aren't

that important. Let donors step up to take care of them. We are worried about police, fire, and those kinds of issues.

One of the things I've tried to do here is position the Portland Center for the Performing Arts as a business. We are a small business. And if you went to City Hall and told them that a half-dozen small businesses are about to go under, they would jump up and down and say, "Oh my gosh, what can we do, we don't want to lose all these small businesses." But if you tell them there is a large number of arts organizations about to go out of business, they would say, "Oh darn! Well, that's the economy, and that's just how it is." So we have gotten really active in being involved in downtown associations, getting them to advocate for us as a small business, and it actually garners a little more attention, because everybody thinks small businesses are a good thing.

Mark Light, president of the Victoria Theatre Association, the Arts Center Foundation, and the Dayton Opera:

Dayton lived in the shadow of Cincinnati and Columbus, and telling the story of how we were not going to have to live in the shadow—not to be ashamed that we were from Dayton, Ohio—was a big deal. That was a story that I told. The way that you could not have to live in the shadow was to support the arts in Dayton so that you didn't have to drive to Cincinnati to see *Les Misérables*— you could see it right here. Because you deserve to see it, and you don't have to take any lip from somebody in Cincinnati who says Dayton's got nothing. Well, that was the big story in our community. That message was a galvanizing force that brought our community together.

Byron Quann, president and CEO of the Whitaker Center for Science and the Arts in Harrisburg, Pennsylvania:

Harrisburg is a small community with limited resources, so people who are active and involved end up getting active and involved in a number of things. When I first got here, I sort of had to embargo things, even though I was asked to be on this board or that board. I really had to dig in here. But at this point, I'm on five or six boards. I was at a board meeting with someone this morning, I have one this afternoon, and then another event this evening. I am interacting with the leaders of the community. And I have a strong board myself consisting of people who are absolutely the top leaders of the community in various walks of life—government leaders, high-net-worth individuals, business leaders, and so on. So I can make any call in this community and someone will return my call. Or I can get someone to help me get that done. And that's important.

NOTES

1. Americans for the Arts, "Arts & Economic Prosperity" (Washington, D.C.: Americans for the Arts, 2003).
2. National Endowment for the Arts, "Survey of Public Participation on the Arts" (Washington, D.C.: National Endowment for the Arts, 2002).

Chapter Thirteen

Managing Historic Theaters

W e felt it would be important to devote a special chapter to the particular joys and challenges of managing an historic theater. Time and time
again, we have seen the restoration, renovation, or adaptive reuse of
historic theaters act as a catalyst for the redevelopment of an urban area. The
very act of investing public and private funds in such a project is a symbol of
a community's determination to save its downtown. The process of reanimat-
ing the theater is also a healthy one. It brings out and engages a broad cross-
section of the community to work together for the common good. But how does
the facility manager operate the facility in such a way as to maximize those
benefits to the community on an ongoing basis? Let's explore that question
and also consider the particular differences and challenges of managing older
facilities.

Historic Theaters in North America

To start with, it is a sad truth that no one has a definitive count of how many
historic theaters there are in North America. There are several organizations
that are paying attention to historic theaters. One is the League of Historic
American Theaters, an organization providing information and support for

groups who have restored and operate historic theaters, plus others who are in the throes of or contemplating restoration. The mission of the League is "to advocate, support, and facilitate the rescue, restoration, reuse, and sustaining of historic theaters and other heritage buildings used for cultural assembly." That addition on heritage buildings is important, as there are more and more examples of the adaptive reuse of old Masonic temples, churches, Grange Halls, and other significant structures into wonderful theaters.

According to Jon Poehlman at the League office, there are 500 active members, with approximately 325 representing operating historic theaters. Poehlman also notes that the League has collected a list of another 6,000 historic theaters in North America that at some point have been considered for reactivation. What that generally means is that a person has called from a community, described the sad situation of an abandoned theater, and inquired as to how the League might help. It is inevitable that many of these structures have been lost, but there is most certainly a large set of old theaters that remain candidates for restoration. Architect Craig Morrison and his wife have been engaged in a multiyear search and survey of all historic theaters in the five boroughs of New York City. So far, they have identified over six hundred facilities originally built as theaters. Even more amazing is the fact that of that total, only fifty are currently active as performing arts venues. The other buildings accommodate everything from hardware stores to nightclubs, with lots of supermarkets and ethnic churches in the mix.

Another organization is the Theater Historical Society, which is much more for individuals who treat historic theaters as a hobby. They collect artifacts and documentation on historic theaters of all kinds, but they seem to be much more interested in historic movie palaces and movie organs than they are in operating historic theaters for the performing arts. This organization also lacks any running tally on how many active historic theaters there are.

A third organization involved in the preservation of historic theaters is the American Theatre Organ Society, a group of passionate devotees of organs and the theaters that house them. They have been instrumental in saving several old theaters as venues for their historic organs, as well as saving the music that was traditionally played many years ago in association with or accompanying live presentations.

The Kiss in the Balcony

One of the great advantages of operating an historic theater is that so many people in the community have a personal connection with the building. Carrie Barnett of the Capitol Theater in Bowling Green captures that sentiment:

> It's intriguing to see how the community surrounds that facility and defines it within their world. We've discovered in the process of the renovation that nothing can happen to the Capitol, because it's the Capitol. I can't tell you the number of times I heard that. The thing that is most intriguing about an old facility is that if this facility were to shut down, there would be a lot of people saying, "Wait a minute, we want this facility to be open!" We have an edge in fundraising because of the history beyond the twenty years we've been running this facility. Many people tell me they had their first kiss in the balcony, or they remember buying popcorn at the concession in the lobby. That creates a strong sense of ownership that we can convert into support.

There is support for the building and its ongoing operations, and the opportunity to turn each sentimental soul into a word-of-mouth marketer for programs in the facility. At the same time, that personal connection often translates into strong feelings and opinions about the building and its programs, such that there is a real risk of alienating those supporters if they disagree with renovation plans or programming. Thus, the manager of the historic theater is often seen as much more of a steward, preserving the asset on behalf of the community. Mark Light operates both a new facility and an historic theater in Dayton, Ohio, and is thus able to speak of the differences:

> We operate the historic Victoria Theater and the new Schuster Center. And while I have a strong affinity for the Schuster, my relationship with the Victoria is much more of a love affair. Everybody loves the Victoria. It is an end unto itself. When it was being built, they believed that they were building a cathedral, which certainly isn't the case in the low-bid public buildings that you see now. You get a low bid, you build a building, and you're done. The Schuster is harder to love. It is easy to work with it, but we don't feel as

close to it. And I've gotten e-mail from people and comments saying they like the Schuster, but they feel like they're coming home to the Victoria.

Cora Cahan is president of the New 42nd Street and the New Victory Theater in New York City. She was also one of driving forces behind the revitalization of that entire block, and is now the landlord for the seven active theaters on the block. As for the joys of managing an historic theater, Cahan says:

> I don't know if it's different, but you do answer to a higher authority. The New Victory is the oldest operating theater in New York. It is probably inefficient in contemporary terms because it was built the way it was built, but that is part of its beauty. We've been very lucky because it didn't have a box office, it didn't have a lobby, it didn't have backstage facilities. Today, through quirks of fate, it has the biggest lobby on Broadway. But is it hard to have an historic building? Yes, because you are dealing with a building that wasn't built to be air-conditioned, cooled, or heated in an efficient way—so you do the best you can. On the other hand, it also gives you something so splendid that it is probably worth the effort. And our facility people are very diligent about keeping it in good condition.

The reference to a higher authority is important. Lots of people tend to have very strong feelings about historic theaters, often framed in terms of the greater good. There are preservationists committed to preserving the building as it once was. There are activists who see the theater as a powerful symbol of the glorious past of the community. And there are all those citizens/voters/taxpayers who connect the building to a deeply personal set of memories. Chris Ball recounts a similar experience at the Astor Theatre in Liverpool, Nova Scotia:

> You'd be amazed at the number of people who come in and say, "I can remember coming here in the 1940s and watching movies," or "I saw my first live show here." Or, we had one gentleman come in who grew up here and he was in his seventies, and hadn't been back to Liverpool in sixty years, and he came in because he just wanted to see the inside of the building again, and really, the inside has not changed a huge amount from that time period. And he came in and he was so happy that it was in operation. And we were having a

show that evening, and he came to the show, and when he left, he was so over-joyed that it was still being used and that it was well looked after that he left us with a $2,000 check.

The Redevelopment Catalyst

The restoration and reactivation of historic theaters is often seen as and used as a catalyst for urban redevelopment. Cora Cahan here speaks of the plan to restore 42nd Street and its theaters:

It was originally imagined that we would have tenants in each of these theaters and that adaptive reuse would be brought to bear on most if not all of these theaters. We imagined that the office building site at 42nd and Broadway and the other four commercial sites would be developed in the early 1990s, and then the mid-block theaters would benefit from those buildings going up, and that we would find tenants falling all over themselves to take over these theaters. Then the real estate market fell apart, and of course those office buildings did not go up, and what happened in a nutshell is that theaters that made 42nd Street what it was at the beginning of the twentieth century reinvented 42nd Street at the beginning of the twenty-first century, and actually drove the development on the rest of the block.

The board did not want us to replicate or do anything that was already thriving in New York City in terms of cultural use. So we came up with three or four models for nonprofit use. One of them was a theater for kids, and it was-n't just to say, We're going to bring kids, it's going to be the pied piper, we're going to bring back the block. It was to fill a perceived void on our part in the cultural and theatrical fabric in the city, which was that there was no place devoted 100 percent to good stuff for the city's young people, their parents, their teachers, the adults who care for them. There was no place to instill in them a passion for the live performing arts, so that when they grew up and they were voting or making decisions in the city, the arts and theater would be an impor-tant part of their quality of life and of living in the city for them.

So the New Victory was hatched as an idea in about 1991-92. We've leased all but one of the other theaters, and we may even have a tenant for that one. Indeed, of those seven theaters on the block, four are in live theatrical use right now, two are part of the big retail development across the street, and the other one is perhaps being leased to a restaurateur/ caterer/disco by our tenant.

Let's be clear on how a reanimated theater can reinvent an urban core. It happens because there are people on the street in the daytime and the evening, which changes the perception of an area from dangerous to safe. Those people on the street are a beacon for commercial development, representing potential consumers. As we've seen, they will eat, drink, and shop as a part of their trip to the theater. More than that, those theater patrons represent a certain type of person attractive to retailers—a relatively well-educated consumer with some affluence and desire for entertainment and/or enrichment. Finally, there has been a trend in cities for people to follow artists into areas previously considered dangerous or, worse, uncool. Some years ago in Montreal, there was a line of graffiti in the Old City that read, "Artists are the Storm Troopers of gentrification." They take the risk of venturing into a new area in search of cheap real estate and bring to it a cultural cachet. The rest of us follow them in, seeking some association with a newly hip image. Thus, a theater reactivated in an urban core can attract artists, audience, development, and a new image.

Physical Constraints

Before we decide to rescue all of the old theaters we can find, let's review some of the physical constraints of these spaces. Here Judith Daykin speaks of the challenges of City Center:

> An old building is different from a new building. City Center was built in 1923. It's a constant maintenance problem—the failure of the HVAC system means that if it's hot, we can't rent the building in the summer, which we tried a few years ago. It was 103 degrees, and the artists and audiences had a miserable experience.
>
> At the same time, people are charmed by this building. It is not ornate, but it is a charming space, and the ghosts that live in this building seem to be happy ghosts. There is a feeling of antiquity, but also of how important City Center has been to the city of New York, and when you read the history and

know how it fits in, our relationship to the Broadway community and Carnegie, it is lovely.

Daykin is also being polite about the fact that the backstage area at City Center is very limited, and the effort required to load shows in and out is Herculean. This is often the case with theaters built for vaudeville or film, as they have shallow stages, limited wing space, very little in the way of support space, and terrible backstage access.

Increasingly problematic is the use of modern performance equipment systems in old theaters. Here's theater consultant Charles Cosler:

> When I first came to New York in 1969, they still used to try to mask the box booms in the Broadway theaters with a big hoop of iron at the top, onto which they tied drapery, and the drapery would hang down behind the lights— frighteningly close to the lights. At some point they stopped doing it, both because there got to be too many lights, and because of the advent of computer boards. When computer boards came along, lighting designers were able to have many more lighting instruments than in the days of old. Back then, 200 to 300 units were a lot of units for a Broadway show. Now, a range of 800 to 1,300 is not unheard of at all. It's a different world.
>
> The other dynamic is that theater people need to do what they need to do. They are being asked by a director to produce a certain effect, and they need to do what they have to do to produce that effect. They will go to great lengths to jerry-rig things to get lights where it's currently not possible to hang them. I tell them, Better to design those positions so that they look right and so that they are integrated, rather than having somebody come along and jerry-rigging a bunch of pipe that may or may not be safe, which is probably going to be pretty unsightly. Just because they are using hardware that is off the shelf and not customized for a particular application.

Many older theaters lack the size and spaces needed to support large-scale performances simply because they were built for movies and/or vaudeville, which required much less in the way of support space or technical areas. But it is also the case that theaters have been accommodating new technologies for a long time. Josh Dachs of Fisher Dachs makes the point well:

My associate Joe Mobilia here likes to say that the future arrives in a truck. You quickly come to realize that the most contemporary, futuristic, ground-breaking, commercial musicals are performed in theaters that are a century old or more. These are shows that use robotic lighting fixtures, and massive stage machinery that does all sorts of physical tricks using projections and lasers and the latest audio equipment, all installed in theaters that were built in 1906. Technology comes and goes and changes over time, and a proper theater design, whether it is a new building or a renovation, needs to anticipate that the technology will come again, and one wants to allow that to happen in a way that doesn't damage the building over the years. But buildings need to embrace change—otherwise they can't survive.

Successful Operation of Historic Theaters

Let's consider some of the specific advantages and disadvantages of operating historic theaters in terms of their financial implications.

Earned Revenues

There are a series of advantages and challenges for historic facility managers as they attempt to build earned revenues:

- One of the real advantages is that some artists and groups prefer to play in a lovely old theater. Hence, the manager is able to negotiate a lower fee to get them there. Michael Currie at the 400-seat American Theater reports: "We did four nights with Marcel Marceau last year, and he loved it. The man is eighty years old and performs all over the world. And he said to me, 'This is one of the finest theaters I have ever performed in. And I want to come back!'"
- Because many historic theaters were built for or adapted for film, there is a more natural affinity with that program. Proctors Theatre runs a weekly film program in their historic 2,700-seat theater, showing classic films and spectacles that are enhanced by the large screen in the large and ornate hall.

- There is the possibility that renters will pay more to access a beautiful old hall, since they believe that the experience of their customers is made better by the historic nature of the structure.
- It is also possible that ticket surcharges are marginally more palatable in historic structures, as managers can frame them as contributing to the worthy cause of restoring the theater.
- On the negative side are all of the physical limitations of the building, including the too-small stage that prevents certain touring productions from coming to town, the lack of support facilities needed to accommodate a local ballet company as a potential renter, or the tiny lobby that limits opportunities for concessions and catered events.

Managing Expenses

The management of operating expenses is also a great challenge for historic theaters, given the following:

- Repairs and maintenance are significantly higher because of the age of the building and the need to preserve that historic quality of the facility. This extends down to the smallest bits of work, such as the effort to replace decorative light bulbs in historic fixtures.
- Basic operating costs are likely higher, given the inefficiencies of the space and how it was constructed, compared to modern facilities. The cost to air-condition the warren of tiny dressing rooms in the tower off stage left will be significant.
- The historic theater is likely to use some older systems for things like air handling and heating that are much less efficient on an operating basis.
- And finally, the capital reserve and the need to replenish that fund are also much higher with a more fragile structure and with those aged systems that must inevitably be replaced.

Contributed Income

In the area of contributed income, historic theaters are in a much stronger position than contemporary facilities:

- First and foremost are the opportunities to raise funds in the community on the basis of the strong connection with the facility. Think back to Carrie Barnett's argument that their historic structure creates a fundraising edge.
- In addition, historic structures have the ability to access different kinds of public-sector support, for example, by selling historic tax credits into the private sector.
- Finally, historic theaters can attract additional financial support if tied to downtown redevelopment efforts. This can come both from the public and private sectors.

All of this is sound advice, but it is often difficult to execute. Community leaders, including arts leaders, tend to agree that reactivating the old theater is a great idea and that lots of people will support the project, but it only makes sense if the theater can be operated successfully over time, supported with an appropriate balance of earned and contributed income.

I am reminded of the story of the Paramount Theater in Rutland, Vermont. It was restored and reactivated as a part of a major downtown redevelopment plan that also included a new downtown shopping plaza, a government office building, a multiplex, a transportation center, and street-scaping. It took years to accomplish and lots of money from the public and private sectors. Matthew Sternberg is head of the Rutland Redevelopment Authority, which drove the project through renovation into operations. But here, he notes how the challenge changes once the theater opens:

> To get the theater renovated, we had to have a person oriented toward the cultural welfare of the community. But once the renovation was accomplished, we had to change gears. Now, success is not based on preserving the cultural integrity of the community. It's about selling tickets, putting bodies in seats.
>
> We just hired a new executive director who I think is going to take the theater in a positive direction. It's a real challenge. Many folks here have had a difficult time shifting gears and recognizing that this building is not going to be all fine arts and culture. What they need to be looking at is things like running a two-week country music festival in the summer that would put bodies in seats. But these folks can't get their heads around the idea of bringing in

something that is, to them, as lowbrow as a country music festival. Well, once they sink far enough in debt, they start to see through that.

I think the reality is that you have to be looking at $100,000 worth of red ink before you get yourself over that one and straighten it out. But our new manager is much more pragmatic and market-oriented. He knows that this theater has to be full and active three hundred days a year in order to do the things we want it to do for the community.

Chapter Fourteen

Managing Campus Theaters

The other kind of theater worthy of note is the campus-based performing arts facility. This generally means a mid-sized to large hall located on the campus of a community or four-year college where there is public access—some combination of audiences and/or community-based arts organizations that use the facility.

From the perspective of the facility manager, there are some tremendous advantages for the manager of a campus-based facility. Colleges are very good at taking care of facilities, and they have very sophisticated fundraising operations. But there are also challenges, such as the need to share facilities with teaching programs and the basic challenge of bringing people from the community onto the foreign territory of a college campus. Let's consider how managers respond to these advantages and disadvantages.

Facility Management Skills

First of all, colleges are skilled at maintaining facilities and planning for the maintenance of facilities. They generally have a large facility management department staffed by individuals who are skilled in facility operations, capital planning, building security, trash removal, custodial services, and so on.

Lance Olson is the manager of the Majestic Theater in downtown Boston, which is owned and operated by Emerson College.

> Emerson College is especially good at taking care of buildings. One of my great joys is the number of people who are here to help me. The facilities maintenance staff does a great job of maintaining the structure of the building, everything from repairs to cleaning. They are very responsive. If I call in a work order, it is taken care of almost always in a very reasonable timeframe. I have a building manager who works with me to address things like walk-off mats and waste bins and wear and tear on the carpet and repair of seats and some of the basic stuff that as an independent theater operator would take up a substantial part of my day.
>
> A theater director I once knew used to say that most of her life was wrapped up in toilet paper. Almost none of my life is wrapped up in toilet paper, nor is that the focus of any of my staff members. If I had those responsibilities, to do them well, to do them anywhere near as well as the college does, I'd need at least two full-time people just for that. I've looked at jobs where those kinds of things would be the responsibility of the executive director, and I realize that what really happens is that you can't afford those two people, so you try to put it into one person, and only half of the job gets done.

Campus-based facilities also have sophisticated campus master plans and capital plans that drive decision-making on the maintenance and improvement of facilities. Here is William Reeder from George Mason University on the planning framework his Center for the Arts fits into:

> One of our great advantages is that our president and our provost are very successful strategists. So we have the benefit of a thirty-year campus master plan that was comprehensive in its formulation. Virtually any artistic facility that you would reasonably aspire to has a site and a physical location on the plan. So there's a very strong integration of strategy and facilities and educational mission between the arts and the university.
>
> The challenge is that they are building a billion dollars' worth of buildings right now, so a very gifted architectural and planning staff is genuinely stretched to the breaking point, and the campus aesthetic really is Virginia brick. So, if there's a challenge here, it is keeping the intention of the

professionals on campus sustained to provide more than adequate responses—to get to great. That's a little trickier, and it's not because the spirit isn't willing; it's just that there aren't enough people to go around, and there are a lot of different priorities. They are integrated in the sense that you can't have another building until you have another water chiller, and you can't have that until you have a parking deck, because the water chiller has to sit on the parking lot that students use Wednesday nights. So it's like building a city.

That's a critical point. There are great planners on campus, but there are also very large plans into which performing arts facilities must fit. An additional challenge is that facility management groups on a campus are rarely faced with buildings as complicated as performing arts centers, so their attempts to fit these facilities into normal maintenance cycles or cost controls is sometimes problematic.

A related challenge is the staffing of campus facilities. Here is Mark Heiser, manager of the State Theater at Lincoln Center and former manager of Cal Presents at the University of California, Berkeley:

At Berkeley, our stagehands were unionized. They were not students, they were not IATSE, but they were part of a union called university technical employees. It's a totally different thing. The stability there is pretty fixed. We had a floating crew, but they don't leave in the middle of work and go to class. The students that work in support positions as production assistants were great. There's a lot of turnover, but that is really part of our mission. You want to be able to engage students at a certain level in the arts, and that is part of the educational mission. Even if they are a psychology major, if you are exposing them to the arts, they are more likely to be a patron later on. So it contributes to your role as a groomer of future audiences or marketing people or future PR people or whatever their particular interest is.

Fundraising for College-based Facilities

Colleges are usually very active raising money to build and sustain facilities. There are advancement departments that are continually seeking and collecting financial support from alumni and others that can be used either to build or operate facilities.

I worked with William Reeder at George Mason University in 2002 on a feasibility study for new performing arts facilities at their campus in Prince William County. The fundraising effort got a big boost when, according to Reeder:

> The University signaled its support for the arts by agreeing to use the services of the foundation and the development staff of the general university to conduct the capital campaigns for new arts facilities. They are willing to use bonding power, with the city and the county to pay the bond off, and then raise $15 million in private funds to endow the operations. That is really amazing, and I doubt that most universities are quite that thoroughly integrated in the way those resources are applied.

The other side of the coin is that if the university's advancement department did not get behind this project and lend its support, it would be dead in the water. There would be no ability for supporters of the project to raise money independently, or even to get the authority to approach anyone for financial support. Fundraising is a very serious business on a college campus, and the typical advancement department generally requires that all development efforts be funneled through its offices. So it's great to have the advancement department's resources and skills, but that doesn't always mean that it can maximize financial support.

As a case in point, we have been working in Bowling Green to help advance the Southern Kentucky Performing Arts Center (SKyPAC) project. Our feasibility study and subsequent efforts suggested that the community should partner with Western Kentucky University on the development and operation of those facilities. When it was time to begin a capital campaign, the university offered moral support and some access to information, but sent the project team off on their own while they completed a $100 million campaign to fund a series of other facilities. To date, the project has had very little success raising funds. The community is relatively small, the economy has been tight, and all of their lead prospects have just made significant pledges to the university.

It's also tough to fundraise with the perception of deep pockets on campus, as confirmed by Mark Heiser:

People have an expectation that if you work on a university campus, the university must fund you, when in fact it doesn't fund us. So, we try to establish ourselves as part of the university. Of course, having an educational program, having something that engages us with the university, is central to our own mission, but at the same time, we are the public face of the university. We were presenting fine arts that have nothing to do with university programs—programs like Alvin Ailey, Bolshoi Ballet, programs that enhance the reputation of the university but are not part of a university program and don't receive direct financial support.

The Campus Environment

Then there is the advantage that to be on a campus is to be in an environment where learning and intellectual curiosity is dominant. Facility programmers thus have the advantage of being able to seek out and book programs that are challenging and provocative. There is also the opportunity to relate what goes on in a performing arts venue to other art forms and social issues. Here is John Haynes, executive director of the Marie P. DeBartolo Center for the Performing Arts at the University of Notre Dame:

One of the dreams that I always had was to use venues to expand the scope of people's understanding and pleasure. Buying a ticket to see a singer, coming to the event, and then walking out and going home—it's a transactional relationship. It's not significantly different in quality from buying a movie ticket. You buy the ticket, you go and see the movie, and you leave. You don't hang around the lobby and discuss with strangers how you felt about the movie. And you don't see that movie and then immediately walk across to the street to an art exhibit that relates to the theme of the movie, or then go see a play on which the movie was based, or go to a concert of music that is either from the film or related to the film.

When you begin with the idea that you've got this audience of people who are seeking, it gives you some opportunities to program in creative and interesting ways that you don't ordinarily have. One of the principal reasons I took this job was because I was very intrigued with doing arts in this environment—for example, the ability to use it to support the work of the Center for

Social Concerns. I am looking at working with Sister Helen Prejean, the subject of the film *Dead Man Walking*, who has had a long relationship with the university through the Center for Social Concerns. Tim Robbins has been working on adapting the screenplay of that film into a stage play, and I've begun to have some conversations with Sister Prejean about the possibility of work-shopping that play as a joint program with the Center for Social Concerns because the whole issue of the death penalty looms very large here. UC Berkley devotes a lot of attention in different areas to questions of social justice and ethics. The arts provide a powerful means to address those issues.

Christopher Beach is the director of the Performing Arts Center at Purchase College. Here he speaks of the pros and cons of operating in this atmosphere:

I've got a lot of colleagues at the college, and it is fun to work with deans and directors of music, dance, and theater. There is a personal element to it. Also, whenever you are around young people, it keeps you young, and it keeps the staff young (although I've got a pretty young staff to start with). Students move quicker than thirty-five-year-olds and forty-five-year-olds, so it keeps us all jumping a little bit.

I would love to be able to say that it's rewarding and exciting for us to put on a great program with a terrific artist or company and see the students banging down the doors, saying, "Please let us in, we want to see these models of excellence!" But they don't, and our new president is deeply committed to changing that. On the other hand, in academia, too much is about the process, not the product. We are about the product. And I could do without the endless committee meetings.

Programming

Colleges are very good at activating facilities, particularly during the daytime. Teaching programs and student-sponsored events bring activity and audiences into the building on a regular basis. But colleges are also interested in activating facilities in a way that reflects well on the institution. Here is Lance Olson on programming:

When I started here, it was all about hitting a budget number. Now my responsibility has gotten far more complex and interesting. That responsibility is much more focused on quality, much more focused on fixing the mission. My most recent instructions were, "We don't care whether you have things in the theater all the time, as long as the things you have in the theater really speak well of the college." That is a huge change—clearly an evolution toward presenting.

This year, for the first time, we will present three weeklong events, something we've done only twice before in the last ten years. These are three very high-quality events; we are talking about $2 million to $2.5 million in presenting, so there is substantial pressure to succeed. But if we are successful, it is likely to make a substantial impact on what we do as part of our operations.

The principal downside to programming campus facilities is that generally they must be shared by some combination of teaching programs, student groups, presenting, and the special events of the college, with perhaps some dates left over for community groups. The facility manager faces quite a challenge juggling all of these competing uses and users, establishing policies and procedures that balance access and minimize conflict. The other related challenge is that teaching programs and student groups enjoy studying in a theater. If access is free or heavily subsidized, they are not inclined to come and go quickly, which limits access to those more likely to contribute to the financial operation of facilities. All of which is fine, as long as budget targets are clear and the expectations of the institution are being met. As Wiliam Reeder says:

> You have to be good at budgeting to manage campus facilities. It is a prerequisite for creativity. If you are careless with the system, then the system will freeze you and lock you down. There is serious political scrutiny, especially at this moment in higher education, where tuition is outpacing general costs and states are losing their financial base. There is tremendous political scrutiny of efficiency and of appropriate use of public dollars. The parents are starting to become much more efficient in choosing where they are going to spend their dollars, so you really must comply. It's a discipline with which you must succeed. We're part of a huge machine that is increasingly transparent to the community.

At the same time, there are many institutions with the resources and the inclination to be risk-takers. Lance Olson describes his experience managing facilities for Rutgers University and Emerson College:

> This college is unusual in that it is remarkably entrepreneurial. At Rutgers, it was an interesting mix of state institution and private college, where we ramped up a program called Rutgers Summer Fest over six months, from zero to about $1 million and then to $4 million over two years. You couldn't do that as a private 501(c)(3). You can't make change that rapidly. No one has the guts to do it, even if you had the resources.
>
> At Rutgers, being able to venture a million dollars was not a big deal. The president was able to approve it without going to the governor; it was very straightforward. And I'm having that same experience here. A strong mission is not constrained by budget. There is an entrepreneurial spirit in most higher education administrations that only comes out when it is presented with an entrepreneurial idea. I'm sure there are people who will argue with me that there is no such thing as entrepreneurialism in higher education, but that has not been my experience.

Command and Control

One of the most unique elements of campus facilities is dealing with the unique command and control structure of an educational institution. John Haynes is getting used to this at Notre Dame:

> I've come from community to campus facilities, and the biggest difference is how control and authority work. As CEO of a freestanding nonprofit, you have a board to answer to. But unless you manage your board poorly, at the end of the day, you still make the decisions. That is not true in a university environment, where authority is diffuse. It really is not even completely invested in the president of the university or in a dean. It is a system that is driven by a desire for consensus without well-developed mechanisms for obtaining it.
>
> I am accustomed to being a CEO, and there is no such thing on a college campus. So I've had to learn not only to be a better collaborator, but also to discover alternative methods of getting decisions actually made. Someone here

once waggishly said to me that a decision at Notre Dame is actually an opportunity for reevaluation, and that is true. From the standpoint of a manager, that is frustrating, but that is really just adapting to a new environment. If those in the arts can't adapt to new environments, then who can? In a university setting, there is a whole set of management issues that makes it different from any other landscape.

Every single impediment to participation has to be removed here, because there is no tradition of arts participation at Notre Dame, of the student body being engaged in the arts. It's a very rich and thoroughgoing history that lives on in the alumni in a way that you underestimate at your peril. Making any kind of significant change at Notre Dame can incur thousands of letters from alumni.

Bridges and Barriers

Perhaps the most intriguing element of campus facilities is the challenge of breaking down traditional barriers between colleges and communities, and the opportunity to use performing arts facilities as a means to that end. According to Lance Olson:

> Emerson College is known for restoring old buildings and sometimes converting them to new uses, whereas some of the colleges up the street are known for tearing down old buildings and building new ones. We used the reopening of the Majestic to highlight the fact that the college is a friend of restoration. The point of that was to talk about the college's relationship to many communities, that we view try to focus our efforts on honoring them individually.

The Center for the Arts at George Mason University was conceived as a bridge to the community, but then evolved into something very different. William Reeder tells that story:

> When it opened, the mandate for the Center was to create connectivity across the campus and across the region for a brand new university. Leadership realized that they couldn't use sports the way many universities do, so they developed the Performing Arts Center to create those connections. At that time,

there was a stated notion that this Center was not for the performing arts students of GMU. They weren't good enough for that yet—they had to earn their way onto stage. Ten years later, they are good enough, and the new administration is very sensitive to strategic outcomes. So they created the college, and then they hired me as the first dean.

I came not from an academic background, but from a nonprofit arts background, only to discover there wasn't a board because the university had not used community resources to build the infrastructure; instead, it had used student fee money. In return, five hundred tickets for every performance are reserved at no cost for the students, since they've already paid for them. But I felt as though we were unnecessarily limiting ourselves by not having a traditional conversation with community leaders, and so I sought the blessing from the president of the university to form a board, and have done so.

What we found was that in fact, hundreds of community members had been seeking and anticipating a way to express their participation in the Center philanthropically. They were delighted to perform traditional board functions, serving on planning and fundraising and artistic advisory committees. People have shown up in volume and have given us a tremendous new point of confidence, with two important results. One is fundraising. We now see an annual fund going from almost zero to $400,000 a year, and we project that will turn into $1.5 million in five years. That is annual money that wasn't available before. The other huge change is in GMU's strategy to remain integrated into the region, so that it doesn't pull away into a classic research tower, but views itself as an aggressive source of economic, social, and cultural development for this region. Having the board makes that real. It's really been a painless development.

In the last three years, our earlier configuration had begun to suffer serious operating losses. Even though it was all subsidized, there was still a budget shortfall of anywhere from $300,000 to $700,000, and that was unsustainable. As the new dean, I asked the provost what he wanted, and he told me to stop the bleeding. It turned out there were some efficiencies and some artistic tweaking that could take place, but the big difference was that we weren't really taking advantage of the capacity of audience volume. By having the university so enthusiastic about starting this network of friends, we have gotten a huge jump in sales. We crossed the million-dollar mark in ticket sales in March 2002, which was our best year ever, and we actually had a $200,000 surplus.

For Lance Olson at Emerson College, the biggest problem is the community perception that the theater is offering "student productions":

> We are in the heart of the theater district. The only difference between my theater and the ones next door is that my theater has a banner on it that says "Emerson College" and the one next door says "*Les Misérables*." I suspect that there is some deterrent every once in a while when people see the Emerson College banner and assume ours are student productions. But we are doing a brand new, fully professional production of *A Christmas Carol*, being produced by Trinity Rep. It's a phenomenal piece, with a production team you wouldn't believe and a great cast. It's an equity production, first-class all the way. So I'm taking the "At Emerson College" out of my ads, because every box office call starts out with, "Is this a student production?"

The significant challenges of managing campus facilities are more than offset by the skills and resources added by a place of learning and the opportunity to operate the facility in such a way as to strengthen the institution and its relationship with the community. Successful managers quickly come to grips with some of these quirks and tricks, and are then in a much stronger position to harness the considerable resources of the institution as it looks outward.

Chapter Fifteen

Final Words

In this our final chapter, let's pull together some of themes that have emerged from our research, then consider how the role of facility manager might evolve into the future.

Complexity

The job if running a performing arts facility is increasingly complex, to the point that the title of facility manager no longer seems appropriate. Among others, Philip Morris of Proctors Theatre in Schenectady took issue with my calling him a facility manager:

> I'm not a facility manager! I see my job as the deliverer of a visual dream—the community has a dream. My job is to appreciate that dream, add to it a little bit, and deliver it. That's what I do.

Whereas thirty years ago facility managers were mostly engaged in taking care of a building, today they are doing anything and everything they can to animate a facility, connect it to the community, and change the world. And if that means producing opera, speaking at Rotary Club meetings, and delivering artists to schools, so be it.

Dealing with Change

The Performing Arts Center of Greater Miami is scheduled to open in 2006, after more than twenty years of hard work by leaders in the public and private sector. Michael Hardy is the president and CEO of the organization that will operate the facility, including the Sanford and Dolores Ziff Opera Ballet House and the Carnival Symphony Hall.

I recently moderated a conference panel that included Hardy talking about preparing to operate these two Western European-style halls in a community that has changed radically since the facility was conceived. There is little that can be done physically to alter the facilities, but Michael is confident that with innovative programming, he can bring the community to the building. He is exploring opportunities such as pay-per-view concerts in partnership with Latin American broadcasters to build earned income (given that 56 percent of the regional population is of Hispanic descent). And he has recently signed a deal with the Massachusetts Institute of Technology to open a digital media center in the Center to explore the boundaries between live and electronic performance.

Looking Outward

The world is changing very quickly, particularly as it relates to performing arts audiences. Facility managers can't wait for change and then react, but must get out in front. How do they do that? The first and most important step is that they adopt an outward perspective. Managers and staff must spend more of their days outside the building, understanding local, regional, and national trends and thinking about the role of the facility in the community. The growth and development of education programs in performing arts centers is one of the outcomes (and benefits) of that outward perspective.

Extending Their Reach

More and more facility management organizations are extending their skills and resources to other arts facilities and programs. There are economies of scale and operating efficiencies when multiple facilities are managed together. And the skills and resources within facility management organizations can have significant and positive impacts on smaller producing and presenting organizations in their communities. More of these arrangements are likely in the future. The big question is whether successful facility management organizations can extend themselves beyond one community to establish regional or national enterprises.

Evolution from Rentals through Producing

Also over the past thirty years, we have seen facility managers become more and more proactive about what's on the stage. The relatively passive act of booking rentals has given way to the risk-taking of becoming a presenter, choosing shows that fit the mission and potentially contribute to financial performance. And now a number of facilities are taking the next step into the world of producing, either by investing in touring product or by actually deploying their resources to create opera, theater, music, or dance.

This trend is likely to continue. There is a desire to take more control for the benefit of the organization and the community. There is an understanding that gaps in the cultural offerings of a community can be filled by the facility. And there is often a mission to serve the community by offering more than simply what the people want.

The High and the Low

One of the most important changes occurring today is the breakdown in the traditional separation of "high" arts and the "lower" forms of entertainment— the rarified versus the popular. Nowhere is this more apparent than in the world of music, where adjectives such as "classical," "modern," "world," "serious," and "popular" are becoming less meaningful. Alex Ross, music critic for *New Yorker* magazine, recently wrote a terrific article on this phenomenon.[1] In it, he describes the journey of a thirty-six-year-old popular music fan who wants to try something different:

> I am now enough of a fan that I buy a $25 ticket to hear a famous orchestra play the *Eroica* live. It is not a very heroic experience. I feel dispirited from the moment I walk in the hall. My black jeans draw disapproving glances from men who seem to be modeling the Johnny Carson collection. I look around dubiously at the twenty shades of beige in which the hall is decorated. The music starts, but I find it hard to think of Beethoven's detestation of all tyranny over the human mind when the man next to me is a dead ringer for my dentist. The assassination sequence in the first movement is less exciting when the musicians have no emotion on their faces.
>
> I cough; a thin man, reading a dog-eared score, glares at me. When the movement is about a minute from ending, an ancient woman creeps slowly up the aisle, a look of enormous dissatisfaction on her face, followed at a few paces by a blank-faced husband. Finally, three grand chords to finish, which the composer obviously intended to set off a roar of applause. I start to clap, but the man with the score glares again. One does not applaud in the midst of greatly great great music, even if the composer wants one to! Coughing, squirming, whispering, the crowd visibly suppresses its urge to express pleasure. It's like mass anal retention. The slow tread of the funeral march, or "marcia funebre," as everyone insists on calling it, begins. I start to feel that my newfound respect for the music is dragging along behind the hearse.

The music ultimately wins him over, but what a struggle! And what a challenge for the facility manager to create an environment in which these potential customers are welcomed, supported, and motivated to return.

Productivity

Amidst all of this change and evolution, the most fundamental challenge remains the same. With productivity accelerating in so many other industries, the economic dilemma of the performing arts as expressed by Baumol and Bowen looms as a growing challenge, here framed by Michael Kaiser:

> Every decade is harder than the decade before. It never gets easier in the arts because we can never improve our productivity. We have the same number of seats, same number of performers. Ten years from now it will be harder than it is today. And twenty years from now it will be even harder, which means that arts administrators have to become better and better and better. I'm sure the arts management training programs do some good, but I believe they are a little bit vocabulary-focused and not necessarily entrepreneurially focused, which is what I believe arts managers have to be. We are all running tiny businesses. Even the Kennedy Center is a tiny business, and it has to be run in an entrepreneurial fashion, finding revenue, finding resources wherever you can and spending them wisely.

The Role of the Arts

In the final chapter of *The Performing Arts in a New Era*, the book's authors present a picture of the future of the performing arts. Key to this is their identification of the three critical functions to be served by the performing arts in the modern world:[2]

1. The arts act as a source of entertainment, enrichment, and fulfillment for individuals
2. The arts serve as a vehicle for the preservations and transmission of culture
3. The arts provide a variety of instrumental benefits to society at the individual, community, and national level

The benefits in that third category are substantial. At the individual level, the arts promote openness to new ideas and creativity, as well as competence at school and work. At the community level, they provide economic and social benefits such as increasing economic activity, creating a more livable environment, and promoting a sense of community pride. And at the broadest level, they promote an understanding of diversity and pluralism, reinforce national identity in our cultural products, and provide a source of the nation's exports. Richard Florida's groundbreaking book, *The Rise of the Creative Class*,[3] is based on the simple idea that economic growth will occur in cities that attract educated and creative people. Many cities have taken this up, refocusing their economic development strategies on investments in cultural facilities and amenities that are attractive not just to artists, but to all of the educated and creatively inclined people who are the fuel of the modern economy.

The underlying idea is that the future of the performing arts depends on providing benefits to individuals, communities, and society as a whole. And it can be said that performing arts facilities are a critical means by which these benefits are delivered. They are the physical place where entertainment, enrichment, and fulfillment are delivered from artist to audience. Managers and their staffs seek out and present works from many different cultures. Education and outreach programs impact the lives of more and more people in their communities. Active facilities attract economic activity and commercial development. And all of these successes become a point of pride and identity for the community and country. Thus, the fundamental challenge for facilities and their organizations is to focus on the delivery of benefits that prove their worth to individuals, communities, and society, and justify ongoing support from both the public and private sectors.

Professional Viewpoint: What Makes a Great Facility Manager?

In our interviews with performing arts facility managers, everyone was asked to identify the characteristics of a great manager. Here are a few of our favorite responses:

Steve Loftin, president and executive director for the Cincinnati Arts Association:

> To be a good facility manager, you are going to have to be a lot more than just a facility manager. I remember when people started figuring out that facility managers had to become presenters and they had to become partners, whereas in the past, it just wasn't something they were doing. But now the dollar is being compressed and fractured into so many pieces that you have to be able to present, create partnerships, and pursue ancillary service opportunities to

make the whole thing work. Great facility managers are also great development officers, they are programmers, they are savvy business people, they are ticketing service providers, and they are merchandisers. You have to have a little bit of all of that, and you have to be entrepreneurial in the way you approach the work.

Christopher Beach, director of the Performing Arts Center at Purchase College:

You've got to be committed to a certain idea—a certain look, a certain style. It's about the artist. It's not about the marketing staff or me—our challenge is to do whatever we can to support the artists' work.

Joseph Golden, author and former managing director of the Civic Center of Onondaga County:

First of all, you need curiosity—a desire to know what's out there that you don't know about. Then you need a community affinity. You have to care about more than just the artists you are bringing in. You have to care about every human living creature in your community, who they are, where they come from, and their demographics. You have to know it. And then you have to trust the staff.

Peter Herrndorf, president and CEO of the National Arts Centre:

What impresses me tremendously about the good ones is how savvy they are. They are savvy about the details of running the operation, but they are also savvy about the business of the performing arts. The people who run more integrated operations—the combination of a facility and various art forms— the successful ones tend to have a real sensitivity to the art form and to the audience and to the artist. So in addition to being a savvy operator, you need that level of sensitivity. The good ones have it, and the other ones had better find it.

Judy Lisi, president and CEO of the Tampa Bay Performing Arts Center:

You have to have an appreciation for art and artists. Recently in our field, there have been a lot of people coming up that are either urban planners or come from city government, and they are being asked to run facilities. I have concerns about that because I believe that in order to be a true arts facility, you have to have people with an appreciation of the arts. They don't have to be artists themselves, but they have to have a true appreciation of it.

The work is very challenging, and you have to juggle a lot of balls at the same time and keep them all in the air. You have to have a wide scope of skills. You have to be able to manage a staff, and often in a very lean way. You have to understand marketing. You have to understand politics and government relations. You have to understand what quality is and what is commercial, and understand that there is also quality commercial product as well. You have to understand how to raise money and all of the ways to really balance earned and unearned income. You have to have eyes in front of you and behind you. And you have to be able to live in five different years, looking at the present but planning for the future.

NOTES

1. Ross, Alex, "Listen To This," *The New Yorker* (16-23 February 2004), 155.
2. Brooks, Arthur, Julia Lowell, Kevin McCarthy, and Laura Zakaras, "The Performing Arts in a New Era" (Washington, D.C.: The Rand Corporation, 2001), 115.
3. Florida, Richard, "The Rise of the Creative Class" (New York, NY: Basic Books, 2002).

Bibliography

Americans for the Arts. "The Arts and Economic Prosperity." Washington, D.C.: Americans for the Arts, 2003.

Brooks, Arthur, Julia Lowell, Kevin McCarthy, and Laura Zakaras. "The Performing Arts in a New Era." Washington, D.C.: The Rand Corporation, 2001.

Bryson, John. *Strategic Planning for Public and Nonprofit Organizations.* San Francisco: Jossey Bass Publishers, 1995.

The Dana Foundation. *Acts of Achievement: The Role of Performing Arts Centers in Education.* New York: Dana Press, 2003.

Fields, Armond and L. Marc Fields. *From the Bowery to Broadway: Lew Fields and the Roots of American Popular Theater.* London: Oxford University Press, 1993.

Florida, Richard. *The Rise of the Creative Class.* New York: Basic Books, 2002.

Golden, Joseph. *Olympus on Main Street: A Process for Planning a Community Arts Center.* New York: Syracuse University Press, 1980.

Grau, Robert. *The Business Man in the Amusement World: A Volume of Progress in the Field of the Theatre.* New York: Broadway Publishing Company, 1910.

Langley, Stephen. *Theatre Management and Production in America.* New York: Drama Publishers, 1990.

Linoff, Gordon. *Data Mining Techniques for Marketing, Sales and Customer Support, Second Edition.* New Jersey: John Wiley & Sons, 2003.

Miller, Clara. "Hidden in Plain Sight: Understanding Nonprofit Capital Structure." Nonprofit Quarterly. Spring 2003.

National Endowment for the Arts. "Survey of Public Participation on the Arts." Washington, D.C.: National Endowment for the Arts, 2002.

Newman, Danny. *Subscribe Now: Building Arts Audiences Through Dynamic Subscription Promotion.* New York: Theater Communications Group, 1977.

Niven, Paul R. *Balanced Scorecard Step-by-Step for Government and Nonprofit Agencies.* New Jersey: John Wiley & Sons, 2003.

The Urban Institute. "The Capacity of Performing Arts Organizations." Washington, D.C.: The Urban Institute, 2000.

U.S. Department of Education. "A Nation at Risk." Washington, D.C.: U.S. Department of Education, 1983.

Wolf, Thomas. *Managing a Nonprofit Organization.* New York: Simon & Schuster, 1990.

Facility Manager Biographies

Rae Ackerman has been director of Vancouver Civic Theatres, Vancouver, British Columbia, since 1990. He worked in theater production across Canada from 1965 until 1989, when he became general manager of the Pantages (now Canon) Theatre in Toronto. He is a board member and chair of several cultural organizations and an honorary lifetime member of Canadian Institute of Theatre Technology (CITT). He was elected Performing Arts Centre Executive of the Year in 1999 by *Session & Tour Guide/ Canadian Music Week.*

Judith Allen is vice chair of the North Carolina Blumenthal Performing Arts Center Foundation in Charlotte, where she oversees a $20 million endowment campaign. From 1990 to 2003, she was president of the Blumenthal Center. She oversaw the design, construction, and opening of the Center, as well as the adaptive reuse, design, restoration, and reopening of Spirit Square. Previously, she served as managing director of the Bushnell Center for the Arts in Hartford, Connecticut, where she oversaw its restoration. She holds a bachelor's degree in psychology from the University of Rhode Island, conducts arts and facilities management seminars and workshops, and consults on theater design, restoration, renovation, and operation throughout the country.

Chris Ball is manager of the Astor Theatre in his hometown of Liverpool, Nova Scotia. Seeking an opportunity to direct his creative energies, Ball began volunteering at the

Astor some years ago. Although he had no formal training in the arts, his potential was quickly recognized, and Bell was offered the theater manager position eight months later. Though the theater had consistently been running a deficit, by the end of his second year, Bell had succeeded in earning a small profit. Seven years later, Bell continues to serve his community by providing quality live entertainment at the Astor Theatre.

Carrie Barnett has a master of arts in community arts management from the University of Illinois-Springfield. In 1998, Barnett joined the Capitol Arts Alliance in Bowling Green, Kentucky, first as its education director. Later, after a promotion to deputy director, she became its president in 2001, responsible for all strategic and daily operations. Barnett then became director of development for University Libraries at Western Kentucky University in January 2004.

Christopher Beach has been director of the Performing Arts Center at Purchase College, New York, since 1989. He was previously production manager for Baltimore Opera Company, production stage manager at Santa Fe Opera, and administrative assistant to the director of production at the Metropolitan Opera. He founded the Santa Fe Festival Theatre in 1980, then returned to the Metropolitan Opera as operations director in 1985. He was managing director of PepsiCo Summerfare at Purchase College campus for ten years. He is a graduate of Johns Hopkins University.

James Brown is manager of Civic Center Music Hall in Oklahoma City, Oklahoma. His career in facility management spans over thirty-one years and multiple venues. His management experience of fairground complexes, convention centers, arenas, college facilities, and performing arts venues includes the oversight and development of new construction and renovation projects. His focus is on audience development, customer service, maximizing utilization, fiscal management, and providing arts education. His leadership has resulted in city government providing management contracts to professionally staff, market, and operate public assembly facilities in other cities.

Cora Cahan began her career as a dancer, and then entered administration. She co-founded and served as executive director of the Feld Ballet, then developed the Lawrence A. Wien Center for Dance and Theater and the Joyce Theater. In 1990, she was named president of the New 42nd Street, a nonprofit organization dedicated to restoring and recreating seven theaters. Cahan serves on the boards of NYC & Company, the New York Foundation for Architecture, and the Times Square Alliance. She is a founder and trustee emeritus of the Joyce Theater. She has been the recipient of a number of awards for public service, including the New York State Governor's Arts Award in 2001.

Brenda A. Neil Carter is the director of human resources at the Cincinnati Arts Association, the nonprofit organization that oversees the programming and management of three performing arts venues: the Aronoff Center for the Arts, Music Hall, and Memorial Hall. With a bachelor's in human resources, Carter has over fifteen years of experience in her field. She is also vice president of the board of trustees of the Arts Consortium of Cincinnati.

Tanya Collier is the director of human resources for the Metropolitan Exposition-Recreation Commission in Portland, Oregon. She has a master's degree in public administration and a bachelor's degree in political science. She also has certificates from the Leadership Skills Institute and the John F. Kennedy School of Government at Harvard University. She spent eight years as a labor relations representative of the Oregon Nurses' Association. Collier also directed the Department of Intergovernmental Relations and Community Affairs for Multnomah County, was the general manager of Portland Energy Conservation, Inc., and was an elected Multnomah County Commissioner and Metro Councilor.

Charles Cosler is president of Charles Cosler Theatre Design, Inc., a full-service theater and architectural lighting design firm. The experience of the firm covers a wide range of performing arts and architectural lighting projects including: new construction, restoration/renovations, higher education, large municipal theaters, professional theaters, school auditoriums, religious facilities, art galleries, and libraries. Recent awards include the 2003 Lumen Citation and a 2003 IIDA Award from the IES for "Rewarding Lives," an exhibition featuring photos by Annie Liebowitz for American Express, and the 2001 USITT Architecture Merit Award for Summerstage, an outdoor stage in New York's Central Park.

Michael Currie has been director of Hampton Arts since its creation in 1987. He oversaw the renovations of the historic Charles H. Taylor Arts Center in downtown Hampton, as well as the purchase and renovations of the historic American Theatre in Phoebus. He established the highly acclaimed Great Performers Series in 1989. Under his direction, Hampton Arts has evolved into a model arts agency, totally unique in the region. Prior to being appointed the director of Hampton Arts, Currie served as founding director of the Fine Arts Foundation of Lafayette for more than thirteen years. He began his professional career as an assistant stage manager at the Chelmsford Civic Theatre in his native England, working in all aspects of theater management and production.

Joshua Dachs is a principal and director of Fisher Dachs Associates, one of the world's leading theater planning and design consulting companies, based in New York. In its thirty years of existence, FDA has helped create over four hundred performing arts projects throughout the U.S. and abroad. A graduate of the High School of Music and Art in New York, where he studied the violin, he holds a bachelor of architecture degree from Cornell University. For the past six years, Dachs has taught a professional development course on theater design at the Harvard University Graduate School of Design. He has been a guest critic at the Cornell University School of Architecture, the Southern California Institute of Architecture (SCI-ARC), and UCLA. He is a member of the American Society of Theatre Consultants (ASTC) and the International Society for the Performing Arts (ISPA).

Judith E. Daykin became president and executive director of City Center (New York) in 1992. Under her leadership, City Center inaugurated its acclaimed "Encores! Great American Musicals in Concert" series. She was previously a principal consultant with Theatre Projects Consultants, Inc., and she owned and operated her own arts-management consulting firm, Daykin Arts Associates. She was also executive vice president and managing director of the Brooklyn Academy of Music and executive director of the Paul Taylor Dance Company. Before coming to New York in the late 1960s, she worked in musical theater in Cleveland and Palm Beach as a performer, stage manager, and press representative, and as assistant to the producer at Musicarnival Theatres.

Stewart Donnell is president of Donnell Consultants, Inc., based in Tampa, Florida, which has operated internationally since 1986, exclusively in project and construction cost management of theaters, opera houses, concert halls, and museums. He has over thirty years' experience in the North American construction market and has been instrumental in developing advanced techniques in the cost planning and control of these facilities. DCI's projects have ranged in cost from $10 million to $300 million. DCI has been engaged directly by private, university, city, state, and federal clients, from early program to the completion of the design stage. He is a fellow of the Royal Institute of Chartered Surveyors.

Eric Fliss is cultural facilities management consultant for the City of Miami Beach, Florida. He is responsible for the operation of the Colony and Byron Carlyle Theatres. He is resident lighting designer for the international contemporary ballet company Maximum Dance and the Florida Dance Festival, as well as president of Anchor Arts Management, where he facilitates productions for organizations such as Miami Light Project, Tigertail Productions, and Miami Dade College Department of Cultural Affairs. From 1987 to 2001, he was facility production manger for the Colony Theatre. In 1986, he co-founded the Acme Acting Company, designed three black box venues, and produced more than fifty productions. Fliss is a graduate of Florida State University.

Steven Friedlander is vice president and principal-in-charge of the New York office of Auerbach Pollock Friedlander Performing Arts/Media Facilities Planning and Design. For more than eighteen years he was a lighting designer and production manager for several ballet and opera companies, including Dallas Ballet, Philadelphia Opera Theater, Lyric Opera of Dallas, Feld Ballet, Houston Ballet, Boston Ballet, and the Boston Shakespeare Company. Recent projects include Atlanta Symphony's new Symphony Center and Zankel Hall at Carnegie Hall. He received a bachelor of fine arts in technical theater and lighting design from Boston University's School of Fine Arts.

Joseph Golden was, for twenty-four years, executive director of the Cultural Resources Council of Syracuse and Onondaga County, New York, and managing director of the Civic Center of Onondaga County. For fifteen years he taught theater history and production at Elmira College, Cornell University, and Syracuse University. He has consulted the New York State Council on the Arts and the National Endowment for the Arts, and is the author of six books on theater history, development, and management. He holds a bachelor of arts from Tufts University, a master of arts from Indiana University, and a doctorate from the University of Illinois.

Teri Freitas Gorman is vice president for external affairs at the Broward Center for the Performing Arts in Fort Lauderdale, Florida, where she oversees new audience development, marketing, and education/community programs. She previously worked as marketing director for the Aotea Centre in Auckland, New Zealand, and as director of marketing for the Maui Arts & Cultural Center in Kahului, Hawaii. A Hawaii native, Gorman is a graduate of the University of California at Los Angeles, where she earned a bachelor of arts in film and television.

Victor Gotesman is managing director at Jaffe Holden Acoustics, president of the Center for Creative Resources in New York City, and former manager of the Cerritos Performing Arts Center. Previous administrative positions include serving as president of Theatre Projects Consultants, Inc.; as director of the Cerritos Center for the Performing Arts, California, from its creation in 1991; and as director of Fine Arts Center Series at the University of Massachusetts Fine Arts Center in Amherst. He has a master of fine arts in arts administration from the University of Iowa and a bachelor of arts in music from the Eastman School of Music, University of Rochester, New York.

Jack Hagler has over twenty-five years of experience as a designer, technician, contractor, and consultant for assembly facilities, including professional/educational/community theaters, convention facilities, and houses of worship. Hagler has provided consulting, design, and project management services for a variety of performing arts and entertainment venues. Significant projects include the Eisenmann Center for Performing Arts, Six Flags Fiesta Texas, Gaylord Palms Resort, the Mesa Arts Center, and renovation of the Jackie Gleason Theater of the Performing Arts. Hagler is a member of the American Society of Theatre Consultants, the International Association of Assembly Managers, and the Illuminating Engineering Society of North America.

Michael C. Hardy is president and CEO of the Performing Arts Center Trust, Inc., the nonprofit corporation that oversees the operation of the Miami Performing Arts Center. Hardy joined the Performing Arts Center of Greater Miami in June of 2002 from Louisville's Kentucky Center for the Arts, that state's premier arts organization, where he was president since 1998. Hardy's distinguished career also includes seven years as executive director of the International Society for the Performing Arts Foundation (ISPA) and five years as president of the Snug Harbor Cultural Center, a national historic landmark on New York's Staten Island. A native of North Carolina, Hardy earned a bachelor's degree in English at Duke University in Durham, a master's degree in dramatic arts and television at the University of North Carolina at Chapel Hill, and a doctorate in theater at the University of Michigan.

John A. Haynes was appointed as founding executive director of the DeBartolo Center for the Performing Arts at the University of Notre Dame in August 2002. He was named the Leighton Director of Performing Arts in January 2003, becoming only the second endowed chair in the arts in the university's 162-year history. Previously, Haynes served as president and CEO of the California Center for the Arts, a twelve-acre regional cultural center located in San Diego county, California, and as executive director of the Children's Theatre Company, America's most prominent producing theater and dramatic conservatory for young audiences.

Mark Heiser is currently managing director of the New York State Theater at Lincoln Center, under the direction of City Center of Music and Drama, Inc. The State Theater is home to the New York City Ballet and New York City Opera. He was formerly general manager of Cal Performances at the University of California, Berkeley. Heiser has a bachelor's degree in drama from UC Irvine and a master's degree in dramatic art from UC Davis. His writing contributions include "The Tao of Stage Management" *(Theatre Design and Technology,* Spring 1991) and "Rebel Without a Clause" (*Facility Management,* December 2003).

Peter Herrndorf is president and CEO of the National Arts Centre in Ottawa, Ontario, Canada. After working in senior management at the CBC and as publisher of *Toronto Life* magazine in the 1970s and 1980s, he joined TVOntario in 1992 as chairman and CEO. He chairs and is on the board of numerous Canadian cultural foundations and organizations. The recipient of many awards, Herrndorf was awarded the prestigious Diplôme d'Honneur for outstanding service to the arts in Canada in June 2000, and is an Officer of the Order of Canada. He holds a bachelor of arts in political science and English from the University of Manitoba, a law degree from Dalhousie University, a masters of business administration from Harvard Business School, and honorary doctor of law degrees from York University, the University of Winnipeg, and Dalhousie University.

Colin Jackson is president and CEO of Epcor Centre for the Performing Arts in Calgary, Alberta, Canada. His career highlights include tenure as executive director of the Confederation Centre for the Arts in Charlottetown, as founding artistic director and executive producer of Winnipeg's Prairie Theatre Exchange, as drama producer for CBC, as a lecturer in arts administration, and as an arts consultant. He currently serves as a member of the Prime Minister's Advisory Committee on Cities and Communities and chairs several significant Canadian cultural organizations. He received the Queen's Golden Jubilee medal and a Canada Council Senior Arts Award. Colin received a master of public administration degree from Harvard University and is the father of two daughters, Emma and Isabelle.

Fred Johnson is vice president of education and humanities at the Tampa Bay Performing Arts Center, where he also oversees the artist-in-residence program. He has a background as a performer of musical theater and classical mime, was involved in a program at the National Center for African American artists in Boston, and has been teaching the performing arts in the community since the early 1970s.

Michael M. Kaiser is president of the John F. Kennedy Center for the Performing Arts. Prior to this, he gained renown as a master in the art of the turnaround with several preeminent arts organizations, including the Royal Opera House Covent Garden, American Ballet Theatre, the Alvin Ailey Dance Theater Foundation, the Pierpont Morgan Library, and the Kansas City Ballet. Before entering arts management, he founded Kaiser Associates, a firm specializing in strategic planning for large corporations. He is the author of three books on strategic planning and positioning. He received a master's degree in management from Massachusetts Institute of Technology and a bachelor's degree in economics from Brandeis University. He has been an adjunct professor of arts administration at New York University and a lecturer at the University of the Witwatersrand in Johannesburg, South Africa.

Claudia Keenan Hough is director of marketing at New York City Opera, where she manages all ticket sales, institutional and brand marketing, advertising, promotions, Web site maintenance, and retail operations. Keenan Hough was previously director of marketing for Manhattan Theater Club, the Spoleto Festival, the Virginia Stage Company, and Festival Marketing. She earned a bachelor of arts from Randolph-Macon Woman's College, where she majored in communications and economics, and studied at the University of London and the London School of Economics. She teaches marketing at NYU's Graduate School for Performing Arts Administration, and serves on the Cultural Committee for NYC and Company and the steering committee for the National Arts Marketing Program.

Michael Kilgore is vice president of marketing at Tampa Bay Performing Arts Center in Tampa, Florida, where he manages marketing, public relations, group services, and publications at the largest performing arts center in the southeastern United States. He joined the Center as vice president in 2001. He formerly worked in news and then marketing for the *Tampa Tribune,* beginning in 1973. He graduated from the University of South Florida in 1973 in mass communications, and received their Distinguished Alumnus Award in 1993.

Mark Light is president of the Victoria Theatre Association, the Arts Center Foundation, and the Dayton Opera. This consortium presents productions to 420,000 patrons, operates venues with a total annual attendance of 900,000, and manages revenues of over $20 million. Mark is also president of consulting firm First Light and a board development associate for BoardSource. His has published two books: *The Strategic Board* in 2001 and *Executive Committee* in 2004. He votes on the Tony® Awards, holds an master of business administration from UCLA and a bachelor of fine arts from Drake University, and is completing his doctorate from Antioch University.

Gordon Linoff is a founder and principal of Data Miners, Inc. He is an expert in the fields of data mining and data warehousing. His experience spans a number of industries, including e-commerce, newspapers and magazines, telecommunications, and banking. With his colleague Michael Berry, Linoff recently authored a new book, *Mining the Web,* about data mining in the new economy. Two previous books, *Data Mining Techniques* and *Mastering Data Mining,* have been translated into many languages. Linoff has a degree in mathematics from Massachusetts Institute of Technology.

Judith Lisi is president/CEO of Tampa Bay Performing Arts Center, Inc. She was previously president/CEO of the Shubert Performing Arts Center in New Haven, Connecticut, for nine years. While there, she founded the Shubert Opera Company in collaboration with the Yale University School of Music. In 1992, she joined the Tampa Bay Performing Arts Center, where she retired a $3.5 million inherited debt, raised a $30 million endowment, and is building a new 45,000-square-foot school for the performing arts. She also founded Opera Tampa and a highly successful cabaret theater program. Prior to arts management, she was a singer, having trained at the University of Minnesota, the Julliard School, and the Metropolitan Opera.

Steve Loftin is president and executive director for the Cincinnati Arts Association (CAA), where he has been since 2000. The CAA is the nonprofit managing organization of the Aronoff Center for the Arts, the Cincinnati Music Hall, and the Hamilton County Memorial Hall. He came to the CAA in 1993 as executive vice president, assisting in the construction and subsequent operation of the Aronoff Center for the Arts. Prior to this, Loftin held similar positions over the previous thirteen years at the Tampa Bay Performing Arts Center and the Tennessee Performing Arts Center in Nashville. He has worked in the performing arts for twenty-six years.

Robert Long is a member of Theatre Consultants Collaborative. He has over twenty-five years of experience with the programming and design of performing arts buildings. He began his consulting career in the office of George C. Izenour Associates. In New York City, Robert worked with Artec Consultants and with Imero Fiorentino Associates. Following that, he was with Theatre Projects Consultants for over twenty years. Long is a member of the American Society of Theatre Consultants (ASTC), and served as president of that organization for three terms.

Bruce C. MacPherson is managing director of the Charles W. Eisemann Center for the Performing Arts in Richardson, Texas. He has over twenty-seven years in the field of arts administration, with the last sixteen specifically involved in the opening and running of new performing arts centers. His past administrative positions include assistant producer for the New Melody Fair Theatre in North Tonawanda, New York; marketing and development director for the Samuel L. Clemens Performing Arts Center in Elmira, New York; assistant director of the Zeiterion Theatre in New Bedford, Massachusetts; and manager of administration for the Meyerson Symphony Center in Dallas, Texas (where he was hired to help open the building). MacPherson is a 1977 graduate of SUNY Fredonia with a bachelor of arts in theater.

Siobhan McDermott is president of Strategic Management Consulting, which she launched in 1998 after serving as a campaign manager for Milano, Ruff & Associates, Inc., a national consulting firm. Representative clients include the New Jersey Performing Arts Center, Prospect Park Alliance in Brooklyn, and Clay Center for the Arts & Sciences of West Virginia. Projects include campaign and annual fund management, strategic planning, and board development. McDermott is a volunteer for the New York City Public School System and a director of the Broadway Mall Association in New York City.

Norbert Mongeon, Jr., is director of finance and programming for the Providence Performing Arts Center, Rhode Island. Prior to joining PPAC in 1985, he was a senior analyst for Ernst & Whinney, a CPA firm. When Professional Facilities Management (PFM) was formed in 1989, Mongeon became vice president/treasurer and principal booker for PFM facilities. He is a graduate of Leadership Rhode Island, a board member of Festival Ballet Providence, and a member of the League of American Theatres and Producers.

Philip Morris is CEO of Proctors Theatre of Schenectady, New York, where he is currently managing a major upgrade and expansion of performance and support facilities that will serve as an anchor to a city-designated cultural district. Before this, as director of the Arts Council for Chautauqua County, he developed a dozen properties as a cultural district linked to the renovation of an historic theater.

Halsey North, chair of the North Group, Inc., has helped arts organizations raise money for over thirty years. He is the former executive director of the North Carolina Arts Council, the Charlotte Arts & Science Council, and New York City's Cultural Council Foundation. He was previously vice president of C.W. Shaver & Company, a fundraising firm, and corporate contributions officer for Philip Morris Companies. For the past seventeen years, Halsey and Alice North have consulted performing arts centers and theaters and taught fundraising for many national and regional arts service organizations. North received the Distinguished Service Award from the North Carolina Association of Arts Councils, the Chairman's Award from the National Assembly of Local Arts Agencies (now Americans for the Arts), and the Fan Taylor Award from the Association of Performing Arts Presenters.

Kathleen O'Brien is the chief operating officer of the Tennessee Performing Arts Center, where she oversees operations, sponsorships, marketing, communications, public relations, customer service, information services, event services, program budgets, administration, and ticketing operations. O'Brien has been employed with TPAC since 1988, and has been part of the senior management staff that was responsible for the Center's growth in attendance and budget. She is also an active member of the League of American Theatres and Producers.

Lance Olson is manager of the Cutler Majestic Theater at Emerson College in Boston. He is also a trustee and past president of the League of Historic American Theatres. Olson has worked in the professional performing arts since 1969. He was previously the presenter at Rutgers University, where he was one of the founders and the executive director of Rutgers SummerFest. He was program manager at Newark (NJ) Symphony Hall and spent four years as director of Performing Arts Facilities at Kean College of New Jersey. He is a graduate of the University of Minnesota and Brooklyn College, holding an master of fine arts in performing arts administration.

Carmen Pietri-Diaz is the executive director of the Nuyorican Poets Café in New York's Lower East Side and co-administrator of the Pedro Pietri Benefit Fund. She comes from a legal background, having worked as a contract lawyer in class action suits and for two decades as a community activist and tenant advocate with the Northwest Bronx Community and Clergy Coalition. She has produced annual variety programs during Puerto Rican History Month at Pace University in New York City and other colleges in the metropolitan area. Pietri-Diaz is on the Advisory Board of Federation of East Village Artists and is an arts advisor to the Select Committee of NYC Council member Alan Gerson. She has a bachelor of arts in liberal arts/urban legal studies from City College, New York, and a juris doctorate from CUNY Law School.

Richard Pilbrow, chair of Theatre Projects Consultants, Inc., is one of the world's leading theater design consultants, a theater, film, and television producer, and an internationally known author and stage lighting designer. His most recent Broadway productions were *Our Town,* starring Paul Newman at the Booth Theatre, and Cy Coleman's musical *The Life,* for which he received a Tony Award nomination. Under his leadership, Theatre Projects has worked on over six hundred projects in fifty countries. Published in 1970, his book, *Stage Lighting,* became an industry standard; his new book, *Stage Lighting Design: The Art, The Craft, The Life,* was published in 1997. In 2001 Pilbrow was elected a Fellow of the United States Institute for Theatre Technology.

Byron G. Quann is president and CEO of the Whitaker Center for Science and the Arts in Harrisburg, Pennsylvania. He was formerly senior vice president of marketing for Election.com, a global Internet election company. Previously he was chief marketing and communications officer for the Mashantucket Pequot Tribal Nation, the owners and operators of Foxwoods Resort Casino. He also was executive vice president for marketing and communications for the ATP Tour, the governing body of men's professional tennis. He spent most of his career with IBM in marketing and communications, conducting advertising and product media relations in the United States.

William F. Reeder is dean and professor of arts management at the College of Visual and Performing Arts at George Mason University in Fairfax, Virginia. Previously he was vice president and general manager of the Washington Performing Arts Society, and he oversaw the Sally Mae Corporation's corporate giving programs and volunteer management. He has also served as executive director of the Levine School of Music, president of the National Foundation for Advancement in the Arts, and executive director of

Opera Music Theater International and the Newark Community School of the Arts. For eight years, Reeder was a leading operatic tenor at the Zurich Opera. He has performed over forty leading tenor roles in fifteen major opera houses throughout Europe.

John Richard is chief operating officer of the New Jersey Performing Arts Center, where he managed the Center's $190 million fundraising campaign, and currently oversees fundraising, marketing, public relations and operations. Richard is co-chair of the Partnership in Philanthropy and a trustee of the Greater Newark YMWCA. He is a fellow of Leadership New Jersey class of 2001. He served on the board (and as president) of the National Society of Fund Raising Executives. He was also a board member of the Muhlenberg Regional Medical Center Foundation, Inc., the Plainfield Health Center, and the Plainfield Symphony Orchestra.

Jeffrey Rosenstock has served as executive director of Queens Theatre in the Park since 1989. During his tenure, he has transformed an abandoned building into a premier performing arts center and increased the operating budget from $500,000 to $2.5 million. Rosenstock is a guest lecturer on fundraising and audience development, and leads workshops and seminars on diversifying and expanding audiences. He is a member of the board of trustees of the Alliance of Resident Theatres/New York and the Queens Chamber of Commerce, and was recently selected as Business Person of the Year by the Queens Chamber of Commerce.

Roderick J. Rubbo is president and CEO of the Cultural Center for the Arts in Canton, Ohio. He received the 2002 Michael Newton Award from Americans for the Arts as recognition for his leadership in the United Arts Fundraising field. His administrative background includes positions at the Pittsburgh Playhouse, Pittsburgh Ballet Theatre, North Carolina Dance Theatre, and Ohio Ballet. He has served on the boards of the Ohio Citizens for the Arts and the Association of Ohio Community Arts Agencies. He is a graduate of the University of Oklahoma, where he received his bachelor of fine arts in scenic and technical design.

Anita Scism is in her sixth year as president and CEO of the Walton Arts Center in Fayetteville, Arkansas. She joined the Center prior to its opening in 1991 as director of financial affairs, bringing over fifteen years of experience in the banking and legal professions. She was promoted to senior vice president, then interim president in 1997, then president and CEO in 1998. In October 2000, she was selected as one of six arts presenters from the United States to participate in the US/China Performing Arts Presenter Cultural Exchange and is on the board of the Association of Performing Arts Presenters.

Kelley Shanley is the executive vice president and general manager of the Broward Center for the Performing Arts in Fort Lauderdale, Florida. He previously worked as general manager for the Coral Springs Center for the Arts in Coral Springs, Florida, and as assistant general manager for Lowell Memorial Auditorium in Massachusetts, while employed by Professional Facilities Management, based in Providence, Rhode Island. He is a graduate of the State University of New York at Geneseo, where he earned a bachelor of arts in communications.

Christine Sheehan is director of education at Proctors Theatre in Schenectady, New York, where she has nurtured an arts career for over ten years. She is responsible for the administration of existing and developing new arts education programming, funding sources, and community partnerships. Christine holds degrees in music education and business administration.

R. Douglas Sheldon, senior vice president and director of Columbia Artists Management, Inc., manages some of the world's preeminent artists and ensembles, including the New York Philharmonic, the Los Angeles Philharmonic, the Kirov Orchestra, Orchestre National de France, the Budapest Festival Orchestra, the China Philharmonic, the Vienna Symphony, Valery Gergiev, Leonard Slatkin, Rafael Frühbeck de Burgos, Anne-Sophie Mutter, Nigel Kennedy, Yundi Li, Beaux Arts Trio, and Marilyn Horne. He is a director of the White Nights Foundation of America, an organization dedicated to the betterment of cultural understanding, cultural awareness, and economic interaction between America and Russia.

Linda Shelton is executive director and a trustee of the Joyce Theater Foundation. She was previously general manager of the Joffrey Ballet and managed tours for the Bolshoi Ballet, Bolshoi Ballet Academy, Moscow Virtuosi, 1000 Airplanes on the Roof, and Sankai Juku, and held management positions at the Twyla Tharp Dance Foundation. Linda holds a bachelor of arts in dance education and has completed work toward a master of arts in arts administration at NYU. She has chaired and been a member of Dance/USA for over ten years. In 1999 Shelton was appointed a Chevalier of France's Order of Arts and Letters for her contribution to furthering the arts. She currently teaches in the graduate program of arts administration at New York University.

Matthew T. Sternberg has been executive director of the Rutland Redevelopment Authority in Rutland, Vermont, where he has led the turnaround of a once failing downtown since 1990. Trained as a stage manager and director, Sternberg started his career managing opera companies in the Baltimore/Washington area. After receiving an master of business administration in marketing, he moved into redevelopment, specializing in the revitalization of older downtown districts. His theater experience came full circle with the renovation of the Paramount Theatre in Rutland, Vermont. For twenty-five years, he has worked to strengthen ties between performing arts and municipal economic development.

Ellen Stewart is the founder and artistic director of La MaMa Experimental Theatre Club. Ellen introduced the works of Tom O'Horgan, Andrei Serban, Jerzy Grotowski, and Tadeusz Kantor to American audiences. She has directed over twenty large-scale performances, including *The Cotton Club, Mythos Oedipus, Romeo and Juliet, The Monk and the Hangman's Daughter,* and *Seven against Thebes.* She is the recipient of honorary doctorates and awards that include the MacArthur Genius Award and the National Endowment for Arts and Culture. She was also awarded the Order of the Sacred Treasure, Gold Rays with Rosette by the emperor of Japan.

Tony Stimac is a graduate of the Royal Academy of Dramatic Arts. He has directed at the McCarter Theatre, CSC, Manhattan Theatre Club, the Roundabout, Lincolnshire Marriott, Papermill Playhouse, the Alliance Theatre, Cincinnati Playhouse in the Park, Coconut Grove Playhouse, MeadowBrook Rep, North Shore Music Theater, and Goodspeed Opera House. He founded Musical Theatre Works in New York in 1983 and was artistic director for fourteen years. Currently, he is the executive producer of the Helen Hayes Theatre Company in Nyack, New York. He is also the producing director of the White Plains Performing Arts Center, New York.

Randy Vogel is the performing arts center administrator for the new Mesa Arts Center, opening in spring 2005. Prior to this, he was director of performing arts for the California Center for the Arts in Escondido, California. He has a master of science degree in arts administration/arts education and a bachelor of arts degree in music (double bass) from Florida State University. He has performed extensively in orchestra, jazz ensembles, and musicals. He is a member of International Association of Performing Arts Administrators, the Association of Performing Arts Presenters, and the Western Arts Alliance, and is on the board for the Arizona Presenters Alliance.

Tom Webster is the director of the University Theatre and entertainment director at the Adams Event Center on the University of Montana-Missoula campus. He is an alumnus of the University of Montana and has worked on the campus since 1994. Webster has been promoting and producing entertainment events throughout Montana and the Pacific Northwest for twenty years. He was a founding member of the Missoula Blues and Jazz Society, and is currently on the boards of the Montana Performing Arts Consortium, the Missoula Cultural Council, and First Night Missoula.

Robyn L. Williams, CFE, has worked in facility management for more than twenty years. She began as technical director at the Lubbock Memorial Convention Center in Lubbock, Texas. In 1990 she became director of theater district facilities in Houston. In 1997, she moved to the Blumenthal Performing Arts Center and Spirit Square Center in Charlotte, North Carolina, as theater and building operations director, and ultimately as vice president of operations and real estate. In 2000 Williams became executive director for the Portland Center for the Performing Arts. She is an instructor and on the Board of Regents for the IAAM Public Assembly Facility Management School.

About the Author

Duncan Webb is founder and president of Webb Management Services, a management-consulting firm serving the arts and cultural industries. In his fifteen years as an arts management consultant, he has published numerous journal articles on arts management and the development, operation, and financing of arts facilities. A professor of New York University's graduate program in performing arts administration, he lives in New York City.

Index

Books from Allworth Press

Allworth Press
is an imprint
of Allworth
Communications,
Inc. Selected titles
are listed below.

Making It on Broadway: Actor's Tales of Climbing to the Top
by David Wiener and Jodie Langel (paperback, 6 × 9, 288 pages, $19.95)

Producing Your Own Showcase
by Paul Harris (paperback, 6 × 9, 240 pages, $18.95)

The Perfect Stage Crew: The Compleat Technical Guide for High School, College, and Community Theater
by John Kaluta (paperback, 6 × 9, 256 pages, $19.95)

Business and Legal Forms for Theater
by Charles Grippo (paperback, 8½ × 11, 192 pages, $29.95)

Career Solutions for Creative People: How to Balance Artistic Goals with Career Security
by Dr. Ronda Ormont (paperback, 6 × 9, 320 pages, $19.95)

Acting That Matters
by Barry Pineo (paperback, 6 × 9, 256 pages, $19.95)

Improv for Actors
by Dan Diggles (paperback, 6 × 9, 224 pages, $19.95)

Mastering Shakespeare: An Acting Class in Seven Scenes
by Scott Kaiser (paperback, 6 × 9, 256 pages, $19.95)

Movement for Actors
edited by Nicole Potter (paperback, 6 × 9, 288 pages, $19.95)

Promoting Your Acting Career: A Step-by-Step Guide to Opening the Right Doors, Second Edition
by Glenn Alterman (paperback, 6 × 9, 240 pages, $19.95)

An Actor's Guide—Making It in New York City
by Glenn Alterman (paperback, 6 × 9, 288 pages, $19.95)

Creating Your Own Monologue
by Glenn Alterman (paperback, 6 × 9, 208 pages, $14.95)

Please write to request our free catalog. To order by credit card, call 1-800-491-2808.

To see our complete catalog on the World Wide Web, or to order online, you can find us at **www.allworth.com**.